# THORNS
## IN THE
# CROWN

# THORNS
# IN THE
# CROWN

## THE STORY OF THE CORONATION AND WHAT IT MEANT FOR BRITAIN

### BARRY TURNER

The
History
Press

First published 2022

The History Press
97 St George's Place, Cheltenham,
Gloucestershire, GL50 3QB
www.thehistorypress.co.uk

British Library Cataloguing in Publication Data.
A catalogue record for this book is available from the British Library.

ISBN 978 0 7509 9813 0

Typesetting and origination by The History Press
Printed and bound in Great Britain by TJ Books Limited, Padstow, Cornwall.

MIX
Paper from
responsible sources
FSC® C013056

Trees for LYfe

# CONTENTS

# INTRODUCTION

# COME THE DAY

Delving into the records and weighing one thing with another, the boys at the Meteorological Office decided that Coronation Day, 2 June 1953, would be warm and dry. It was cold and wet. Not that this was in any way a deterrent to those determined to see what they could of the great event. A film of the procession route three days before shows crowds camping out twelve deep on both sides of the Mall. By coronation eve, some 30,000 were bedded down.

Buses started bringing more spectators into the coronation area at 4.30 in the morning and the underground started at 3.00 a.m. They came equipped with spirit stoves, stools, blankets and tinned food. Portable radios and wind-up gramophones helped to pass the time. London's famous buskers – dancers, acrobats, singers – worked all hours.

The doors at Westminster Abbey opened at 6.00 a.m. for the first guests to take their places. They sat huddled together against the chill. The more privileged, including foreign royals and other overseas dignitaries, followed after 8.30 a.m. Though most went unrecognised by onlookers, they were all given a hearty cheer.

The excitement mounted with the procession into the Abbey, led by royal chaplains followed by a host of all that was esoteric in the orders of chivalry, the royal household, the Commonwealth prime ministers, Sir Winston Churchill looking distinctly grumpy in the Tudor vestments worn by Knights of the Order of the Garter, and the senior clerics of the Church of England.

The 4-year-old Prince Charles, in tow with his nanny, entered by a side door to sit between the Queen Mother and Princess Margaret. Proudly, he announced that he was wearing his father's hair oil. Anyone who showed an interest was invited to take a sniff.

By 11.00 a.m. the full congregation of 8,000 was squeezed into the Abbey, the least fortunate seated so high on the temporary galleries they were able to give close attention to the mouldings on the ceiling. The Queen arrived at 11.15 a.m. in the Gold State Coach – magnificent to look at, but a byword for discomfort. At the Queen's side was her husband Philip, Duke of Edinburgh, in the uniform of Admiral of the Fleet.

Across the country 20 million television viewers, many of them sharing sets with friends and neighbours, were tuned in to freckled screens. The greatest royal show ever, almost certainly never to be repeated, was about to begin.

# 1

# A MONARCH IN
# THE MAKING

Bordered by privilege, the childhood of the future Queen Elizabeth was narrowly confined. Soon after her birth on 21 April 1926, the first daughter of the Duke and Duchess of York was handed over to the care of a nanny of the old school. A spinster daughter of a tenant farmer, Clara Knight was of dictatorial disposition with unbendable rules on behaviour in the nursery. But whatever her limitations, she came to the royal household with impeccable credentials having served as nanny to the mother of her latest charge.

The other great influence on Elizabeth's early years was her grandfather, George V. When her parents set off on a six-month tour of Australasia, she was often in his company. The effect of the relationship was as great on the King as it was on his granddaughter. As a parent, he was insensitive and autocratic, not even allowing his children to address him unless he spoke to them first. But he was devoted to Elizabeth, his 'Lilibet', as he called her, adopting her own garbled pronunciation of her name. The Princess called him 'Grandpa England'.

With her parents' return to London, the family moved into 145 Piccadilly, now the site of the InterContinental Hotel but then a spacious mansion in what had long been the preserve of the fabulously rich. The staff at 145, with its twenty-five bedrooms, comprised a butler, an under-butler, a telephonist, two footmen, a valet, a dresser, a cook, two kitchen maids, nightwatchman and an RAF orderly as a general dogsbody.[1] A close neighbour was the 7th Duke of Wellington at Apsley House, known as No. 1 London.

Others of the old aristocracy, all family friends, lived nearby, though it was a sign of the times that Devonshire House, with its apron wall surrounding a 3-acre garden, had been sold by the Duke to pay off death duties. The house was demolished in 1924 to make way for a nine-storey office block. Likewise, Grosvenor House in Park Lane, home of the Duke of Westminster, fell to the wrecking ball in 1927 to be replaced by the Grosvenor House Hotel, while the nearby Dorchester House, thought by some to be so strongly built as to be virtually indestructible, went the same way in 1929 to create a site for the Dorchester Hotel. The Duke of York was not best pleased by these changes to his domestic surroundings.

A second home for the Yorks was Royal Lodge in Windsor Great Park. It was in the 98 acres of pasture and woodland that Elizabeth nurtured her love of animals (the King gave her a pony for her 4th birthday) and all things rural. Her sister, Margaret, born in 1930, was to mature quite differently, a sparky, mischievous child, and a contrast to Elizabeth who liked to be organised and tidy, eager to meet the approval of her elders.

In 1933, she and Margaret acquired a governess. Marion Crawford, or 'Crawfie' as she came to be known, was a 22-year-old Scotswoman who had trained as a teacher. She was a good all-rounder but, true to the Presbyterian lower middle class in which she grew up, the standards she set in the fourteen years of her employment were none too taxing for two bright girls. A restricted curriculum ran parallel to a closeted existence with no friends or even acquaintances outside the aristocratic magic circle.

Elizabeth's earliest ambition was to marry a farmer who had plenty of dogs, horses and cows. 'She was happiest when riding or running about outside Royal Lodge with her father's dogs.'[2] Setting a trend in books about the young royals, in 1936 there appeared a collection of photographs by Lisa Sheridan called *The Princesses and their Dogs*. It was a bestseller. The image of sweet innocence was reinforced by the way the princesses appeared in public. For George V's Silver Jubilee in 1935, they were turned out identically in pale pink dresses and pink bonnets. Always, the stress was on presenting a family ideal of dutiful children beholden to their caring and wiser mentors.

The childhood fantasy of a life of bucolic contentment faded for Elizabeth after the abdication of her uncle, Edward VIII, in 1936 and the accession of her father as George VI. If, at age 10, the Princess could hardly be expected to understand the connotations of being next in line to the throne, it was clear to those responsible for her upbringing that it was no longer enough for her to be coached as a future wife and mother with the usual quota of social accomplishments.

To broaden the education of the destined first citizen, Henry Marten, Vice Provost of Eton College, was called in to give lessons on constitutional history. His fellow tutor was the Vicomtesse de Bellaigue, who taught both princesses French, French Literature and European History. Elizabeth came to speak fluent French without a trace of an English accent.

It was from Marten, who was knighted for his efforts, that Elizabeth acquired an understanding of what was expected of a monarch. The image created for Queen Victoria as the Great Queen Empress, mother of a world-wide family of diverse countries, was adapted to the somewhat reduced circumstances of post-war imperial Britain, with the sovereign at the hub of a Commonwealth of free nations with the add-on of an assortment of colonies aspiring towards independence.

There was emphasis too on Victoria's philanthropic initiatives, with her wish to give 'support to works of mercy among the sick and suffering and to anything which may tend to brighten the lives and ameliorate the condition of Her Majesty's poorer subjects'. It was a policy enthusiastically adopted by Victoria's eldest son after he was crowned as Edward VII. Patron of some 250 charities with contributions to another 250, Edward tapped into his moneyed friends who could rely on an honour of some sort as long as they gave generously, in return, to one of the King's pet projects. As a recent commentator has observed, 'Nothing arouses a philanthropist more than the expectation of a knighthood.' And the benefit to the monarch? 'No other role offered such rich returns in publicity and deference for so little effort.'[3] It was a lesson the young Princess was not to forget.

If philanthropic patronage strengthened the Crown, so too, said Marten, did the ability of the monarchy to adapt to social and political evolution. Credit here went to Elizabeth's grandfather. Nobody except his biographers ever described George V as an intelligent or even likeable man. Given to expressing antiquated views without fear of contradiction, he was ill-tempered and callous to those brave enough to cross him. 'He is a tyrant in his own circle,' wrote the politico socialite Henry 'Chips' Channon, a 'most severe father and frequently irascible, although subject to fits of camaraderie and good-natured fellowship'.[4] Head of state for twenty-five years, he was happiest when reducing the bird population (he was said to be Britain's finest shot) or contemplating his stamp collection. His appreciation of art barely extended to portraits of his ancestors and heroic battle scenes while music was only music when played, loudly, by a military band. The point of having a Poet Laureate or a Master of the King's Musick was entirely lost on him – as, in fairness, it was to most of his subjects.

Where George V made all the difference was in responding to the changing mood of the country. He had, in abundance, a talent for reaching out to his subjects or, as his eldest son put it, he managed, 'without apparent design, to resolve the internal contradictions of the monarchy that requires it to be remote from yet, at the same time, to personify the aspirations of the people'.

There was nothing new in royal visits to factories and mines. Prince Albert and Edward VII set aside several days a year for venturing into the industrial heartland. George V more than doubled their efforts. We cannot know what examples Marten might have given Elizabeth of the King's common touch, but she might well have heard of the occasion in 1912 when the King and Queen visited Cadeby coal mine after series of explosions had killed ninety-one miners. The royal couple, who were on an official visit to the area, made a point of going to the mine to express their sympathy. It was hardly an extravagant gesture, yet few earlier kings would have done as much.

Always available for opening public buildings such as Manchester's Central Library and Liverpool's Mersey Tunnel, no ceremony over which George V presided was complete without an uplifting speech extolling the virtues of working together for the common good. Charities, notably those for disabled servicemen, benefited from the King's patronage blazoned on their letterheads. In the years of the Depression and mass unemployment, the public appearances of the King and Queen symbolised unity in troubled times.

The poor came to regard George V as their friend. As George Orwell recalled of the 1935 Silver Jubilee, the slogan 'Poor but Loyal' was popular in the slum districts of London. Other slogans coupled loyalty to the King with hostility to the landlord with 'Long Live the King. Down with the Landlord', or, more often, 'No Landlords Wanted'.[5]

On a lighter note, in 1916 the King and Queen Mary were at Drury Lane Theatre for a production of *Julius Caesar* – which probably bored him rigid. In the cast was Frank Benson, a leading actor of his day, whose knighthood had been announced but not yet bestowed. The resident producer at Drury Lane, Arthur Collins, came up with the idea of the King performing the ceremony in the theatre. Attendants of the royal couple were aghast. 'It can't be done – it has never been done.' The King, however, was all in favour. 'A nervous Benson was sent for, in the ante-room the ceremony was quickly rehearsed, the King entered from the royal box, Benson in his Julius Caesar robes knelt and the accolade was confirmed.'[6] The sword, hastily brought in from a theatrical costumier, was later presented to Benson.

But it was in relation to the monarch's constitutional role that the paramount lessons from her grandfather were handed down to Elizabeth. Though given to a blunt expression of his views, George V could switch on the charm in dealing with politicians. He stuck by whatever government came his way, always taking care not to step beyond the bounds of expediency.

This is not to say he was without influence. For good or ill, in 1931 he played his part in creating the cross-party National Government to cope with the economic depression and financial crisis. It made a hash of the job but, in handing power to the Tories for the rest of the decade, it presumably gave the King satisfaction.

His toughest test as a constitutional monarch came at the start of his reign after the attempt by the House of Lords to decimate the 1909 People's Budget with its unprecedented tax increase on the rich. The response of the Liberal Government was to introduce legislation to remove the power of the Lords to veto money bills and to limit delay on other bills to two years. This only became practical after the King made it known that he would agree to the creation of a sufficient number of peers to outvote the Tory majority. He did not like it but he did it.

It was a pivotal event for the monarchy. In acting against his private convictions, George V won popular support while leaving his natural allies among the hereditary peers to take the flak. Distancing his family from the House of Saxe-Coburg and Gotha by adopting the thoroughly English name of Windsor bolstered his image as a King for all his people, one who was 'raised above all private and local interests, to think of all, to care for all, to unite all in one fellowship of common memories, common ideals, common sacrifices'.[7] It was a grand vision, altogether too much for common consumption, though it came close to realisation at the funeral of the Unknown Warrior in Westminster Abbey. In the company of

100 winners of the Victoria Cross, George V walked behind the coffin for a service described by *The Times* as 'the most beautiful, the most touching and the most impressive … this island has ever seen'.

The death of George V in 1936 sent the nation into shock. Though no friend of royalty, Kingsley Martin, editor of the *New Statesman*, was struck by the public mood:

> No one who talked to his neighbour on a bus, to the charwoman wash-ing the steps, or to a sightseer standing at the street corner, could doubt the almost universal feeling of loss, nor could any perceptive observer fail to notice the peculiarly personal character of this emotion. People who had never seen the King and only heard his voice on the wireless talked about him as if he were a personal friend or a near relative cut off in his prime. Propaganda, no doubt, accounts for much, but no propaganda can create this type of personal emotion unless the conditions are particularly favourable. Propaganda can exploit, spread, intensify existing emotion. It cannot create when the materials are lacking.[8]

Later, A.J.P. Taylor was to write, 'No King tried harder to do his duty. He made constitutional monarchy a whole time occupation.'[9]

In tracking Elizabeth's reign, with its endless duties of public appearances, support for good causes and coping with politicians and foreign dignitaries, not all of them otherwise acceptable in polite society, it is easy to see the guiding spirit of her grandfather. If much of this was imparted by Henry Marten in his tutorials with Elizabeth, she would certainly have picked up more from her grandmother Queen Mary, more cultured than her husband, who was strong on national and family history.

The only lesson handed down to Elizabeth from the brief reign of Edward VIII was how not to be head of the royal family. Surrounded by aco-lytes to bolster his self-esteem, the young, debonair Edward saw himself, like his father, as one with the people, while failing to realise that it took more than an advanced sense of entitlement to operate independently of the politi-cal elite. He had a 'one-track mind', wrote Chips Channon. 'His complete absorption is in the interests of the moment.'[10] Admiring the strong leaders in Fascist Europe, he pitched himself against the fumbling inadequacies of democracy, maybe even seeing himself as the white knight who would come to the rescue of a nation brought low by recession and mass unemployment.

In the event, he was powerless even to choose his own wife. When he made it known that he intended to marry the twice divorced Wallis Simpson, a plain-spoken American, who showed scant respect for old-world conventions, the serried ranks of constitutional diehards lined up against him and, more particularly, against her. The parallel today with Prince Harry and his wife, Meghan, an American divorcee of forthright views, is hard to miss.

The political rumpus that led to Edward's departure put the monarchy under a harsh spotlight. Fortunately for the Windsors, the reserves of goodwill were strong enough to see them through a transition that made Edward's younger brother and Elizabeth's father the new head of state. It helped that George VI was the opposite of his sibling. With him, it was back to business as usual. Duty came first, devotion to family a close second. Painfully shy and with no outside interests beyond field sports, his social skills were further constrained by a severe stammer. Ill-disposed to public ceremonial, he was a monarch by default. His mother confessed that he had been appalled when he succeeded: 'He was devoted to his brother, and the whole abdication crisis made him miserable. He sobbed on my shoulder for a whole hour.'[11]

Eight years later, he was still not quite reconciled to the unexpected turn of events. 'How I hate being King,' he said. But he was right for the time. 'Had he been clever, he would have been censored for meddling. Had he been highbrow, he would have caused resentment. The public came round to George VI precisely because he was vulnerable, unpretentious, decent and dogged.'[12]

But this was to be generous to the King or, rather, to his admirers. There was no getting away from the fact that George VI 'was surrounded by courtiers and equerries whose world-views were, if anything, more blinkered and reactionary than his own'. His private secretaries, Alexander Hardinge and his successor, Alan Lascelles, were 'snobbish, narrow-minded, obscurantist and completely lacking in flexibility and imagination'.[13]

Though inclined to be an overprotective parent, George was devoted to his daughters and took strength from his wife, whose charm and sense of fun carried him over the awkward moments. An acute observer of the first family, Chips Channon encapsulated the contrast between the public façade and the private reality:

All his mature life [George VI] has been entirely under the dominion of his wife. He is dull, he is dutiful and good-natured. He is completely uninteresting, undistinguished and a godawful bore! … He likes shooting and hates society and people, particularly witty or elegant or fashionable people who bring out his dullness. So does she, but she is mildly flirtatious in a very proper romantic old-fashioned Valentine sort of way … She makes every man feel chivalrous and gallant towards her, but, of late, she has been growing much too fat.[14]

The war was the making of the King. By choosing for his family to stay in Buckingham Palace and, overnight, at Windsor Castle throughout the Blitz, he and Queen Elizabeth came to symbolise Britain's determination to survive, though there were those who pointed out that Windsor was well out of the danger zone. Joe Kennedy, the American Ambassador in London who had a bolthole near the castle, earned himself the nickname Jittery Joe.

The King was lucky in having Churchill as his Prime Minister. His first choice to follow Neville Chamberlain had been his friend, the Foreign Secretary and arch appeaser Lord Halifax. If he had had his way, it is a near certainty that Britain would have suffered a humiliating submission to Hitler's territorial ambitions.

Initially suspicious of Churchill as an untrustworthy chancer (he was not alone in thinking this), he soon came to recognise Churchill's qualities as a leader. It helped that Churchill was a fervent royalist who kept the lines open to the Palace and was only too happy to adopt the King as the standard bearer of ultimate victory.

A recurring theme throughout the hostilities was togetherness. It was put at its simplest in the King's Christmas broadcast in 1941: 'It is serving each other and in sacrificing for our common good that we are finding our true life.'

The message was championed by the press and the BBC, and while there were critics who pointed out that the sacrifices were not evenly distributed, the doctrine was broadly accepted and the royal messenger applauded for delivering it. From then on, 'togetherness' was adopted as the royal rallying call for coping with a national crisis, most recently in response to the coronavirus. 'Together we are tackling this disease. I want to reassure you,' said the Queen in 2020, 'that if we remain united and resolute, then we will overcome it.'

It could have been her father speaking.

Elizabeth began her formal training as heir apparent with her appointment as a Counsellor of State. This meant that, together with her mother, she was empowered to act on behalf of the King when he was unavailable. From 1944, aged 18, she took on royal duties such as launching HMS *Vanguard*, the longest ship ever built in Britain, though also, as it turned out, the whitest of white elephants, which had to be taken out of service in the late 1950s, broken up and sold for scrap. From 1950, Elizabeth had access to Cabinet papers.

By now she was a practised broadcaster. Her first exposure to the airwaves had come in 1939 when she and Margaret spoke to their parents in Canada over the transatlantic telephone – a first for the royal family. The children finished their end of the rehearsed conversation by pinching the Queen's corgi to make him bark.

Seventeen months later, in October 1940, when Elizabeth was 14½, she undertook her first independent broadcast, a message to the children who had been sent abroad to escape the Blitz. Heard throughout North America, she told her listeners how she and her sister knew from experience 'what it means to be away from those we love most of all'. Margaret was allowed to join in at the end. 'My sister is by my side and we are both going to say good night to you. Come on Margaret.'

'Good night,' said a smaller voice. 'Good night and good luck to you all.'

Jock Colville, who was later to be Private Secretary to Elizabeth, was 'embarrassed by the sloppy sentiment' but 'her voice was most impressive' and it was what the public wanted.[15] So successful was the broadcast that the BBC put it on a gramophone record which sold impressively in America and across the Empire. No one was unkind enough to mention that the Princess had been addressing herself exclusively to the children of those wealthy enough to send them abroad, out of harm's way. Young evacuees in Britain, of which there were over a million in 1940, many of them living in deprived circumstances and also missing their parents, were not similarly favoured. But then, the chief purpose of the broadcast was to inspire America to join the fight.

A closer experience of how the other half lived came at the end of the war when Elizabeth signed on for training in driving and vehicle maintenance at No. 1 Mechanical Transport Training Centre at Aldershot. It was mainly a propaganda exercise:

While she was driven back every evening to spend the night at Windsor, the other women slept in dormitory huts. At lectures she was surrounded by officers, with the lower ranks sitting behind. At the intervals between lectures she was 'whisked away' by the officers and lunched in the officers' mess [though] later she managed to extricate herself from her praetorian guard and join the other women for a break.[16]

Photographs of her posed activities were in every newspaper and she was on the front cover of *Time*. The course ended on 16 April 1945, just before her birthday; she told her new friends how sorry she was that it was over.

The 1945 general election, which ousted Churchill in favour of Clement Attlee leading a Labour Government with a thumping majority, came as an unpleasant surprise to the King. But neither Attlee nor his senior ministers were revolutionaries intent on overthrowing the monarchy. Rather, they saw in the King the virtues of stability in an uncertain world. As Herbert Morrison, Labour's Deputy Leader, said later of Elizabeth, 'When the people cheer the Queen and sing her praises, they are also cheering our free democracy.' Or, as the nineteenth-century economist and constitutionalist Walter Bagehot put it more soberly, 'A family on the throne is an interesting idea … it brings the pride of sovereignty to the level of petty life.'

In relations with the Palace, Attlee was a smooth operator. He listened politely to any royal advice that came his way while making known his respect for the King's sense of duty and dedication to hard work: 'I knew that I would always get from him a well-balanced judgement.'[17]

On matters that the Prime Minister felt were of no great constitutional significance, he was happy to give way. It was without argument that he agreed to take the Order of the Garter out of politics and to place it in the King's gift. Whether he made good use of it was open to question. As A.J.P. Taylor observed:

The first list of his nominations contained the obvious war leaders. There followed in 1948: the Duke of Portland, Lord Harlech, the Earl of Scarborough, and Lord Cranworth. In 1951 there was a further batch; the Duke of Wellington, Lord Fortescue, and Lord Allendale. Who were these men? What had they done to deserve any honour, let alone the highest in the land? Did they even exist?[18]

They most certainly did, if only as personal friends of George VI.

It was not in the nature of the King to rock the political boat, though he did take issue over the suggestion that Hugh Dalton was to be appointed Foreign Secretary. One of the brightest of the Labour leadership, Dalton was the son of the chaplain and tutor to Prince George, later George V. As such, he might have been expected to show respect. Instead, 'My relations, as a minister, with the King, though perfectly correct, were quite cold and formal. Nor did he ever show any inclination to make them less so.'[19] From his stance on the left of the party, Dalton made no secret of his antipathy to hereditary privilege. After he lobbied for taking over at the Foreign Office where, he believed, he would be best placed to come to an accommodation with the Kremlin, the King made strenuous objection to the elevation of a class traitor.

When, in the event, Ernest Bevin went to the Foreign Office, George was convinced that he had forced the decision, though it is more than likely that Attlee himself decided to put a strong man, one who would stand up to the Russians, in charge of foreign affairs. A master of veiled intent, the Prime Minister let the King believe he had real influence. A clever economist, Dalton was thought by Attlee to be more suited to the Exchequer. While Elizabeth was not directly involved in these exchanges, the family gossip must have given her more than an inkling of the games politicians play in their relations with the Palace.

It was the royal tour of South Africa in early 1947 that gave Elizabeth her first opportunity to project her personality in a way that suggested she might have a mind of her own. To coincide with her 21st birthday, she delivered a broadcast, which would have met with Henry Marten's approval, celebrating 'our great imperial Commonwealth to which we all belong', a close-knit community of free nations with a common heritage and a shared future. It was an ideal that appealed to all progressives in the imperial camp, though not an entirely new concept. As early as 1943, a clear and compelling case for a new spirit of imperialism was made by the Army Bureau of Current Affairs for the benefit of the troops who might want to know more about what they were fighting for:

We no longer regard the Colonial Empire as a 'possession', but as a trust or responsibility. 'Imperialism' in the less reputable sense of that term is dead: there is obviously no room for it in the British Commonwealth of equal nations, and it has been superseded by the principle of trusteeship for Colonial peoples, in which the interests and welfare of the native peoples are regarded as paramount. The conception of trusteeship is already passing into the more active one of partnership, and we have declared that our aim for all the Colonial peoples is to help them towards the goal already attained by the Dominions, namely full self-government. We are the only Colonial Power (if we exclude the United States) which has declared such an objective for its Colonies, and we are already actively implementing that policy.[20]

As was soon to emerge, the devil was in the detail, not least in South Africa where racial harmony was distinctly out of fashion. But the message of Unity in Diversity was taken up enthusiastically by the press at home and by the Palace, where Alan Lascelles, the King's Private Secretary, declared the speech to be of such quality as to leave him 'completely satisfied [with the] feeling that not a single word should be altered'.

Aside from Elizabeth's contribution, the South African tour was a disaster. The timing was unfortunate. When the royal party set sail from Portsmouth on 1 February, heading for two months of bright sunshine, Britain was suffering the worst winter on record. With heavy snowfalls and temperatures down to sub-zero, ordinary life was reduced to a stultifying grind. Bread rationing was introduced for the first time in British history.

When the King heard of the publicity backlash he began to regret ever having agreed to the tour. There was talk of making a hurried return to Britain, until the Queen pointed out that he could do nothing to ease the crisis and Attlee signalled his opposition to a cancellation which would 'magnify unduly the extent of the difficulties we are facing … especially in the eyes of foreign observers'.

More trouble followed closely on arrival. Though it is hard to believe, it came as a surprise to the royal visitors that the division between the races was rigorously enforced. A diplomatic embarrassment threatened when, on presenting medals to Black South African servicemen, the King was told he could not speak to them or shake their hands. The rule did not apply to white South African servicemen. Never an easy-tempered man, the King made his displeasure known but was told that he had no choice but to follow the instructions of the South African Government. Everywhere the royal party went, white policemen, heavily armed, were present in force.[21]

Dissembling wildly, Britain's High Commissioner reported 'a complete absence of unfortunate incidents' and credited the tour with a softening of Nationalist animosity towards those who, half a century earlier, had fought the Dutch settlers into submission. The real state of affairs was not lost on the heir to the throne. After the Nationalists entered the long nightmare of apartheid, Elizabeth was not to visit South Africa again until racial discrimination had been abolished.

If the guiding spirit for Elizabeth's intellectual awakening had been Henry Marten, the next stage of her development was influenced by Dermot Morrah, who had written the script for her South African broadcast. Morrah was a *Times* journalist, a romantic royalist who was Arundel Herald Extraordinary, an honorary appointment that gave him access to royal ceremonials where his expertise on heraldry and genealogy was highly regarded.

Having made his mark in South Africa, Morrah was called upon to put together an illustrated biography to celebrate Elizabeth's coming of age. In this, he presented his subject as the 'foremost representative of the younger generation' who looked to her as 'the personification of their aspirations and ideals'. It was a fanciful image with less appeal to the target audience than to the middle aged and elderly, who wanted to keep the lid on a rebellious spirit that was beginning to show itself among teenagers.

As far as it is known, Elizabeth made no objection to the role model allotted to her, though it came back to haunt her later in the decade when her innate conservatism was called into question.

# 2

# THE KING IS DEAD, LONG LIVE THE QUEEN

The all-pervading gloom of post-war Britain was dispersed, if only temporarily, by the marriage of Princess Elizabeth to Lieutenant Philip Mountbatten in November 1947. The couple had been on nodding acquaintance for some time. It was said that Elizabeth had been only 13 when Philip had caught her eye. Fanciful though this may be, as early as 1941, the politician and socialite Chips Channon confided to his diary that a marriage was forthcoming.

However, it was another five years before Philip made the traditional request to the father of his future bride. The response from the King was for a postponement of a formal engagement until Elizabeth's 21st birthday the following April. Doubtless he genuinely believed his daughter to be too young to commit to a lifelong partnership, but there were other matters to be addressed, not least Philip's mixed Greek and German ancestry.

His father was Prince Andrew, the youngest brother of King Constantine of Greece, both of whom were banished in 1927 following their country's defeat by Turkey. After his parents split up, Philip, aged 8, was sent to Britain to live with his Mountbatten relatives and subsequently to be educated at Gordonstoun, famous for fresh air and cold showers, before going to Dartmouth Naval College in 1939. A commendable war record was all well and good but Philip was lacking in one vital respect. He did not have British nationality.

The restoration of the Greek monarchy with the assistance of British troops to put down communist opposition brought further complications and unfavourable press comment. It was no help that four of Philip's sisters had married Germans. Courtiers who had the King's ear warned of a matinee idol fortune hunter who could not be trusted with the palace silver.

If this was not aggravating enough, a further irritation for the King was the persistent lobbying of Lord Louis (Dickie) Mountbatten, second cousin once removed of Elizabeth, and Philip's uncle, guardian and mentor, who made no secret of his mission to blend the two sides of his family. As a naval hero and last Viceroy of India, Mountbatten had an aura of glamour, but he could be duplicitous and his pushiness was much resented in the royal family as it had been among his fellow officers.

Though admired for his war record and his efforts in bringing about independence for India, he was inclined to behave as if his colleagues, no matter how senior, were his underlings. In his pithy style, Field Marshal Sir Gerald Templar told Mountbatten, 'If you swallowed a nail, you'd shit a corkscrew.' Not surprisingly, the King was wary of this self-appointed marriage broker.

The prospect of a royal wedding excited more press attention than any other event in Elizabeth's formative years. In January 1947, the *Sunday Pictorial* conducted a poll of its readers asking if 'our future Queen' should wed Philip, a foreigner of uncertain lineage. On the first count, 55 per cent favoured the marriage as a love match, a figure that rose to 64 per cent in the second week. Women readers were overwhelmingly supportive. Mountbatten worked tirelessly on his Fleet Street connections to ensure that his ward was portrayed as a clean-living, fun-loving dashing young naval officer. In March 1947, Philip was granted British nationality and received into the Anglican Church.

Three weeks after the royal party returned from South Africa came the official announcement of Elizabeth's engagement to the newly created Duke of Edinburgh. The newspapers were enchanted. Even the *Express*, an inveterate opponent of any expenditure regarded by Lord Beaverbrook as extravagant (he opposed the 1948 London Olympics and came out fighting against the 1951 Festival of Britain), championed a gala wedding as an antidote to the years of post-war austerity.

Not everyone was happy. Hostile questions from the republican element in the House of Commons put the government under pressure. In October, a Labour Member wanted to know how many clothing coupons had been allotted to Elizabeth's trousseau. He was told that 100 coupons had been granted to Elizabeth while the bridesmaids and pages had been allocated twenty-three and ten coupons respectively. As to decorations, only those in Whitehall and outside the Palace would be funded by the taxpayer, all else would have to be paid for by the Civil List. As it happened, this did not include the participation of the Household Cavalry in full dress uniform or the refurbishment of the State carriage.

Political point-scoring touched absurdity with the rumour that a consignment of silk from Lyon had been ordered for the bride's dress. From the Palace came the waspish response that while Chinese, not French, silkworms were providing the new material, the dress was to be woven in Scotland and Kent. The going-away dress would contain 4 or 5 yards of Lyon silk but this was to come from stock held by the dressmaker (Norman Hartnell) and thus would not have to be specially imported.[1]

Fears that Elizabeth would be deprived of her trousseau were much exaggerated, reported the *New York Times*, tongue in cheek:

Princess Elizabeth ... will have a new wedding gown fresh from the hands of one of London's smartest designers. This will enable her to fulfil the old tradition of wearing 'something old, something new, something borrowed, something blue'. Moreover, for Elizabeth there may still be a few garments left over from the South African trip to make up for the empty hope chest. Only last winter the British press brimmed over with descriptions of that glamorous hot-weather outfit, evoking some unpleasant, sullen murmurs from the labor ranks. Now the royal decision to suffer the same privations as 'Arry and 'Arriet should at least shame into silence [those] who don't 'give a tinker's cuss' what happens to anybody in England but the working man.[2]

As the big day approached, Philip gave signs of pre-marital nerves, a presentiment that maybe he was getting into something that was beyond his capacity to manage. Given the antipathy, even hostility, towards him from much of the royal household, his sentiments were understandable. According to a recent biographer, he shared his worries with the romantic novelist Daphne du Maurier when he stayed with her for a weekend in her Cornish home. There was no question of a sexual relationship with du Maurier, who was married in an on/off sort of way to General Sir Frederick 'Boy' Browning. The following year, Browning was to become

Comptroller and Treasurer to Princess Elizabeth. Du Maurier told Philip not to be silly, adding, if improbably, 'Your country needs you.'[3]

While Elizabeth tried to keep a low profile, Philip allowed himself to be portrayed as a fun-loving celebrity. On the eve of his marriage, he gave a bachelor party at the Dorchester. After the paparazzi had taken their pictures, Philip decided that he and his guests should reverse roles with the photographers. The following morning, the *Daily Mirror* ran two pictures, one of Philip and company, the other of the photographers snapped by Philip. It was a break with convention that delighted readers.

Predictably, there were tense meetings between the King and his bête noire, the Chancellor of the Exchequer. Hugh Dalton complained of the cost of adding Philip to the Civil List and renovating Clarence House, where the couple were to take up residence. Relations with the Exchequer improved markedly later in the year after Dalton, having let slip to a journalist a detail of his budget before it was presented to the House of Commons, was compelled to resign. The King got on well with Dalton's successor. Though outwardly austere, Sir Stafford Cripps was keen to move on from the distractions of royal funding. And he and the King had something in common. Both were addicted smokers who shared a passion for fine wine.

A souvenir book listed 2,428 wedding presents sent from all parts of the world. They ranged from a gold tiara from the Emperor of Ethiopia to a 'fringed lacework cloth' from Mahatma Gandhi. Queen Mary thought it was a loincloth of the sort habitually worn by the Indian leader, judging it to be almost indecent. One can imagine her giving a Lady Bracknell impersonation in the manner of Edith Evans. 'A LOINCLOTH?'

Among the general public there were a few grumbles at the outlay, but if the files of the opinion sampler Mass Observation are to be believed, the occasional resentment at wealthy privilege was heavily outweighed by a 'perception of national renewal'. Typical were the comments of a 46-year-old woman from Birmingham:

> I feel the royal wedding has put us back in the world's estimation before the Duke of Windsor threw his crown away. I feel it is the beginning of a new era. Already the impetus to do better, to create, to start to live, not exist from day to day has begun to manifest itself.[4]

A reminder that royal ceremonial could do with updating came with a protest from the Vatican that loyal addresses were limited to the Anglican Church, the Free Churches and two Jewish organisations. This was to exclude the representatives of 3.5 million Roman Catholics. Understandably, the Catholic hierarchy felt aggrieved.

There were few other complaints but some of the gilt on what was widely regarded as a momentous occasion came off a month after the wedding when the *Express* serialised the memoirs of the Duke of Windsor. He said little that was not already well known, but readers were happy to re-engage with a right royal scandal, an example of the contradictions inherent in the popular presentation of a family delegated to set standards that they themselves found impossible to meet. In its first month of publication, *A King's Story* sold 80,000 copies.

The last word on the royal wedding was left to the *Literary Gazette* in Moscow. The only Soviet mention of the celebration was headed 'A National Tragedy'. A creative Russian journalist reported 2,500 casualties among drunken revellers.[5]

While Clarence House was being made fit for habitation, the newlyweds moved in with the bride's parents. Lesser mortals on the waiting list for a semi-detached council house might have seen this as an enviable solution to a short-term problem. Philip would have set them right. With its 775 rooms and miles of corridors, Buckingham Palace was about as user friendly as the Taj Mahal. Retainers round every corner made privacy a rare privilege.

Philip found the atmosphere stifling, the more so for the offhand treatment he had to endure from prissy courtiers who had yet to be convinced that he was not an unscrupulous fortune hunter. The relationship with his mother-in-law was not easy. The Queen had a view on everything and was inclined to give her daughter unsolicited advice. Ever the dutiful child, Elizabeth listened and generally obeyed.

For now, however, Philip at least had a job to go to. Each morning he made his way to the Admiralty, a short way along the Mall, returning in the late afternoon, just like, it was suggested, any other young breadwinner. It helped to keep frustration at bay but it was not to last.

Elizabeth found it easier to slip into her new role, with a first notable decision on how to organise the distribution of the hundreds of tons of tinned food sent from communities abroad as wedding presents to be handed on to the needy. The Palace high command was inclined to shuffle off the responsibility to the Ministry of Food. Elizabeth was having none of that. With the help of the Women's Voluntary Service and requisitioning the kitchens in Buckingham Palace, thousands of attractively packed and well-assorted food parcels were dispatched to widows and pensioners throughout the kingdom, each containing a personal message from the Princess. The cost was reduced to almost nothing after the Post Office agreed to send the parcels free of charge.[6]

By late 1947, for those closest to the political heartbeat, the King's health was of growing concern. Suffering leg pains, yet impatient with medical fussing, it was the best part of a year before he could be persuaded to consult his doctors. In November 1948, they decided to call in Professor James Learmonth, the foremost specialist in vascular problems. Having diagnosed serious arteriosclerosis, the fear was of gangrene setting in, making it necessary to amputate the King's right leg.

Decisions now had to be made about the forthcoming royal tour of Australia and New Zealand. This had long been a highlight in the King's calendar and he was strenuously opposed to a cancellation or even a postponement. But with the Queen supporting the doctors, he agreed to a complete rest. With little regard for veracity, the medical bulletin insisted that the King's general health 'gives no reason for concern', though 'the strain of the last twelve years has appreciably affected his resistance to physical fatigue'.

He attended the christening of Charles, his first grandchild, at Buckingham Palace on 15 December, and was up to broadcasting the now traditional Christmas message. But while there could be no immediate return to full life, it was under protest. He chose, or was persuaded, to believe that the treatment he was undergoing would soon restore him to vigour. Meanwhile, he agreed to a 'right lumbar sympathectomy operation' to increase the blood supply to his leg. Carried out on 12 March 1949, it was judged to be successful as long as the patient cut back on his chain smoking and took things gently.

The faint hope for the King and Queen to visit Australia and New Zealand in 1952, albeit with a much reduced programme, receded in favour of sending Princess Elizabeth and the Duke of Edinburgh to carry the royal banner. The last occasion for George VI and his Queen to be at the centre of public attention was the 1951 Festival of Britain. Launched in the dying days of the Labour Government, the Festival was billed as a 'tonic to the nation', a pick-me-up for a weary people barely emerging from the doldrums of austerity while, at the same time, setting standards in design, technology and architecture for a golden future.

As the Festival's impresario, the former newspaper editor Gerald Barry was an energetic promoter of social innovation. But he was convinced equally that pride in the past was the prerequisite for national renewal. So it was that the Festival had to be got under way with a royal seal of approval. A service of dedication in St Paul's Cathedral was led by Geoffrey Fisher, Archbishop of Canterbury, who never missed an opportunity for a dedication to the Almighty with the King as his representative on earth.

A *Times* reporter described the scene outside the Cathedral:

> On either hand, running the length of the west portico and then down the steps to a lower terrace, was a scene of pageantry, with the scarlet and red and gold of uniforms, the tall white plumes, and the glister of helmets asserting the presence of the Honourable Corps of Gentlemen-at-Arms, the King's Body Guard of the Yeomen of the Guard, and Yeomen Warders of the Tower.
>
> On a lower level stood the state trumpeters of the Household Cavalry, in their slashed gold coats, and in front of the dais pursuivants and heralds in their richly worked tabards had taken up their stations ... In a place of prominence the Lord Mayor of London, in his robes, bore high the Pearl Sword of the City ... These formed the tableau of which the King became the centre.[7]

After the service, attended by a 3,000-strong congregation, the opening ceremony was on the steps of St Paul's, where a pigeon-proof dais had been erected.

The King, in naval uniform, spoke confidently: 'I see this Festival as a symbol of Britain's abiding courage and vitality ... we look back with pride and forward with resolution.' Unfortunately, few of those present heard a single word. At the behest of the BBC, the microphones could not be used to amplify the King's voice for fear of creating an echo on the nationwide broadcast.

There were those who found it odd that an occasion for looking forward should start with a recreation of medieval pageantry. But too much can be made of the Festival as a crusade for modernism. Linked events across the country were predominantly nostalgic with maypole dancing, bowls tournaments and cricket matches on the village green. One of the Festival team who chose to remain anonymous detected the first sign of the British Disease, when 'we stopped trying to lead the world as an industrial power and started being the world's entertainers, coaxing tourists to laugh at our eccentricities, marvel at our tradition and wallow in our nostalgia'.

The King and Queen were on parade again for the opening of the Festival Hall when George led the audience in a standing ovation for Malcolm Sargent's boisterous arrangement of 'Rule, Britannia!', soon to be a staple of the annual Promenade concerts at the Albert Hall. Afterwards, the King told Sargent that 'Rule, Britannia!' should be played at every concert. It had to be put to him, tactfully, that this would not always be appropriate.[8]

Later in the year, Elizabeth and Philip set off on a tour of Canada and the United States. By now it was known to all in the Palace circle that the King was gravely ill. Well, not quite all. The King himself was kept in ignorance. X-rays revealed a malignant cancer in his left lung, making another operation a matter of urgency. To soften the blow, the King was not told the true reason for his incapacity. The shroud of secrecy was accepted by a submissive press which stuck to upbeat reporting on royal affairs. Even when it was announced that Elizabeth and Philip would take on the royal tour of Australia and New Zealand the following year, speculation was muted.

Across the Atlantic, Elizabeth was under increasing strain. Criticised for rarely smiling at public functions, the French community in Canada found reason to voice its opposition to a symbol of British sovereignty. But Elizabeth could be forgiven for her preoccupation. At the time of her marriage, she might confidently have expected to remain next in line to the throne for at least twenty years. Now, intimations of her father's mortality were bringing the prospect of succession ever closer. For a 25-year-old, still working her way into her role as a wife and mother, this must have been a daunting prospect.

If the Canadian tour fell short of expectations, the royal visit to Washington was a great success, largely because President Truman was determined to make it so. Piling on the compliments, he described Elizabeth as a 'fairy princess'.

The family was reunited for Christmas at Sandringham, where spirits were lifted by the presence of 6-month-old Princess Anne. As the doctors had declared themselves 'very well satisfied with the King's progress', he was seen out on a shoot. On the morning of 31 January, the King and Queen with Churchill, now back in office after the October 1951 general election, gathered at London Airport to see off Elizabeth and Philip on the first leg of their journey to New Zealand and Australia. Also in the party was Lord Ismay, Churchill's former Chief of Staff and now his Secretary of State for Commonwealth Relations. Though looking gaunt and skeletal, the King was in good spirits:

> Although it was a bitterly cold and windy morning, His Majesty walked out to inspect the aeroplane and then climbed to the roof of the Royal waiting-room to wave good-bye. On his return he suggested to his Prime Minister that in view of the intense cold, a little whisky might be permissible. Mr Churchill said that he had already taken precautions. 'Already?' asked the King. 'Yes, sir,' the Prime Minister replied: 'When I was younger I made it a rule never to take strong drink before lunch. It is now my rule never to do so before breakfast.'[9]

As a preliminary to the chief business of the royal route, the royal couple stopped off in Kenya for what was billed as a five-day holiday. Their hosts saw it as more than that. Though not officially acknowledged, here was a country on the edge of insurrection. The warning signals had been put up by Arthur Creech Jones, Colonial Secretary under the Labour Government. 'There is in Kenya,' he declared, 'a civilisation of the dominant race, supported by cheap labour and that kind of society is intolerable.'

It was not the view of Sir Philip Mitchell, who served as Governor from 1944 to 1952. A colonial administrator of long standing and a gifted linguist who spoke several African languages, Mitchell, having started out as a progressive, was ending his career as a hardline white supremacist. His response to Creech Jones was to accuse him of losing touch with reality, 'as if there was yet any reason to suppose that an African can be cashier to a village council for three weeks without stealing the cash'.

Mitchell pushed hard for a royal visit to boost the confidence of white settlers. They could stay at Sagana, a fishing lodge that had been given to them as a wedding present, and at Treetops, a three-bedroomed hotel, 20 miles away in the Kenyan forest where elephants, baboons, warthogs and other exotic wildlife could be viewed from a safe height. But the dangers were not from animals. Sagana Lodge and Treetops were in the heart of Kikuya homeland where civil unrest, led by a secret society known as Mau Mau, was threatening to get out of hand.

Bearing in mind what happened not long afterwards, with a native uprising leading to thousands of lives lost, property destroyed (Treetops was burned down), savage repression and multiple executions, protecting the heir to the throne might have been given a higher priority. As it happened, events 4,000 miles away soon took precedence over concerns about security.

Elizabeth was at a state dinner at Treetops the night her father died. The news was cabled to Government House in Nairobi the following morning. After a delay in decoding the message (the codebook was locked in a safe and there was some difficulty in finding the key), Philip was told the news and it was Philip who had to console his wife as the couple walked together in the garden. The Queen did not break down nor show any strong emotion but made a conscious effort to apologise to those around her for spoiling the rest of their visit to Kenya.

George VI had died in his sleep. It was his valet, bringing his morning cup of tea, who found him. The official announcement from Sandringham stated that he had retired to rest 'in his usual health', a pronouncement that must surely have given his doctors a twinge of embarrassment. Churchill was still in bed when he was brought the news from the Palace. 'When I went to the Prime Minister's bedroom,' recorded Jock Colville, now Joint Principal Secretary to the Prime Minister:

> ... he was sitting alone with tears in his eyes, looking straight in front of him and reading neither his official papers nor the newspapers. I had not realised how much the King meant to him. I tried to cheer him up by saying how well he would get on with the new Queen, but all he could say was that he did not know her and that she was only a child.[10]

In fact, Churchill had met Elizabeth at least once, albeit when she was only 2 years old. In 1928, after a visit to Balmoral, he told Clementine that the princess was 'a character' with 'an air of authority ... astonishing in an infant'.[11]

While Elizabeth was flying home, the blueprint for national mourning at the death of George V, sixteen years earlier, was adopted without fuss. As carpenters at Sandringham built a coffin of oak from the estate, the House of Commons and House of Lords adjourned for the Accession Council when MPs and peers took the Oath of Allegiance.

All cinemas and theatres were closed, BBC programmes were cancelled except for news bulletins and solemn music, public functions and most sports fixtures were postponed, and flags were flown at half-mast. As Earl Marshal, responsible for public ceremonies involving the royal family, the Duke of Norfolk made it known that for the three days of mourning all men should wear black armbands and black ties. Many, if not the majority of citizens, followed his instructions.

George's elder brother and predecessor, the Duke of Windsor, arrived on the 13th. He travelled alone, having left his Duchess, the former Wallis Simpson, to sit out the royal funeral in New York. This concession to his sister-in-law, who was unforgiving on the matter of the abdication, was not enough to secure him an invitation to Buckingham Palace. Instead, he stayed with his mother, the 85-year-old Queen Mary, at Marlborough House, where he heard the unwelcome news that his £10,000 a year allowance, paid as a personal favour by the late King, would now cease.

The new Queen and the Duke flew from Entebbe to El Aden (now Tobruk International) in Libya, then an RAF station, where a British Overseas Airways Argonaut jet was waiting to carry them to London. During the journey a radio message from the Queen Mother was copied on to a BOAC signal form and handed to Elizabeth:

To Her Majesty, all my thoughts and prayers are with you. Mummie.

A statement from Downing Street appealed for the public to stay away from London Airport.

The first indelible image of the new reign was of the young Queen stepping off the plane to be met by Churchill and a bevy of elderly, black-suited Privy Councillors. She had had warning of what to expect. As the younger brother of the King, it fell to Prince Henry, Duke of Gloucester, to board the plane to be the first to greet the Queen. Thus briefed, she descended the passenger stairs in a brisk, businesslike manner.

At her first Privy Council she made her Accession Declaration, resolving to follow her father's example of service and devotion. And in a broadcast to the nation, she looked forward to her coronation, for which she was preparing 'with prayer and meditation'. She appealed to her audience to 'Pray for me on the day. Pray that God may give me wisdom and strength to carry out the solemn promises I shall be making.'

The King's lying-in-state at Westminster Hall attracted huge crowds. On the first day, 12 February, close to 80,000 filed past the catafalque. Many had waited in queues the entire night. 'In the hours before dawn those without blankets stamped on the frosty pavement to keep warm.'[12] It was originally intended to close the doors at 10.00 p.m., but such was the crush, it was 2.00 a.m. before the doors at the northern exit were shut behind the last of the mourners. A *Times* reporter wrote:

> The scene within Westminster Hall was at once majestic yet simple in all its impressive solemnity. The lying-in-state was majestic as befits a king; the people's homage was a simple and ready expression of their affection towards a man who had passed from among them. The many thousands who entered Westminster Hall did not feel that they had come merely to see the King lying in state; rather did they know that they were taking part in the common tribute to a beloved Sovereign.

In all, over three days, some 300,000 people attended the lying-in-state.

For those who were not eyewitnesses, a memorable account was provided by the radio commentary of Richard Dimbleby. A rotund, avuncular figure with a seductive delivery of carefully modulated diction, Dimbleby had honed his broadcasting skills as a war reporter for the invasion of Europe. Sad or jolly as circumstances dictated, he found favour with the Palace where his mellifluous tones and overly reverential manner were thought to give royalty the required lustre. Malcolm Muggeridge dubbed him 'Royal Microphone in Waiting'.

The first part of his radio commentary transmitted on 12 February gives the flavour of his delivery:

> They are passing, in their thousands, through the hall of history while history is being made. No one knows from where they come or where they go, but they are the people, and to watch them pass is to see the nation pass.

It is very simple, this Lying-in-State of a dead King, and of incomparable beauty ... There lies the coffin of the King.

The oak of Sandringham, hidden beneath the rich golden folds of the Standard; the slow flicker of the candles touches gently the gems of the Imperial Crown, even that ruby that King Henry wore at Agincourt. It touches the deep purple of the velvet cushion and the cool, white flowers of the only wreath that lies upon the flag. How moving can such simplicity be. How real the tears of those who pass and see it, and come out again, as they do at this moment in an unbroken stream, to the cold, dark night and a little privacy for their thoughts ...

He ended:

For how true tonight of George the Faithful is that single sentence spoken by an unknown man of his beloved father: 'The sunset of his death tinged the whole world's sky.'

Three days later, on a cloudy and misty morning, a mile-long cortege began its slow journey from Westminster Hall to Paddington Station. Big Ben rang fifty-six chimes, one for every year of the King's life. Artillery salutes of fifty-six guns were fired in Hyde Park and at the Tower of London.

In a carriage behind the coffin came the Queen, the Queen Mother, Princess Margaret and the Princess Royal, all in black, followed on foot by the four royal dukes – Edinburgh, Gloucester, Windsor and Kent. It was a study in contrasts. A top hat sat uncomfortably on the head of the 17-year-old Duke of Kent, his long hair poking out under the brim. Bringing up the rear were heads of state, foreign royals, ambassadors and other dignitaries.

From Paddington, the coffin was taken by train to Windsor for burial in St George's Chapel. The government sent a wreath of white lilac and carnations. The card attached was in Churchill's writing. It read, simply, 'For Valour', the inscription on the Victoria Cross.

In his broadcast tribute, Churchill rose to the considerable heights of his flowery rhetoric, ignoring any strict regard for the truth. Who would have imagined that the King had been kept from knowing the seriousness of his illness hearing Churchill's rich tones? 'The King walked with death as if death were a companion, an acquaintance, whom he recognised and did not fear. In the end, death came as a friend.'

He finished on an ecstatic note:

I, whose youth was passed in the august, unchallenged and tranquil glories of the Victorian era, may well feel a thrill in invoking once more the prayer and the anthem, 'God Save the Queen'.

# 3

# OPENING MOVES

Five days after the death of George VI, while Britain was in the throes of one of its periodic financial crises, the Cabinet found time to discuss the date of the coronation. As housing minister and soon-to-be contender for the party leadership, Harold Macmillan noted in his diary, 'There was general agreement that it should not be this year. This year the bailiffs may be in; the Crown itself may be in pawn.'

'It'll have a steadying effect next year,' said Churchill. 'Anyway it will beat the Festival of Britain.'

Churchill was on good form, having apparently made a quick recovery from his grief over the loss of his royal soulmate. A tease of James Stuart, Secretary of State for Scotland, as to whether Elizabeth should be the second or first north of the border led on to the future of the Stone of Scone, stolen from Westminster Abbey at Christmas 1950 by four young Scottish nationalists and recovered four months later. 'We decided,' wrote Macmillan, 'to take it out of the cellar in which it is now guarded and put it back in its place.'[1]

Memories of the Festival of Britain rankled with Churchill. By securing the endorsement of the Palace, he felt that the Labour Government had used the King to support socialist propaganda. But he objected even more strongly to the Festival as an exclusively civil affair with no role for the Commonwealth and Empire or for the armed forces. It was a stunted Britain on display, argued Churchill. He was not about to commit the same mistake with the coronation. This was to be his swansong and he was determined to make the most of it.

The proclamation signed by the Queen on 6 June 1952 put the date of the coronation one year ahead, 2 June 1953. At the same time, forty-two members of the Privy Council were appointed to an exclusively male Coronation Committee. Two royal dukes, Edinburgh and Gloucester, were supported by a dozen hereditary peers. The archbishops of Canterbury and York spoke for the Church, while senior government ministers had the right of attendance along with spokesmen for the opposition parties, Attlee, Herbert Morrison and former Home Secretary James Chuter Ede, who were considered closest to the man in the street.

Not that they were asked to contribute very much. The coronation was to be an almost exclusively upper-class affair presided over by the old-school political elite. There was a contradiction here. Was not the aristocracy supposed to be a thing of the past?

At a critical stage in Britain's fortunes, George Orwell had predicted that the war would sweep away the old class system to make way for a society in which equality counted for more than hereditary privilege. 'The war,' he wrote, 'and the revolution are inseparable.' In castigating a decaying and stupid ruling class ('the half pay colonel with his bull neck and diminutive brain'),[2] Orwell rejected Soviet totalitarianism. What he anticipated was a new kind of democratic 'English Socialism' which made freedom from want the basis for all other freedoms.

The second half of the 1940s was strong on evidence that Orwell had got it right. With punitive taxation rising to 93 per cent on incomes above £15,000 a year, Britain was well on the way to an egalitarian society. The gap between the highest and lowest paid had never been narrower. In 1952–53, there were only thirty-five people in the entire country who had a net income after tax of £6,000. Death duties, set in 1915 at 20 per cent for fortunes over £2 million, increased to 65 per cent in 1940 and to 80 per cent on estates over £1 million after 1949.[3]

The financial battering of the landed aristocracy was nothing new. Its troubles pre-dated the war with the collapse of agricultural prices. Noël Coward satirised the trend with 'The Stately Homes of England', written for his 1938 show, *Operette*. Four 'scions of a noble breed' sang of 'those homes serene and stately, which only lately, seem to have run to seed … the fact that they have to be rebuilt and frequently mortgaged to the hilt is inclined to take the gilt off the gingerbread'.

The gentry had more to worry about in the wake of the 1939 Emergency Powers Act. This allowed for the requisition at short notice of country mansions and their surrounding land for relocated government departments, evacuated schools, convalescent centres and military quarters. Compensation, based on the low rentals of the 1930s, was bogged down, often for years, in a bureaucratic quagmire.

Those who came off worst were deposed by the military. Impatient for action, the rank and file were none too respectful of grand architecture and manicured gardens. At Melford Hall in Suffolk, described by *Country Life* as 'one of the most perfect Tudor houses that have come down to us', the entire north wing was destroyed by a fire started by junior officers the worse for drink.[4] It was by no means an atypical example.

Requisitioned by the army in 1939, Rolls Park in Essex was occupied by eighteen different regiments. The Tudor staircase was chopped up for firewood, paintings were defaced beyond repair, and an enemy V1 flying bomb took off part of the roof. The government offered a grant of £8,000 for repairs reckoned to cost seven times as much. In 1953, the house was demolished.[5]

The owners who did regain possession were not at all sure that the government was granting any favours. Even where there was money for restoration, building restrictions hampered work. But all too often, money was not on tap. With farm rents pegged below the rate of inflation, the return to the family home was, for many, hardly worth the effort. The last straw was to find that once loyal retainers had moved on to more remunerative careers. The servant class, over a million strong in 1939, had all but vanished.

The option for coping with over-large houses that could not be kept up was to knock them down. The highly visible evidence of a feudal class on the verge of extinction was the wrecking ball burying history under piles of rubble. From 1946 to 1950, seventy-eight houses that today would qualify for preservation were sacrificed, the contents sold off at bottom prices before the wreckers took over. Over the next five years, the peak period, the annual loss jumped to 204. In coronation year, country mansions were falling at a rate of one every two and a half days.

The implications were not lost on the royal family, stationed as it was at the pinnacle of what many saw as an outmoded social structure. In his darker moments, George VI sensed his world collapsing around him. When in 1947 he honoured Vita Sackville-West, author, poet, gardener and wife of Harold Nicolson, with the Companion of Honour, he asked after Knole, her childhood home and one of England's grandest country mansions. As Nicolson recorded, 'She said it had gone to the National Trust.' The King had raised his hands in despair. 'Everything is going nowadays. Before long, I shall have to go.'[6]

And yet, despite its disabilities, proof that the aristocracy had staying power was there for all to see in the composition of the wartime government. An aristocrat in all but title, Churchill was the grandson of a duke and related to a string of hereditary titles. When he took power in 1940, his administration was shaped by upper-class luminaries with, notably, Anthony Eden, described by Beatrice Webb as 'an aristocratic country squire', as Foreign Secretary and presumed successor. In Whitehall and across the country, jobs of national importance went to the entrenched elite, while in the military even Bernard Montgomery, the self-styled soldiers' friend, was descended from a long line of Ulster squires. Alan Brooke, Chief of the Imperial General Staff, was similarly privileged. Churchill's favourite general, the urbane Harold Alexander, son of the 4th Earl of Caledon, rose to be Supreme Allied Commander Mediterranean and, as Earl Alexander of Tunis, served in Churchill's post-war government as Minister of Defence. 'It is not altogether fanciful,' concludes David Cannadine, 'to see the European war as the reassertion of upper-class leadership against the upstart corporals and petty duces of the Fascist powers.'[7]

A helping hand to the aristocracy to keep going was unexpectedly provided by the post-war Labour Government, committed, in theory, to putting an end to hereditary privilege. On the principle that the best things in life should be shared with ordinary citizens, Hugh Dalton, as Chancellor of the Exchequer, set up a National Land Fund to accept historic houses and land in lieu of death duties. At the same time, the National Trust was encouraged to adopt historic houses to be leased or rented back to their previous owners. By 1950, there were fifty-two houses in the care of the trust.

The nobility was further emboldened by legislation introduced by the outgoing Labour administration and adopted by its Tory successors. The 1953 Finance Act extended the concession whereby stately houses could be handed over to pay for death duties to include works of art and other contents. Moreover, the National Land Fund was empowered to put money upfront to buy houses and contents on the understanding that these would be handed over to the National Trust. With the Historic Buildings and

Ancient Monuments Act came Historic Buildings Councils for England, Scotland and Wales to advise the Ministry of Works on the payment of restoration and conservation grants to owners of historic houses. The machinery set up is essentially the same today with the addition, from 1975, of tax exemptions to owners who open their houses to the public for sixty days a year.[8]

To support their way of life, several of the aristocracy revealed an unsuspected talent for showmanship. Having inherited Longleat, a 118-roomed mansion, the Marquess of Bath opened the house to paying visitors. It was a huge success. In the first year, 135,000 people came to view, a figure that speedily increased to 250,000. Others of the nobility with a flair for business soon followed. Lord Montagu of Beaulieu turned his home into a motoring museum while the Duke of Bedford made Woburn Abbey a centre for all the fun of the fair. It was a form of reaching out to the public that had lessons for the royals.

The rising profession of accountancy was quick to sign up aristocratic clients to advise on claiming against tax on what might loosely be described as business expenses. For one stately home owner, this included a swimming pool, technically open to the public, but in reality used exclusively by the family. A kitchen equipped to provide sandwich lunches and cream teas for paying visitors could also meet the more substantial needs of the private dining room. By the time of the coronation, there were more private houses open to the public than in the National Trust.

There were other ways in which fortune favoured a revival of aristocracy. By handing over family wealth to the heirs three years ahead of death, estate duty could be avoided altogether. The period of grace was soon extended to five years and later to seven. Even so, with sensible planning, estate duties became almost voluntary. When they were imposed, for the landed gentry there was comfort to be had in the knowledge that, from 1949, agricultural land qualified for 45 per cent relief.

More good news came with the revival of the art market, though the beneficiaries were slow to catch on to this abundant source of income. As custodians of national treasures, the aristocracy had a poor record. The typical occupant of a stately home was more interested in shooting and fishing than in rare paintings or books. Ancestral art collections, with pictures too numerous to be put up on the walls, were often stowed away, unloved, in the attics. At Kenwood, bordering Hampstead Heath, its fabulous art collection, including Turner's *Lee Shore*, Vermeer's *Guitar Player* and Rembrandt's *Self-Portrait*, now all on public view, was in the charge of a caretaker who left the key to the depository under a dustbin.

Early post-war collectors were short of funds, but with economic recovery and the reappearance of wealthy American buyers, the art market began to take off. The big auction houses, Christie's and Sotheby's, were able to demonstrate that the hard-up gentry had hitherto unsuspected assets in plain sight. At Eaton Hall, the Duke of Westminster's massive Victorian pile, taken over by the army for training National Service officers, there hung over the main staircase *The Adoration of the Magi*. Used as a target for bread rolls to enliven mess dinners, the painting was valued at a mere £7,500 in 1950. Less than a decade later, it was sold for a record £275,000 (£5.225 million in today's money). The buyer, a property tycoon, found a more congenial home for the Reubens masterpiece by presenting it to King's College, Cambridge.

The massive death duties landed on the Devonshires after a quick succession of fatalities – the 9th Duke in 1938, the heir to the 10th Duke in 1944 and the 10th Duke himself in 1952 – were eventually covered by the handing over of Hardwick House and contents, and by selling half a dozen of Chatsworth's treasures. Later, the Duke raised an endowment fund of £215 million for Chatsworth by disposing of a couple of paintings ('not his best') and duplicates from his library.[9]

With the rise in land values, selling off part of an estate to support the rest became commonplace. At the lower end of the scale, a patch of land sold with planning permission to a speculative builder, this in the days before capital gains tax, was a handy supplement. Moreover, the loss of land through enforced sales was often more than outweighed by the increased worth of that which was left. Of the great landed estates of the nineteenth century, over half were still in place in the 1950s, albeit with a reduced acreage. With farming qualifying for subsidies from 1947, the countryside became something of a tax haven.

The aristocratic influence on government was cut back after 1949 when the delaying power of the House of Lords was reduced from two years to one (the privilege whereby a peer accused of treason and felony had the right to be tried by his fellow peers had gone the year before). But abolishing the hereditary right to sit in the Upper Chamber was put on the back burner and the Lords continued to provide a platform for the antediluvian element to sound off against any progressive measures while the upper-class hold on the Tory Party remained strong. 'Beyond question, Churchill's 1951 administration which brought back many of his cronies from the Second World War was more authentically aristocrat than any since the National Governments of the 1930s.'[10]

By the early 1950s the aristocratically led social round was back to full strength. After the Royal Academy's summer exhibition came the Chelsea Flower Show, the 4th of June at Eton, Royal Ascot, Henley Regatta, Harrow Speech Day, the Eton and Harrow match at Lords, Cowes Week, Goodwood, the International Horse Show at White City, the Dublin Horse Show and the St Leger, with the celebrity magazines working overtime to give full coverage to the parade of the class elite.

For 1953, the event that was to outshine all else in the London season was the crowning of the young Queen, a triumphal confirmation of all the aristocracy stood for or, at least, that was the hope of those who had most to gain. One of the first tasks of the Coronation Committee was to set up an executive committee to do the hard work. This was to be chaired by the Duke of Edinburgh, with the Duke of Norfolk as Earl Marshal, his deputy. A florid and portly 45-year-old, the senior Catholic peer had seen out the war as Agricultural Secretary.

Trading on his experience of organising the coronation of George VI, he took control of all to do with the coronation service, though he had to contend with being upstaged by David Eccles, Minister for Wales, an ambitious career politician who combined elegance and arrogance, earning the tag 'Smarty Boots'.

Ironically for one who was to become an imaginative education minister and arts minister, the first task for Eccles under Churchill's 1951 government had been to remove any visible sign that the Festival of Britain had ever existed. It counted against his best instincts but he was not about to sully his first weeks in office by picking a losing battle with the Prime Minister. The Festival was a lost cause, while the coronation was his opportunity to make his mark as a political high-flier.

A stage manager, Eccles made sure that he was constantly in the public eye. The joke was of a general uncertainty as to who was being crowned, Elizabeth or Eccles. His unguarded reference to the Queen as his 'perfect leading lady' was picked up by Randolph Churchill, who used it to belittle a rival for his father's attention.

Throughout the preparations for the coronation, Churchill remained high spirited. Knowing full well there were voices in his government, not least those of the supporters of Anthony Eden, for the Old Man to stand aside for a younger leader, he also knew that no one would dare to try forcing him out in a year of renewal and celebration.

But there was more to it than that. Here was his chance to end his career in a blaze of glory while giving his party a kickstart that would carry it through to victory in the next general election. The coronation was to be the biggest, grandest event ever staged for a royal celebration. If the Festival of Britain had been planned as a 'tonic to the nation', the coronation was to be more like a massive injection of adrenalin.

Churchill was besotted with Elizabeth. He saw himself in the role of counsellor and friend to the young Queen, much as Lord Melbourne had served as a surrogate father to the 18-year-old Queen Victoria. Both were charmers, given to sentimental overdrive, both were witty and urbane, and both were addicted to the royal cause. But there the similarities ended. Melbourne had been 58 when he entered Victoria's life. Though his judgement was often faulty and his private life hardly beyond reproach, a winning personality kept him by Victoria's side rather longer than was strictly necessary for effective government.

Churchill, on the other hand, was 78 and losing his grip. Stories abounded of how incomprehensible appointments were made because Churchill forgot faces and muddled up names. Men called to Downing Street found themselves addressed as someone else, and some, though they served in his ministry, never did succeed in establishing in the mind of the Prime Minister who they actually were. 'I have sent for you,' Churchill told Sir William Hayter, Britain's Ambassador to the Kremlin, 'in order to make your acquaintance.' But this was the third outing for Sir William and the third occasion on which Churchill had said the same thing.[11]

Though it was not obvious to the people who voted him back into office, Churchill was simply not up to the job. While six years of opposition had sharpened his appetite for power, and while his oratory was still feared by politicians who incurred his wrath, his capacity for government had been diminished by a sybaritic lifestyle, ill-suited to an overweight septuagenarian:

He was going deaf and losing his once formidable powers of memory and concentration. He smoked and ate and drank too much. The arteries which fed the brain were closing up, the nerves in his back had been affected, and according to Lord Moran [his doctor] had never fully recovered from a stroke which he had sustained some eighteen months earlier while staying with Lord Beaverbrook in the South of France.[12]

As one of the more recent of Churchill's biographers, Roy Jenkins rejects the parallel of Churchill and Melbourne. While Churchill was 'imbued with romantic feelings … for the person of his new Sovereign', the fact that 'Queen Elizabeth was a little older [than Victoria at the start of her reign], already had a husband and because he had more other things to do, [the relationship] was less cloying than that of Melbourne with the young Victoria'.[13] But this is to underestimate Churchill's craving for attention and his denial of the penalties of old age. His infatuation with his literary agent, the vivacious Wendy Russell, proved his capacity for making a fool of himself with a young woman.

Churchill's devotion to the Queen knew no bounds. He had her photograph by his bedside and was ever eager to attend the Palace in frock coat and top hat for a lengthy weekly audience with the young woman he hailed as 'wife and mother … heir to all our traditions and all our glories'. The Queen returned the compliment by appointing Churchill to the Order of the Garter which, thanks to her father, was exclusively in the royal gift. So it was that the Prime Minister became Sir Winston Churchill.

We can only guess what Elizabeth made of Churchill. There can be no doubt that she respected him for all he had achieved. But for a spirited 25-year-old, even one who had been brought up to defer to her elders, the weekly audiences with an elderly man given to rambling anecdotes about his life as a young cavalry officer in India and as a war correspondent in South Africa must have stretched her patience. When asked for his version of what they found to talk about, Churchill said it was mostly about horses. Perhaps that subject, dear to the Queen's heart, was her contribution to keeping the conversation going.

While his ministers got on with the job of implementing the Tory manifesto pledge to 'set the people free' by dismantling wartime controls, Churchill focused on the coronation and on his grandiose scheme to bring peace to the world by acting as honest broker between America and the Soviet Union. It seemed to him that the circumstances were propitious. In the wake of Stalin's death came the novice Georgi Malenkov, while

America had just elected President Dwight Eisenhower, a soldier of high military and a natural politician, but an innocent in the ways of international diplomacy. By making an appeal direct to Malenkov for an informal summit with himself and Eisenhower, Churchill saw the chance of laying the foundation for world peace, a crowning glory that would be followed by another crowning, that of a young queen with Churchill standing proudly by her side.

It turned out that the two superpowers felt no need for an intermediary who, quite clearly, had lost the plot. Churchill had to make do with the coronation. He was not unhappy with the prospect.

The way forward was not entirely trouble free. Refusing to take a back seat, Philip protested vigorously at his adoption by the House of Windsor. What the alternative might be was made clear two days after the accession when Queen Mary was informed by one who had attended a dinner at Broadlands, the Mountbatten home, that the host had raised a glass to the House of Mountbatten. It was a typically cavalier gesture which confirmed the worst fears of those who saw no limit to the ambitions of the high-born warrior diplomat.

Churchill had been a fan of Mountbatten, sharing with him an addiction to imaginative but often impractical schemes for hastening the end of the war. But the relationship had soured when, as Viceroy of India, Mountbatten had presided over what Churchill saw as a humiliating 'skuttle'. There was no way he was about to allow Mountbatten to usurp the royal brand. With the exception of Philip, the Palace coterie led by the Queen Mother was equally averse to a change of identity.

When it was made clear that the family name of Windsor would be retained, Philip took umbrage: 'I am the only man in the country not allowed to give his name to his children.' He had no choice, but this confirmation of his secondary role continued to chafe. Harold Macmillan confided to his diary:

It is clear that the Duke has the normal attitude of many men towards a mother-in-law of strong character, accentuated by the peculiar circumstances of his position ... It is more than likely that he has been told that we are suspicious of him on political grounds. It is still more probable that the Mountbattens are exercising their influence pretty strongly. Altogether, it is rather tiresome and had it happened at a time when the

Crown had more real power, might prove very dangerous. In present conditions, it should not be worse than 'tiresome' ...[14]

A more contentious issue centred on how the Queen should be styled as the sovereign of many and varied peoples across the world. The title agreed for 1927 was 'George V, by the grace of God, of Great Britain, Ireland and the British Dominions beyond the Seas; King, Defender of the Faith, Emperor of India'. The same formula was adopted for Edward VIII and George VI, though come the independence of India, he could no longer be emperor.

What was assumed to be a simple amendment opened a Pandora's box. Canada was unhappy with the reference to British Dominions since there was no distinction between colonies and the self-governing members of the Commonwealth. The complications mounted when India demanded a form of words that allowed it to be a republic and part of the Commonwealth. There was more trouble with the proposal to replace Ireland with Northern Ireland. A committee headed by the Cabinet Secretary eventually came up with a formula whereby Elizabeth would be 'Queen of the Realm and of all her other Realms and Territories, Head of the Commonwealth, Defender of the Faith', thus sidestepping the question of what her realms actually were.

This raised more problems than it solved. The matter was discussed at the Commonwealth Economic Conference in December 1952, when it was agreed that each member country should 'use for its own purposes a form of title which would suit its own particular circumstances' but that 'the title of the Queen should include a reference to Her Majesty's other realms and territories and her title as Head of the Commonwealth'.[15]

It only remained for a Royal Titles Bill to be passed into law. It wasn't until March 1953, just three months before the coronation, that the House of Commons gave its verdict. The second reading of the Bill was introduced by the Home Secretary, Sir David Maxwell Fyfe. A politician confident of his powers of persuasion, Maxwell Fyfe took it for granted that the Bill would receive unanimous approval. The Labour leadership fell into line, welcoming 'a period in which there will be a steady rise in the dignity, the stature and the states of the Crown ... as a symbol of the free association of independent nations'.

There followed a short debate as to where Scotland fitted in, before Enoch Powell, the stormy petrel of the Tory Party, intervened to devastating effect. Slapping down attempts to stop him in mid-flow, he condemned the Bill as meaningless nonsense. For the first time, he thundered, and without proper deliberation, the unity of the Empire under the Crown had been abandoned for 'a fortuitous aggregation of a number of separate entities'. Moreover, 'British' was no longer applied to the Queen's territories.

'Why is it,' asked Powell, 'that we are so anxious … to eliminate any references to the seat, the focus and the origin of this vast aggregation of territories?' The formula was a sham – 'essentially something we have invented to blind ourselves to the reality of our position'. Worse still, 'we are doing this for the sake of those to whom the very names Britain and British are repugnant'.[16]

There was no chance that the Bill would be defeated. It was passed by 328 votes to 39, with Powell abstaining, presumably because he had no wish to be lumped together with the republicans on the Labour benches. But while Powell exaggerated (he was never one for nuances), there was force in his argument that the Royal Titles Bill was no more than a camouflage for the fragile threads that held together the British family of nations.

The tensions that threatened the break-up of the Commonwealth and Empire were plain to see after Ceylon (Sri Lanka) won its independence with dominion status, and Burma (Myanmar) reached the same objective but as a republic outside the Commonwealth. In 1949, Eire had cut the last constitutional link with Britain by becoming the Republic of Ireland. Leaving the Commonwealth was welcomed by the salutes of guns, the ringing of church bells and a celebration that attracted 50,000 revellers to the centre of Dublin.

While India and Pakistan remained grudgingly in the Commonwealth, their association with each other spoke less of brotherhood than of hostility over Kashmir. Apartheid South Africa had slammed the door against the international community, communist insurgents were occupying the British Army in Malaya, Kenya was in the throes of a tribal revolt, trouble was brewing between Greek and Turkish separatists in Cyprus, and the Gold Coast (Ghana) and Nigeria were heading towards independence and an uncertain relationship with Britain.

What held together the Commonwealth, those parts of the Empire that were soon to join the Commonwealth, and the remaining colonies was as mysterious as the monarchy itself. Tradition, language and trade had their role but, to be more precise, opened up an argument to which there was no end.

Undaunted, Churchill was determined on the coronation as a demonstration to the world of Britain's imperial might, testimony to its claim to be counted with the great powers. The Queen was the essential focus, giving the appearance of strength and purpose to a delusion of grandeur. After her South African broadcast, it was a fiction that she and her advisers were happy to adopt.

# 4

# THE MOULDING OF
# TRADITION

As the BBC's lead commentator on the coronation, Richard Dimbleby paid tribute to the 'pageantry and grandeur of a thousand-year-old tradition', a soundbite that was as memorable as it was deceptive. The centrepiece of the ceremony, the Recognition of the newly crowned Queen by the people, is the oath by which the monarch promises to protect the established laws and customs and the anointing with holy oil, indeed had lengthy antecedents. But all else had been adapted down the years. Most obviously, while the Plantagenet and Tudor monarchs were consecrated according to the medieval rite in Latin, by the time of James I, an English version had allowed for substantial amendments. The process continued as political and religious fashions came and went.

Almost every coronation held since the earliest records has had its share of distinctive features, by no means all to the credit of the institution:

Dunstan, abbot of Glastonbury, was appalled by the behaviour of King Eadwy immediately after his anointing in 955. He noted that 'the lustful man suddenly jumped up and left the happy banquet and the fitting company of his nobles for the caresses of loose women'. Dunstan and another cleric were sent to drag the king back to the ceremony. When they entered his apartment, they found the royal crown carelessly thrown down on the floor and the king wallowing between the two ladies 'in evil fashion, as if in a vile sty'.[1]

As an act of reconciliation, bringing the people together, the coronation of William I hit low base. The Conqueror of the Saxons was, at the time of his coronation on Christmas Day 1066, still an enemy among enemies. On hand to quell any disturbances, mounted troops loyal to the King lined the approaches to Westminster Abbey, or as it then was, the Abbey Church of St Peter's of Westminster.

A mixed congregation of Saxons and Normans, neither of whom spoke the other's language, required a doubling-up of the service with Geoffrey, Bishop of Coutances, and Ealdred, Archbishop of York, doing duty for their respective flocks. When it came to the Recognition, instead of a clear unanimous acclamation, what was heard outside the Abbey was a babble of the two languages which sounded like a hostile demonstration. This prompted the Norman cavalry to wade in on the crowd of onlookers who were assumed to be part of the trouble. Houses were set on fire as the street battle gained strength, and the congregation abandoned the Abbey to join the fracas. Left to himself with only his immediate circle, the crowning of the Conqueror was completed with hardly anyone to witness it.

William was the first sovereign to be crowned at Westminster Abbey. Before then, there had been several coronation sites. Arthur of the Round Table was invested at Stonehenge. Edward the Elder and many of his successors held their coronations at Kingston upon Thames, while other pre-Norman rulers were crowned in Oxford, Winchester or St Paul's Cathedral. Westminster came to eminence as the burial place of Edward the Confessor, the last great Saxon monarch, who had also ordered the building of the Abbey, with a palace adjoining so that he could supervise the construction. William's choice of the Abbey for his coronation was intended to confirm him as the rightful successor to his Saxon forebears.

If William's coronation was remembered chiefly for the violence that erupted, an even worse turmoil disgraced the coronation of Richard I in 1189:

Among the vast concourse which the coronation had attracted to the metropolis, many wealthy Jews had flocked from every part of the kingdom, to consult with their friends in the City about presenting a liberal freewill offering to the king on his accession. Richard had issued a proclamation prohibiting all persons of that nation to enter the Abbey or Westminster Hall on the day that ceremony was performed. Some of them were, however, detected pressing among the crowd into the Hall. This brought upon them, at first, a torrent of abuse of language, which soon changed into the more formidable assaults of brickbats and bludgeons. Perceiving too late their imprudence, and the danger in which it had involved them, the poor Jews endeavoured to make good their retreat into the City, pursued and pelted by a furious multitude. In this state of fermentation it was easy to give out, and as easily believed, that the king had issued orders to destroy all Jews. Never were real orders more promptly and more ferociously executed. Many of those unhappy creatures were inhumanly massacred in the streets; such as were able to escape to their habitations, or had stayed at home, were not the more secure. The houses were broken into and plundered or burnt over their heads. Those who were shut up perished in the flames; those who forced their way out fell by the sword.[2]

The wording of the coronation oath sworn by King Ethelred in 978 ('to keep and by your oath confirm to the people of England the laws and customs to them granted by the Kings of England, your lawful and religious predecessors') was retained by the Normans, but as others succeeded an attempt was made to strengthen the King's commitment to conform to the established laws and customs. This held to the time of Henry VIII, who made numerous amendments to the oath in his own handwriting, to give him greater freedom to rule as he pleased. As a foretaste of Henry's falling out with Rome, his promise to maintain the rights and privileges of the Holy Church was tempered by the addition of the words 'not prejudicial to his jurisdiction and dignity'.

The coronation of Charles I was distinctly lacklustre, with the congregation failing to respond to the invitation to recognise the King. As recorded by Sir Simonds d'Ewes:

The bishop said in my hearing to this purpose: 'My Masters and friends, I am here come to present unto you your king, King Charles ... and therefore I desire you by your general acclamation to testify your consent and willingness thereunto.' Upon which, whether some expected he should have spoken more, others, hearing not well what he said ... or the presence of so dear a king drew admiring silence, or that those which were nearest doubted what to do; but not one word followed till my lord of Arundel told them they should cry out, God Save King Charles. Upon which, as ashamed of their first oversight, a little shouting followed.

Given his unhappy end, it was not surprising that the credulous fastened on to the bad omen of the coronation, the King choosing to wear a white satin robe, a colour associated with sacrificial victims. The unluckiest portent of all was the earthquake felt while the coronation was in progress.

As a Catholic convert, James II insisted on changes to the corona-tion service to satisfy his beliefs and to hasten matters along. Archbishop Sancroft was instructed to 'take out the communion service and to abridge ... the extreme length of the rest'. It did not bode well for the future when the royal standard over the Tower of London tore in two. Like some others who succeeded him, James had difficulty in holding his crown firmly in place.

When, after the expulsion of James II in 1688 and the return to Protestantism with the accession of his daughter Mary and her Dutch hus-band, William, Prince of Orange, in 1689, the coronation oath was again revised with the sovereign promising to maintain 'the Protestant Reformed Religion established by law'. This was reinforced by the 1701 Act of Settlement which excluded any Roman Catholic or one who was married to a Catholic from the royal succession 'for ever'.

Preparing for his coronation in 1901, Edward VII attempted to amend the oath. He felt it would be divisive and offensive for the new head of state to promise to uphold the 'Protestant religion'. But it was to no avail; the Established Church was adamant. George V took the oath to uphold Protestantism as did George VI and Elizabeth II. The 1701 Act of Settlement remained unaltered until 2013, when it was at last permitted for a member of the royal family to marry a Catholic and still succeed to the throne. But the law remained that no Catholic could wear the crown.

The coronation of William and Mary in 1689 took place under threat of invasion. It was while the royal couple were being robed for the ceremony that they heard that James, Mary's father and predecessor, had landed at Kinsale in Ireland and that most of that country was under his control. From this vantage point, he wrote to Mary threatening that 'if she was crowned while he and the Prince of Wales were living, the curses of an outraged father would light upon her'.

Not surprisingly, the news from Ireland cast a blight over the coronation, which was delayed for over two hours. A notable absentee was the Archbishop of Canterbury. Though a firm Protestant and no friend of James II, William Sancroft felt unable to swear allegiance to William and Mary, who had overthrown a divinely appointed monarch. Sancroft's understudy was the Bishop of London.

Once under way, the coronation was carried out with only minor hitches. When the King and Queen were kneeling at the altar to make their first offering, the King found that the envelope which should have contained 20 guineas was empty. The Queen had no money either and a long pause ensued, 'which everyone began to deem excessively ridiculous', until Lord Danby drew out his purse and placed 20 guineas in the gold basin on the King's behalf.

A large pearl and several pieces of plate 'bearing the royal arms were lost or stolen at the coronation' and 'a notice had to be placed in the *Gazette*, inviting those who had them to return them to the board of green-cloth'. It is not known if there was any response to this appeal.

After Mary died in 1694, William reigned alone until his death in 1702, when he was succeeded by Mary's younger sister, Anne. An enthusiast for royal ceremony, it was humiliating for her, at the time of her coronation, to be afflicted with a severe attack of gout. Carried to Westminster in a sedan chair, she acquired the dubious distinction of being the only infirm monarch to ascend the throne.

The coronations of the first two Georges were uneventful but that of George III in 1761 was memorable, for all the wrong reasons. Horace Walpole hoped never to see another such spectacle, grand in the 'richness and variety of habits' but defective in implementation:

In the morning they had forgot the sword of state, the chairs for King and Queen, and their canopies. They used the Lord Mayor's for the first, and made the last in the Hall; so they did not set forth till noon; and then, by a childish compliment to the King, reserved the illumination of the Hall till his entry, by which means they arrived like a funeral, nothing being discernible but the plumes of the Knights of the Bath, which seemed the hearse. My Lady Townshend said she should be very glad to see a coronation, as she never had seen one. 'Why,' said I, 'Madam, you walked at the last?' 'Yes, child,' said she, 'but I saw nothing of it; I only looked to see who looked at me.'

Prize fighters were engaged to keep the peace between beleaguered guests. Outside the Abbey, recorded William Hickey, there was 'much confusion' as carriages 'ran into each other whereby glasses and panels were demolished without number, the noise of which, accompanied by the screeches of terrified ladies was at times truly terrific'.[3]

In the Abbey, no one seemed to know what they were supposed to do. Senior clergy were kept waiting for over an hour outside the north door while an attempt was made to put things right. Amazingly, George remained in good humour and in control, giving instructions to those who were at a loss:

> When the King approached the communion-table, in order to receive the sacrament, he inquired of the Archbishop, *whether he should not lay aside his crown?* The Archbishop asked the Bishop of Rochester, but neither of them could say what had been the usual form. The King determined within himself that humility best became such a solemn act of devotion, took off his crown and laid it down during the administration.

After the crowning, the Archbishop of Canterbury attempted to deliver a sermon but:

> ... as many thousands were out of the possibility of hearing a single syllable, they took that opportunity to eat their meal, when the general clattering of knives, forks, plates and glasses produced a most ridiculous effect, and a universal burst of laughter followed.

The subsequent banquet in Westminster Hall was equally chaotic with:

> ... baskets, handkerchiefs and garters let down by hungry onlookers in the galleries to friends at the tables below, who filled them with chicken legs and bottles of wine to be hauled aloft for eager consumption.

His patience exhausted, the King complained to the Deputy Earl Marshal. Lord Effingham turned aside the criticism, none too tactfully: 'It is true, Sir, that there has been some neglect, but I have taken care that the next coronation shall be regulated in the exactest manner possible.'

Wisely settling for a relatively passive role in political life, George III was an incidental beneficiary of the Napoleonic Wars when he came to represent a country united in patriotic endeavour against the threat of a French invasion. But the popularity of the monarchy was not guaranteed. By the time George IV came to the throne in 1820, having served as regent in the period of his father's mental deterioration, he was already a byword for reckless extravagance and a decadent lifestyle. For his coronation, he aimed to outshine that of the recently deposed Napoleon. With this in mind, he sent his tailor to Paris to replicate the emperor's coronation robe. As a result, his lavishly ornate costume required eight train bearers.

This was the least of his indulgences. Settling on a celebratory theme of medieval and Tudor pageantry, George spent wildly on creating a Gothic setting. An unintended light note was added to the proceedings with the sight of elderly courtiers struggling to appear dignified in outmoded finery. As the arch romantic, Walter Scott was 'astonished and delighted to see its revival of feudal dresses and grandeur', but if this sentiment was at all widespread it was dissipated by the farce that ensued when Queen Caroline, George's discarded consort, was refused entry to the Abbey. The Annual Register takes up the story:

> The door-keeper repeated that his orders were peremptory – and said, however reluctant he might be, he could not suffer her Majesty to pass without a ticket.
>
> Lord Hood: 'I have a ticket.'
>
> Door-keeper: 'Upon presenting it, I will permit you to pass.'
>
> Lord Hood then took from his pocket one ticket for the Abbey, for a Mr. Wellington, which he tendered to the door-keeper.
>
> The door-keeper said that would admit but one individual.
>
> Lord Hood then asked her Majesty, if she would enter alone. Her Majesty hesitated – upon which Lord Hood asked, whether there had not been some preparation made for her Majesty's reception.
>
> The door-keeper answered in the negative.
>
> Lord Hood: 'Then I am to understand you refuse your Queen admittance to Westminster Abbey?'

The door-keeper said he was ready to admit her Majesty with a ticket, but not without.

After a short consultation with her Majesty, whether she would go into the Abbey alone, or not – her Majesty declined – and it was resolved that she should return to her carriage.

As she was quitting the spot, some persons in the door-way burst into a vulgar laugh of derision. Her Majesty looked at them contemptuously, and turning about, passed through a group of fashionable women who were going to the Abbey with tickets, but who did not take the slightest notice of her. She was followed by a crowd to the platform, some of whom were approving, and some disapproving of her conduct. On entering her carriage, there was considerable disapprobation, intermingled with cries of 'Shame, shame', 'Off, off', while other parts of the populace repeated the cries of 'The Queen, the Queen', with great enthusiasm.

Meanwhile, the King was causing offence by nodding and winking to his mistress, Lady Conyngham, which he continued to do throughout the service. To add to the confusion, at the singing of 'God Save the King', a coronation first, part of the congregation demonstrated their support for Caroline by changing the words to 'God Save the Queen'.

For the banquet in Westminster Hall the two thousand wax candles were lit. 'The very great heat', wrote one observer, 'was nowhere more visible than in the havoc which it made upon the curls of many of the ladies, several of whose heads had lost all traces of the friseur's skill long before the ceremony of the day had concluded.' Sartorial splendour was lost when the candles melted and great drops fell 'without distinction of persons' on the dresses of the peers and peeresses. Escape was impossible 'for the wretched tenants of a slave ship were never more closely packed together. If a lovely female dared to raise her look to discover from what quarter the unwelcome visitation came, she was certain of receiving an additional patch on her cheeks, which in order to disencumber herself of, obliged her to wipe away also the roseate hue which had been imparted to her countenance at her toilette, thereby obliging her to wear a double face, of nature on the one side, and of art on the other.'

The vast expenditure on the coronation, forty times higher than for George III, did at least turn the event into a national celebration with bonfires and feasts across the country. It was noted, however, that attempts to engage the public were successful only as long as the copious supplies of free beer held out.

As the next in line, George's younger brother, who succeeded as William IV, was well aware that another extravaganza, just ten years after the last, would not go down well with cost-conscious politicians or with the public. In any case, he was averse to elaborate ceremonial. While accepting that a coronation, though not essential to his royal legitimacy, was desirable as confirmation of his rule, he insisted on a modest affair, ordering that 'no ceremonies are to be celebrated at the Coronation, except the sacred rites attending the administration of the royal oath in Westminster Abbey. The usual procession and feast are to be dispensed with.'

However, a cut-price coronation did allow for the King and Queen to journey to the Abbey in the Gold State Coach, by wide consent the clumsiest conveyance ever built for a royal progression. Trundled out for every subsequent coronation, William said it was like being on board a ship 'tossing in a rough sea', while Queen Victoria complained of the 'distressing oscillation', and for George VI the journey from the palace to the Abbey was 'one of the most uncomfortable rides I have ever had'. A concession to modernity came with rubber overlay to the iron wheels. Even so, the most recent occupant described the coach as 'horrible'.

A distinctive feature of William IV's coronation was the opening of the 'New Avenue', now known as the Mall, with night-time illumination. But, as for the service, Horace Walpole dismissed it as 'a foolish puppet show' and Charles Greville endured what he described as 'the greatest of all bores'.

It was at this time that the coronation service was given a radical overhaul:

The annotated copy of the 'Form and Order' for William IV resembles a battlefield. The anthem 'The king shall rejoice' is dropped altogether, the litany and the creed are to be said, not sung, no oil is to be wiped away from the king's head after his anointing, he was not to be girt with the sword, no armils were to be used and, as regards vestments, he was only to be clothed with a royal robe. Psalm 23 was substituted for the anthem 'Praise be the Lord'; the words accompanying the delivery of the Bible were truncated and two more anthems cut, with Handel's Hallelujah Chorus substituted.[4]

New prayers were introduced to reflect the reform of the franchise and remove 'divers abuses' of the electoral system. God was called upon to give William 'a faithful Senate, wise councillors and magistrates, loyal nobility, dutiful gentry, pious, learned and useful clergy, an honest, industrious and obedient commonality' – a tall order, even for the Almighty. 'Precious little respect was shown for what remained of an ancient liturgical rite,' notes Roy Strong.

Victoria's coronation was another hazardous affair. The clergy lost their place in the order of service, the choir sang out of tune and two of the trainbearers talked throughout the ceremony:

> The different actors in the ceremonial were very imperfect in their parts, and had neglected to rehearse them. Lord John Thynne, who officiated for the Dean of Westminster, told me that nobody knew what was to be done except the Archbishop and himself (who had rehearsed), Lord Willoughby (who is experienced in these matters) and the Duke of Wellington, and consequently there was continual difficulty and embarrassment, and the Queen never knew what she was to do next ... she said to John Thynne, 'Pray tell me what I am to do, for they don't know'; and at the end, when the orb was put into her hand, she said to him, 'What am I to do with it?' 'Your Majesty is to carry it, if you please, in your hand.' 'Am I?' she said, 'it is very heavy.' The ruby ring was made for her little finger instead of the fourth, on which the rubric prescribes that it should be put. When the Archbishop was to put it on, she extended the former, but he said it must be on the latter. She said it was too small, and she could not get it on. He said it was right to put it there, and, as he insisted, she yielded, but had first to take off her other rings, and then this was forced on, but it hurt her very much ...[5]

Near the end of the service, the Bishop of Bath and Wells turned over two pages at once, told Victoria the service was finished, then realising his error, had to call her back from St Edward's Chapel. The Queen was shocked to find that the Chapel altar or 'what was called an altar was covered with sandwiches, bottles of wine, etc'.

As a throwback to earlier coronations, unseemly behaviour was quick to surface. When, following custom, medals were scattered, peers wrestled with military brass hats to retrieve them from the Abbey floor. During the Homage, Lord Rolle, nearly 90, was the subject of cruel laughter when he caught his robes on the steps of the throne and rolled to the bottom. With more sensitivity, the 19-year-old Queen leaned down to save him from another fall.[6]

Outside the Abbey, it was party time. 'There never was anything seen like the state of the town,' wrote Charles Greville:

It is as if the population had been on a sudden quintupled; the uproar, the confusion, the crowd, the noise are indescribable. Horsemen, footmen, carriages squeezed, jammed, intermingled, the pavement blocked up with timbers, hammering and knocking, and fallen fragments stunning the ears and threatening the head; not a mob here or there, but the town all mob, thronging, bustling, gaping and gazing at everything, at anything, or at nothing; the Park one vast encampment, with banners floating on the tops of the tents, and still the roads are covered, the railroads loaded with arriving multitudes.

Hyde Park was turned into an enormous fairground with conjurers, acrobats, jugglers and freaks such as the 'living skeleton' and the 'pig-faced lady' (always a draw in Victorian England) putting out the hat. Food stalls did a roaring trade despite inflated prices. Penny loaves were sold for sixpence while a pot of beer fetched the unheard of price of a shilling.[7]

Dense crowds lined the coronation route. Recognisable guests were loudly applauded with the warmest welcome given to the Duke of Wellington, the greatest living Englishman. Good humour extended to a friendly reception for Marshal Jean-de-Dieu Soult, the French soldier who had fought for Napoleon and acted as his Chief of Staff at Waterloo.[8]

The celebratory mood was less in evidence outside London. Widespread poverty in the industrial north served to point out an unfavourable contrast between them and us.

It was in the second half of the nineteenth century that Britain began to acquire a reputation for organising world-beating events. The trend was set by the 1851 Great Exhibition, inspired by Prince Albert as a festival of commercial and artistic creativity to support peace and prosperity.

The dramatic improvement in the planning and preparation of royal occasions owed much to the organisational talents of Viscount Esher, Secretary of the Office of Works from 1895 to 1902 and Lieutenant Governor of Windsor Castle from 1901 to 1928. As the mastermind of every state pageant from Victoria's Diamond Jubilee to the funeral of Edward VII, Esher supplanted, albeit tactfully, the Duke of Norfolk, hereditary Earl Marshal who, by tradition, was responsible for royal ceremonial.

Efficient as he was, Esher was unable to compensate for the frailty of Archbishop Temple, who presided over the coronation of Edward VII. With failing eyesight, Temple had problems reading his lines, while stiffness of joints made it hard for him to get up from a kneeling position. At the actual crowning, according to George Kennion, Bishop of Bath and Wells, the Archbishop 'put on the crown the wrong way to the front and, endeavouring to alter it, made it worse and I had to … help put it straight on his head'. The sudden blaze of electric light, recently introduced at the Abbey, and switched on at the moment of crowning, was sufficiently dramatic to distract attention from the confused ritual. Worse was to follow when the Archbishop collapsed while doing homage. The King had to pull him to his feet and haul him off to the disrobing room where he was revived with a cup of soup.

The embarrassment was all the greater for the King himself being in poor health. His coronation had had to be postponed to allow him to recover from an emergency operation for appendicitis. Though Edward remained ebullient, changes had to be made to the service to reduce the strain.

A mark of Britain's growing reputation for state spectaculars was the renaissance of English music. In Germany, Britain was known as the country with no music. This was not entirely fair since there was a great appreciation of music, even if it was German composers who were appreciated. For most of Victoria's reign the only English composer of note was Henry Purcell and he had died in 1695. The transformation was led by Hubert Parry, Edward Elgar and Arthur Sullivan. For the coronation of Edward VII, Parry composed the anthem 'I was Glad', which has since been incorporated into every coronation.

Elgar composed the ever-popular 'Imperial March' for the 1897 Diamond Jubilee and the 'Coronation Ode' for the accession of Edward VII including, at the King's request, the choral setting of 'Pomp and Circumstance Number One', soon to be adopted as a second national anthem as 'Land of Hope and Glory'. Elgar was to the fore again for the coronation of George V with the 'Coronation March'. In 1924, Elgar was made Master of the King's Musick.

Abbey choirs and orchestras matched the upsurge in musical compositions. For the 1902 coronation, the orchestra had eighty players and a choir of 400. The Abbey itself, notoriously ill-managed for a generation or more, was given a makeover that included a new organ and electric lighting. From 1897, choristers wore distinctive red cassocks.

Victoria's Diamond Jubilee of 1897 and the 1935 Silver Jubilee of George V were the royal celebrations that came closest to matching the coronation of Elizabeth II. Nine months in the preparation, Victoria celebrated her reign of sixty years with a procession through 6 miles of cheering crowds:

> Beneath blue skies and in glorious sunshine, the old Queen drove slowly through the flagged streets to the Cathedral, in a procession which was a blaze of colour. Once more the horse was among the chief actors in the London scene. The great swaying landau drawn by the famous Hanoverian creams, in their panoply of purple and gold; the postillions and outriders in scarlet and gold; the escorting princes radiant in uniforms of every hue, glittering with gold lace, their plumes waving, the mailed Household Cavalry, their helmets and cuirasses focusing and reflecting the sun's beams; the Guards in scarlet and gold; the glossy chargers, caparisoned in gold, and the golden sunshine over all, blending and softening the mass of brilliant colour into one glowing splendour – such was the apotheosis of the Victorian age.[9]

With echoes that resounded across the years to the 1953 coronation, the Jubilee was presented as an act of 'national communion', reaffirming the universal commitment to the family, the nation, the monarchy and the Empire.[10] But then, as later, every sector of society had its own take on the anniversary. For the aristocracy, it was a confirmation of hereditary privileges; for the middle class, it represented order and stability; while for many workers it was a welcome day's holiday, a warning for those who cared to note it that the outward appearances of loyalty and devotion could be deceptive.

The homage paid to Victoria in death, as in life, was not expected to be repeated for her son and heir. But after a shaky start, when Edward VII had to live down his deserved reputation as a playboy lecher, he settled into his role as a father figure with a popular following at home and abroad, where his efforts as a freelance diplomat, particularly in easing relations with France, were entirely to his credit. But it was Edward's love of pageantry that set the tone for the monarchical grandeur of subsequent reigns, not least for the 1953 coronation. Reviving the street procession for the state opening of Parliament, he appeared in full regalia to read the speech from the throne – a curtain-raiser his mother had avoided for forty years.

The march of democracy called for a wider representation at the coronation. For the crowning of Edward VII, places had to be found for London's elected councillors, the chairmen of the recently created county councils and senior members of the legal and medical professions. And that was just the start. Since 1887, the year of Victoria's Golden Jubilee and of the first Colonial Conference in London, the Empire had been central to every key royal event. Ten years later, for the Diamond Jubilee, it was axiomatic that the monarch was central to holding the Empire together. When Edward VII was crowned, 300 seats in the Abbey were reserved for imperial premiers and governors with pride of place going to Indian princes.

With a congregation over 7,000 strong, there had to be a cutback of those on the fringe of entitlement. For the crowning of George V in 1911, the daughters, widows and eldest sons of the peerage were omitted from the invitation list.

Royalty had a more wide-ranging function thrust upon it with the realisation that in competition with its commercial rivals, Germany, France and the United States, Britain had need to bang its own drum. To build on the grandeur of a monarchy befitting a world power, a triumphal ceremonial to rival the Arc de Triomphe in Paris and the Brandenburg Gate in Berlin was planned early in the new century. The objective, said Prime Minister Arthur Balfour, was to create a monumental ensemble 'of the kind which other nations have shown example and which we may well imitate and can easily surpass'. The result, unveiled between 1906 and 1913, was a widening of the Mall, the building of Admiralty Arch and the re-fronting of Buckingham Palace with the Victoria Monument in front of the main gates. The work on the new Portland stone façade for the Palace, which brightened up its appearance, was completed within three months.

g thus exalted at this most solemn moment above common humanity, mind's eye may catch, beyond all the pomp, another vision. It is a on to hush the enthusiasm, but only in order to deepen the feeling oyalty and turn good will into prayer. The king is on his way to be roned, indeed, and acclaimed. The trumpets will sound and the le will cry out 'God Save King George!'. But he is on his way also consecrated to be dedicated. Once that is done, he is no longer an ry man. He is a man dedicated.[17]

o the Abbey service was Bernard Marmaduke Fitzalan-Howard, e of Norfolk and hereditary Earl Marshal, now reasserting his le in organising ceremonial state occasions. His father having died was 9 years of age, he was a mere 29 when he was called upon e Executive Committee for the 1937 coronation. Apart from Norfolk estates in West Sussex, his only qualification for event t was a briefly held commission in the Royal Horse Guards and ial Army officer.

cessor had not shone in the role of coronation supremo. After nce in 1902 and 1911, George V had said bluntly, 'As a man e is absolutely impossible.' There was even talk of supple- Duke by creating an office for state ceremonies but, in the triumphed. It then came as a welcome surprise that the ved to have all the skills of a high-class showman, not least n punctuality. At the 1937 coronation he offered to pay a or every minute the actual crowning was too late or too ly £5.

curiosity of the role of Earl Marshal that, as part of the hierarchy, his Church is excluded from the coronation. To iculty, an Act of Parliament passed in 1824 permitted the an office held with brief interregnums, since 1483, despite tions.

every effort went into mounting a spectacle that would llective memory the shame and embarrassment of the the reluctant monarch dreaded the occasion, he came 'most important ceremony of my life'. There were a few the King's diary:

With a few minor changes in the service, George V thoroughly enjoyed his coronation. His diary entry for 22 June 1911 started with the journey from the Palace to Westminster Abbey in the coronation coach:

There were ovr 50,000 troops lining the streets under the command of Lord Kitchener. There were hundreds of thousands of people who gave us a magnificent reception. The Service in the Abbey was most beautiful, but it was a terrible ordeal. It was grand, yet simple & most dignified and went without a hitch.

He was full of praise for Queen Mary who, he said, 'looked lovely', adding, 'It was a great comfort to me to have her by my side.' After the service they drove back to the Palace by way of the Mall, St James's Street and Piccadilly:

On reaching B.P. just before 3.0 May & I went out on the balcony to show ourselves to the people. Downey photographed us in our robes with Crowns on. Had some lunch with our guests here. Worked all afternoon answering telegrams & letters of which I have had hundreds. Such a large crowd collected in front of the Palace that I went out on the balcony again. Our guests dined with us at 8.30. May & I showed ourselves again to the people. Wrote & read. Rather tired. Bed at 11.45.

The next day, the King and Queen drove in an open carriage through central London. Then came the naval review at Spithead and, on 29 June, a thanksgiving service at St Paul's. Finally, there was a tea party for 10,000 London children at Crystal Palace. 'Their cheers,' wrote the King, 'were quite deafening.'[11]

But it was the 1935 Silver Jubilee that raised the monarchy to a peak of acclaim. Public affection for the King was genuine and spontaneous. The day after receiving addresses from both Houses of Parliament, George V and Queen Mary drove through the poorer quarters of London. 'The greatest number of people in the streets that I have ever seen in my life,' the King wrote in his diary. 'The enthusiasm was indeed most touching.'

By the accession of Edward VIII, precedent and practice had sharpened the royal act. Though the young King was not much interested in the plans for his coronation, all eventualities had been anticipated – except for the absence of the star of the show. When Edward decided to forsake the opportunity to preside over a hidebound nation unable to accept an American divorcee as Queen, the coronation was put on hold.

Among those who had hoped for better things in the new reign was Cosmo Gordon Lang. As Archbishop of Canterbury from 1928, he magnified the religious dimension to royalty and the spiritual significance to the crowning in Westminster Abbey, making it much more than a constitutional formality in a holiday setting. It was all part of his Recall to Religion campaign, a national effort to revitalise the Church of England and its mission.

The Church and monarchy had long been in harness. The link between earthly and heavenly power (Christ as King of Heaven) reinforced loyalty to the medieval nobility as well as emphasising the obligations and duties of a Christian society. Miraculous powers were attributed to the royal person. The 'royal touch', a form of laying on of hands, was believed to offer a cure for various diseases. From 1633 to 1715 the Book of Common Prayer included a service for the healing of the sick by the monarch.[12]

Charles II 'touched' 23,000 people in the four years following the Restoration in 1660. His nephew, William of Orange, who became William III, took a more practical view, telling one supplicant for the King's touch, 'God give you better health and more sense.'[13]

If the popular conception of the divinity of the king or queen extending to healing powers had all but disappeared by the nineteenth century, the coronation was seen by the Church of England as underlining 'the essentially spiritual and sacred nature of British monarchy'.[14] The reverence for the monarchy and the worship of God strengthened in parallel. After the dog days of the eighteenth century, when the Church had sunk into lethargy, the Victorian religious revival took in a raft of young, dedicated clergy. Their energy extended to an ambitious programme of church building and rebuilding and to the revival of colourful ceremonial and sacred music, all of which gave substance to the Queen's role as Defender of the Faith while sanctifying royal pageantry.

Observing Victoria's coronation, the writer and critic Harriet Martineau noted sharply that it endowed the Queen with divinity and the Almighty with royalty. As a close adviser to George V, Cosmo Lang wove religion into the royal fabric. At his urging, the King revived the practice of personally

officiating at the rites of Maundy Thursday, a cere the Last Supper. He was the first monarch to do so

As the most visible symbol of nationhood, th by Cosmo Lang and the Church hierarchy as t the leader of a movement to restore the Church life. Lang wrote four of George V's broadcasts a address, all of which stressed the Christian mes

But the Archbishop's ambitions for the accession of Edward VIII, a sceptic who di for emotional language. The feeling of m part, it turned to active hostility when it be planning to marry a divorcee. Contrary t biographer shows convincingly that the A the political shenanigans that led to the a

It was in the aftermath that Lang cou radio address in which he belaboured E circle whose standards and ways of l and traditions of his people', and his duties as a Christian monarch'.[15]

Public hostility to Lang from f that the Church could all too easi However, undeterred, Lang put George VI:

By his anointing – regarded of the ceremony – the King itual character – that care, pr Religion of his people whi The King does not crown and placed upon his hea committed to him by Go

It was a theme taken up

Nothing is heard no the Stewarts, Queer with the magical 't

officiating at the rites of Maundy Thursday, a ceremony originating with the Last Supper. He was the first monarch to do so since James II.

As the most visible symbol of nationhood, the monarch was idealised by Cosmo Lang and the Church hierarchy as the 'head of our morality', the leader of a movement to restore the Church to a central role in British life. Lang wrote four of George V's broadcasts and most of his 1935 Jubilee address, all of which stressed the Christian message.

But the Archbishop's ambitions for the monarch fell short with the accession of Edward VIII, a sceptic who did not take to Lang's fondness for emotional language. The feeling of mistrust was mutual. For Lang's part, it turned to active hostility when it became apparent that Edward was planning to marry a divorcee. Contrary to received opinion, Lang's latest biographer shows convincingly that the Archbishop played an active part in the political shenanigans that led to the abdication.

It was in the aftermath that Lang courted controversy, with an ill-judged radio address in which he belaboured Edward for his attachment to a 'social circle whose standards and ways of life are alien to all the best instincts and traditions of his people', and his 'craving for private happiness over his duties as a Christian monarch'.[15]

Public hostility to Lang from fans of a matinee idol king suggested that the Church could all too easily fall out of step with popular opinion. However, undeterred, Lang put his indelible stamp on the coronation of George VI:

> By his anointing – regarded from the early days as the central feature of the ceremony – the King is consecrated and invested with that spiritual character – that care, protection and supervision of the Church and Religion of his people which has always been an attribute to his office ... The King does not crown himself. His crown is brought from God's Altar and placed upon his head in token that his Kingship is a solemn trust committed to him by God.[16]

It was a theme taken up in a *Times* leader on the day George was crowned:

> Nothing is heard nowadays of the 'divine right'; and not since the last of the Stewarts, Queen Anne, has any sovereign of England been credited with the magical 'touch' for the cure of the 'King's Evil'. Yet seeing the

king thus exalted at this most solemn moment above common humanity, the mind's eye may catch, beyond all the pomp, another vision. It is a vision to hush the enthusiasm, but only in order to deepen the feeling of loyalty and turn good will into prayer. The king is on his way to be enthroned, indeed, and acclaimed. The trumpets will sound and the people will cry out 'God Save King George!'. But he is on his way also to be consecrated to be dedicated. Once that is done, he is no longer an ordinary man. He is a man dedicated.[17]

Critical to the Abbey service was Bernard Marmaduke Fitzalan-Howard, 16th Duke of Norfolk and hereditary Earl Marshal, now reasserting his family's role in organising ceremonial state occasions. His father having died when he was 9 years of age, he was a mere 29 when he was called upon to chair the Executive Committee for the 1937 coronation. Apart from heading the Norfolk estates in West Sussex, his only qualification for event management was a briefly held commission in the Royal Horse Guards and as a Territorial Army officer.

His predecessor had not shone in the role of coronation supremo. After his performance in 1902 and 1911, George V had said bluntly, 'As a man of business he is absolutely impossible.' There was even talk of supplementing the Duke by creating an office for state ceremonies but, in the end, heredity triumphed. It then came as a welcome surprise that the 16th Duke proved to have all the skills of a high-class showman, not least his insistence on punctuality. At the 1937 coronation he offered to pay a colleague £1 for every minute the actual crowning was too late or too early. He lost only £5.

It remains a curiosity of the role of Earl Marshal that, as part of the Roman Catholic hierarchy, his Church is excluded from the coronation. To get over this difficulty, an Act of Parliament passed in 1824 permitted the Duke to exercise an office held with brief interregnums, since 1483, despite his heretical affiliations.

For George VI, every effort went into mounting a spectacle that would wipe from the collective memory the shame and embarrassment of the abdication. Though the reluctant monarch dreaded the occasion, he came to think of it as the 'most important ceremony of my life'. There were a few hitches, recorded in the King's diary:

Trouble began when the Dean tried to put on the *colobium sindonis* inside out and the King had to firmly resist him. When it came to the oath neither of the supporting bishops could find the place so that the archbishop stepped in and, George VI writes, 'held his book down for them to read, but horror of horrors his thumb covered the words of the oath'. On that occasion the Lord Great Chamberlain was so shaky that the King had to vest himself, added to which, as he left the chair of St Edward, one of the bishops stepped on his train, pulling him. 'I had to tell him to get off it pretty sharply as I nearly fell down.'[18]

But by common consent, the coronation was a success beyond all expectations:

The panorama was splendid, and the spectators, at least those in the galleries, felt they were sitting in a frame, for the built-in stands suggested Ascot, or perhaps – more romantically – the tournaments of medieval days. The church atmosphere had gone; the chairs were covered with blue velvet, and the people were decorative. I looked about me; on all sides were MPs I knew, and their be-plumed, be-veiled, be-jewelled wives. Some were resplendent with their own or borrowed jewels.[19]

But for Chips Channon, the service seemed endless:

Then at last the procession formed itself and we watched spellbound, as it uncoiled slowly and processed down the nave … There was a long wait after the royalties and procession left, and impatience broke out in the very splendid crowd! Chocolates were munched, and flasks shyly produced … And then the most famous moment of all, that we had looked forward to, that swirl when the peeresses put on their coronets; a thousand white gloved arms, sparkling with jewels, lifting their tiny coronets and at the same moment, like fluttering swans in [a] swannery, was very white, graceful and lovely. Now at the end, one of the gold staff officers, losing his humour and his head, called out 'A baron has got out before the viscounts,' and there was a general uproar of laughter.

Half a million people had spent a night in the rain just to see the dress rehearsal of the coronation procession from Buckingham Palace to

Westminster Abbey. That same Sunday night, 9 May, there was a crowd of 50,000 outside the Palace to cheer whoever stepped out on to the balcony.

London was a sea of colour. Gilded crows, lions and unicorns were joined by red, white and blue bunting. The large stores gave over their window displays to patriotic themes, with Selfridges taking the prize with its huge sculpture depicting 'The Empire's Homage to the Throne'.

On coronation eve, the city was awake for most of the night. One of the Mass Observation team was at Marble Arch at around 3.30 a.m. to see multitudes of sightseers making their way to the processional route:

> … carrying parcels, boxes, rugs, children, flags, rucksacks etc. Lots of shocked comment on discovering that they are not first on the scene. I walk very quickly through Hyde Park section of route – identical scenes as Oxford Street – and here, in addition, the crowds are camping on the grass verge as well as the footway, so a few may sleep in a little comfort. By now a pathetic and sordid spectacle: everyone's weariness is apparent, couples mutter in each other's ears, close-folded in one another's arms under rugs and coats, children weep or mutter sleepily, young girls of twelve or so run about to keep warm and shout irritably to one another.[20]

The mood brightened with signs that the show was soon to begin. Police on horseback provided a welcome diversion along with the road sweepers who had to clear the way of aromatic mounds of manure. The workers were greeted with some of the loudest cheers of the day.

Among those who enjoyed the procession was the theatre historian Walter Macqueen-Pope. He and his family had a ringside seat in the window of a department store on the corner of Piccadilly and Regent Street:

> It was not a bright morning, but dull and inclined to rain, but crowds were there even as early as 7.30 and many had been there all night. We came by our car to as near a point as allowed and then walked the short distance … We all wore our best and I had my morning coat and shining topper … We had magnificent seats and Swan and Edgar's did us proud. Breakfasts were served from 8.30 to 10.30 and there was a deliciously served buffet luncheon from 11.30. The most expensive dish, Scotch salmon, cost 2/9d. and a variety of cocktails cost only 1/- each. We had a bottle of Pol Roger

in honour of the day … Well fed and completely comfortable we saw the pageant of England pass by.

It was the longest ever coronation procession with a military presence of 32,500 officers and men either marching or lining the route. 'The Navy drew the biggest acclaim,' said Macqueen-Pope:

And there was a great and warm welcome for the new King and his delightful wife as he passed by, a little still and upright in his crown and finery. There came from him a feeling, even then, that this was going to be a good and a great monarch. He seemed to radiate reliability; that day was his and his people rejoiced with full hearts and cheering voices as another King George passed along Regent Street which his ancestor, the fourth of his name, had created.[21]

The press was unanimous in its praise, with *The Times* declaring the Crown to be 'the necessary centre, not of political life only, but of all life'. Even the left-leaning *Daily Herald* was impressed, describing the ceremony and procession as 'the greatest spectacle of its kind the world has yet staged'.[22]

Princess Elizabeth presented to her parents her own account of the coronation, written in pencil on lined paper with pink silk ribbon, 'To Mummy and Papa. In Memory of Their Coronation, from Lilibet By Herself'. 'Papa [was] looking very beautiful,' she wrote. His actual crowning passed 'in a haze of wonder'. She was only surprised that 'Grannie' (Queen Mary) did not remember much of her own coronation – 'rather odd,' she commented.[23]

There was a collective sigh of relief when the King managed to overcome his stutter for a royal broadcast, the first after a coronation, in which he gave special reference to the dominions, 'now free and equal partners with this ancient kingdom'. The message, as indeed the message of the entire coronation, was essentially soft-centred. While overseas it went down well with the democracies, there was contempt from the Fascists and Soviets for what they saw as a demonstration of British decadence: a country so beholden to its past that it was unable to see the reality of modern power – the efficiency and drive of a centralised, all-embracing authority exercised by a charismatic leader.

Sandwiched between the 1936 and 1937 Nuremburg Nazi rallies, where the military precision of marching thousands could not be seen as anything other than a threat to the established order, the easy harmony of the coronation was upheld two weeks later at the opening of the Exposition Internationale in Paris where the British pavilion was dwarfed by the aggressively assertive profiles of Germany, Italy and the Soviet Union. For Germany, there was a 54m tower topped by an eagle embraced by a swastika. The equally grandiose Soviet display featured a stainless steel figure of an excessively muscular worker bearing a hammer and sickle built to the height of a six-storey building.

The contrast with the British pavilion spoke volumes:

> When you went in, the first thing you saw was a cardboard prime minister [Neville Chamberlain] fishing in rubber waders and, beyond, an elegant pattern of golf-balls, a frieze of tennis racquets, polo sets, riding equipment, natty dinner jackets and, by pleasant transition, agreeable pottery and textiles, books finely printed and photographs of the English countryside. I stared in bewilderment. Could this be England?[24]

Well, yes, it could. In the month of the coronation, May 1937, Neville Chamberlain became Prime Minister intent on leading the country down the path of appeasement, giving the dictators all they wanted in the vain hope of achieving a lasting peace. For those who shared Chamberlain's delusions, the coronation was part of the comfort package, an assurance that all would be made good in a best possible world. It took a world war to prove otherwise.

# 5

# A YEAR TO PREPARE

The makeover of Westminster Abbey to create space for a congregation of 8,000, four times the usual maximum, took the best part of a year. A workforce of 200 fitted together 1.35 million feet of tubular scaffolding to build tiers of seating almost to the roof. Statuary, wall tablets, choir stalls and the organ screen were all boarded over. To soften the acoustics, the floors were laid with felt. In and around Parliament Square, sixty-eight stands requiring 4,300 tons of steel tubing were erected by the Ministry of Works to seat 110,000 official guests. The work also required 1,750 standards of timber, each, claimed the press, as high as Nelson's Column.

The Earl Marshal set up his headquarters in Berkeley Square, a Mayfair address where the upper class could feel at home. It was here that a multitude of press reporters from home and abroad descended to check out the archaic functions of such as the Rouge Dragon Pursuivant (a junior officer at arms of the College of Arms), the Portcullis Pursuivant (ditto) and Bluemantle Pursuivant, in charge of 'Dress, Press and Ceremonial'. It was revealed that a pursuivant, the lowest rank of heraldic officer, derived from old French *poursuivre*, 'to follow'. There was a lively debate at the BBC on how the word should be pronounced.

Leading lights of the old aristocracy were schooled in performing their antique duties. Four Garter Knights, the Dukes of Portland and Wellington, and Lords Allendale and Fortescue, were to hold the Queen's canopy during the anointing of the monarch, the most solemn part of the service. Lord Alexander was to carry the Orb, the Duke of Richmond the Rod with the

Dove, the Marquess of Salisbury the Sword of State. The dowager Duchess of Devonshire was designated Mistress of the Robes.

Along with the Earl Marshal (ranked above the Lord High Admiral but below the Lord High Constable, it should be noted), the prime mover in deciding how the coronation service was to be conducted was the Archbishop of Canterbury. A former private school headteacher, the 66-year-old Geoffrey Fisher had a justifiable reputation as an administrator and organiser but by no stretch of imagination could he be described as a thinker or innovator. His conviction that we are all part of a masterplan drafted by the Almighty closed his mind to any constructive engagement with social and political challenges.

Like Cosmo Lang, Fisher put great emphasis on the spiritual dimension of the monarchy. It was for whoever wore the crown 'to lead, to inspire, to unite' by force of character and by 'personal example'. It now fell to the Queen to uphold the 'pillars of society, domestic fidelity and united homes', no matter how much suffering this caused by trying, nearly always unsuccessfully, to stitch together broken relationships.

If Lang had put his stamp on the coronation of George VI, Fisher was determined that his imprint on the 1953 coronation should be even stronger. Elizabeth had inherited the throne from her father but only the Church could anoint her and only the Archbishop could perform that sacred duty. Self-importance was second nature to Fisher. Throughout the planning of the coronation he was a floating presence, ever ready to bounce forward if there was any suggestion of straying from the accepted norms.

He did not have it all his own way. As Garter Principal King of Arms, the highest heraldic office in England and Wales, Sir George Bellew had the advantage on matters of detail. Described by his successor as a 'temperamental combative Irishman, not easy to live with', Bellew had an eye for design and was responsible for the heraldic statues at the doors of Westminster Abbey. He was certainly not one to mask his disagreement with a cleric, however senior, intent on leaving an indelible impression on every aspect of the coronation.

Studiously ignored by Fisher was a reasoned appeal in *The Times* for fresh thinking. A leading article called for a complete revision of the coronation order of service. 'With so long a time for preparation [this was in May 1952], it is to be hoped that the Ecclesiastical Authorities will at last undertake the thorough revision of the Rite itself.' Their aim would be to move on from the medieval and feudal mindset to a service that had more relevance to the modern and largely secular society.[1]

Similar views were relayed back from Canada, where a visiting Church dignitary recorded the strong opinion that 'on the last occasion the pageantry was wholly out of date and lacking any sort of relevance to the world today'. It was a sentiment shared by the Queen's Consort but he, along with other critics, was brushed off by Fisher, who made it known that 'he would not readily be a party to dismantling the structure of the ancient Rite, however out-of-date its pageantry might be'.[2]

Slight revisions introduced at the behest of Edward Ratcliff, Professor of Divinity at Cambridge, actually reinstated elements from the medieval rite while removing much of the language and some of the features introduced at the coronation of James II and William and Mary.[3] The 'obscure excursion into the legendary past' wrapped in a 'mysterious jargon which delights specialists in heraldry and ecclesiastical tradition' were all but incomprehensible to the average citizen.[4]

Fisher was undeterred. He had control and he knew it. 'Never did the Church of England dominate the public stage more majestically than in the Queen's coronation,' remarks Brian Harrison in his survey of post-war Britain.[5]

At the request of the Queen, Fisher was prepared to make adjustments to the service to give Philip a more prominent role. This amounted to the Consort walking behind the Queen at the processional entry, to sit on a folding chair on the right of the Sovereign in the sanctuary and to join her as she received Communion. Whether this satisfied either the Queen or her husband went unrecorded.

Fisher was prepared to offer a further concession. It appeared that he was 'entirely willing to forego his claim, in favour of the Duke to do his homage before anybody else even if it meant the Church consenting to act second to a layman'.[6] At which point some of those involved must have wondered just how much more of this nonsense they could take.

Breaking precedent, a peace feeler was put out to the Roman Catholic Church but Cardinal Bernard Griffin, Archbishop of Westminster, declined on behalf of himself and his bishops to attend the ceremony while suggesting representatives of the Catholic laity as stand-ins. At that, Fisher drew back, with the result, a delicious irony, that the only official Catholic presence at the coronation was the Earl Marshal who, technically speaking, was running the entire show.

Church and Palace were in total agreement on one point. The Duke of Windsor would not be invited. The question was whether Edward would accept the ruling. No one put it past him to simply turn up. A flurry of correspondence between Sir Alan Lascelles, the Queen's Private Secretary, and the Duke's lawyers brought reassurance that the 'Pretender' would spare his niece embarrassment by toeing the official line.

In the lead-up to the coronation Fisher was a frequent visitor to the Palace. Whether his ministrations were helpful is open to question. His constant harping on the religious significance of just about everything to do with the ceremony must have stretched the nerves of a young Queen already the recipient of much unsolicited advice from her Prime Minister. When Fisher came up with a small 'Book of Devotions' for Elizabeth to use daily during the last months before the coronation it was left to the Queen Mother to thank the Archbishop, describing the book as 'quite perfect, so helpful and lovely and simple'.[7] Is it entirely fanciful to imagine her tongue firmly pressed against her cheek?

The cost of the coronation was a running sore with the Labour Party. Having come under intense scrutiny for every item of expenditure for the Festival of Britain, Labour MPs of radical persuasion were now in the happy position of turning the tables. In January, Emrys Hughes, MP for South Ayrshire, demanded to know from David Eccles, as Minister of Works, if the construction of the annexe to Westminster Abbey was diverting labour and finance from the building of council houses for those who would otherwise be homeless. Eccles conceded that ninety-five workers were engaged on the annexe at a total cost of £50,000, adding, 'I do not think that the public begrudge this modest expenditure of materials on the preparations for the coronation.'

Hughes disagreed. The Minister of Works was setting a bad example, given that it was he who had urged economy for the housing programme, adding, mischievously, that the Festival of Britain had benefited from closer oversight of expenditure. The criticism was dismissed. Eccles could see no comparison.[8]

In the weeks following, a succession of barbed questions were put to Eccles. Would the timber used for the stands built in Parliament Square be recycled? (Yes, it would.) What was the cost of the coronation dinner service ordered from Wedgwood? (£825.) How could such extravagance be justified? (The service was to be used for a dinner for the Queen given by the Foreign Secretary – a coronation tradition. That caused some laughter.)[9]

Other topics of concern ranged from the provision for disabled ex-servicemen to view the procession to the licensing of corn sellers in Trafalgar Square. Eccles assured the House that the pigeons would be well catered for.

A recurring theme was the comparison between the coronation and the Festival of Britain. The Festival budget of £11 million provided for a five-month celebration enjoyed by 10 million visitors to the Thames South Bank and to the Battersea Pleasure Gardens. By contrast, as revealed by the Financial Secretary to the Treasury on 10 March 1952, in addition to the £925,000 voted for the coronation in the Civil Estimates, something over £1 million would fall under supplementary votes – all this for a single week of events. It did not take advanced maths, said the critics, to calculate the relative value for money.

Then again, the coronation budget did not take account of the hidden costs such as giving the military a prominent role. All three services from home and Commonwealth were represented. Of the British armed forces, the army provided 16,100, the RAF 7,000 and the navy 3,600. In addition, there were 2,000 troops from the Commonwealth and 500 from the colonies. 'More than enough to start a small war,' said one observer. The East Yorkshire Regiment put its representatives for the coronation parade on a boat at Singapore. They spent four weeks at sea, followed by six weeks drilling in preparation for the day, then four more weeks on the boat back to Singapore. For some officers in the Household Division, the coronation was the most significant event of their post-1945 military careers. A national serviceman in the Life Guards stationed in Germany reckoned that two-thirds of the regiment had been sent back for the coronation.[10] Three military bands were allocated to the coronation procession through London.

To give full representation to the Commonwealth and Empire, one suggestion was to enact the Enthronement in the more commodious Westminster Hall. But while there was a precedent in the coronation of George IV, the Cabinet rejected the idea, fearing that any changes in the service to increase the number of imperial guests would cause endless jockeying for extra seats. Moreover, to stage the Enthronement in Westminster Hall and the coronation in Westminster Abbey all on the same day would, according to Lord Salisbury, Secretary of State for Commonwealth Relations, 'place an intolerable burden on the Queen'.

As it was, the pressure of coronation planning bore heaviest on the Colonial Office, which had to balance the conflicting claims of overseas politicians who were mindful of their prestige at home. An order of precedence was requested by the Earl Marshal for 300 guests from the colonial territories. The smaller the country, the greater the sensitivity. As Prime Minister of Malta, an island with fewer than half a million inhabitants, Dr Borg Olivier boldly asserted his claim to a 'rightful place alongside other prime ministers of the Commonwealth'.

It fell to Oliver Lyttelton, as Colonial Secretary, to seek a compromise. He was not helped by the Governor of Malta, Sir Gerald Creasy, who sided with Olivier, pointing out that Malta had achieved self-governing status and that the Prime Minister and his wife had been invited to the Queen's wedding in 1947.

When Philip came in for intense lobbying by those he had met in Malta when stationed there between 1949 and 1951, it was inevitable that the Queen should get involved. It was her decision that Olivier and his wife would be treated as 'Distinguished Guests' with seats in the Abbey. But they would have to cover their own expenses. Olivier was still not happy. Why, he asked, had he not been included in the procession of Commonwealth Prime Ministers to and from the Abbey, and why was he to be seated among the colonial representatives? The answer was that Malta, though self-governing, was not a full member of the Commonwealth.

In the end, Malta was put on par with Southern Rhodesia in recognition of the award to the island of the George Cross for gallantry in the war.[11] Even then, Olivier held to a threat to boycott the ceremony unless the Maltese national flag emblazoned with the George Cross was flown, even though it had not been formally recognised by the Crown. He got his way, though when he raised further difficulties, Churchill lost patience, telling Lyttelton that if, 'after all the trouble we have taken he threatens to go back to Malta, we should help him in every way'.[12]

Another confrontation was anticipated with the Gold Coast (Ghana). As Prime Minister of a colony well on the way to independence, Kwame Nkrumah might have expected to be invited to the coronation. Some thought was given as to where he might fit into the order of precedence, but before any conclusions were reached, Nkrumah took the initiative. Made aware that he would not be part of the Commonwealth Prime Ministers' Conference, he decided not to come to London, having no wish 'to call attention to the inferior status of his premiership'.

More diplomatic gyrations were required for Kenya where, in April, Jomo Kenyatta, a future Prime Minister and President, had been found guilty of masterminding the Mau Mau insurgency (a blatant miscarriage of justice, as it turned out) and sentenced to ten years' hard labour. For the coronation, the dominant white minority was happy to have a Black African as one of their representatives as long as he supported the status quo. As Governor, Sir Evelyn Baring managed to square the circle by persuading London to allow a moderate African politician to join the Kenyan party on a non-official basis. The European settlers acceded reluctantly.

The height of absurdity was reached with the proposal from Pitcairn Island in the Pacific to send as their emissary a self-styled Princess to give a touch of 'Oriental and exotic splendour', even though she had never set foot on the island. A letter of objection from the Chief Magistrate was gently turned aside and the Princess, a descendant of Fletcher Christian of mutiny on the *Bounty* fame, was accommodated in the Abbey while the Chief Magistrate had to make do with a seat on the processional route.[13]

Called in to advise on gun salutes, the Admiralty fell back on the programme for the 1937 coronation of George VI. On that occasion, the Queen of Tonga and the Sultan of Zanzibar had both been awarded twenty-one guns. In 1953, Tonga was reckoned to be closer to independence than Zanzibar so the Queen kept her twenty-one-gun salute while the Sultan had to be satisfied with sixteen guns.

Commonwealth celebrations started early with a lunch for the Commonwealth Parliamentary Association held in Westminster Hall on 27 May. As Chairman of the Association, Harold Holt, Australian Immigration Minister and heir apparent to Prime Minister Robert Menzies, was first to be presented to the Queen, with David Eccles making the introductions. A fanfare of trumpets began the proceedings:

The luncheon itself was an exclusively Commonwealth affair – Scotch salmon, New Zealand lamb cutlets, Ceylon pineapple, Canadian maple syrup – Kenyan coffee. The food, all served cold – intentionally – that is because we were hundreds of yards from the Parliamentary kitchens.

It could have been sawdust for all the attention it got from me. South African Sherry and Brandy, Australian Chablis, Burgundy and liqueur, Jamaican cigars, Southern Rhodesian cigarettes. The Queen was very easy to talk to, completely natural, charming. I told her we were both sitting on the spot where Charles the First was tried for treason, but she seemed more interested in what I had to say about the picture pulling the kids through the window, which I'd seen published in every country we had passed through. Yes, the Crown is something more than a symbol she agreed. What with her to the left and Lady Churchill on my right, there were no awkward pauses. Zara [his wife], looking very attractive in her grey shantung suit, was between Attlee and the House of Commons Speaker, 'Shakes' Morrison. The Queen told me it was the first time she'd been in the hall other than on an errand of sorrow. It had always seemed so cold and dark to her then. It was certainly a contrast to-day with the colourful assembly, the festive tables, and the surge of noise from the conversation.[14]

Holt was among the coronation honours with his admission to the Privy Council. After the announcement on 1 June, he was on duty again at a reception in Buckingham Palace for Dominion ministers. This gave him the chance to chat with Philip ('He looks just as good and talks just as intelligently as his pictures would suggest'). But it was Mountbatten who made the strongest impression. His 'appearance and personality even in that galaxy of talent seemed overpowering'.[15]

Meanwhile, the thirty-four-strong Coronation Joint Committee, with Commonwealth representatives, headed by the Earl Marshal and the Archbishop of Canterbury, took on the detailed planning, with many hours spent discussing ways and means of maintaining the dignity of the occasion with admonitions to television viewers to desist from 'unseemly behaviour' such as watching a solemn moment in the service while enjoying a cup of tea and a sandwich.

Showing respect was a preoccupation of the Earl Marshal's office. Bordering on kitsch, a Central Souvenirs Committee sifted applications to produce officially recognised memorabilia. Among the approvals was a pennant with the royal cipher for cyclists and a home safe with a gilt-lettered engraving promoting 'Savings in the New Reign'. Sharp's Toffee was granted permission to produce a tin with the Queen's image on the lid. Of the rejects, the vote against crown-embroidered knickers was unanimous.

On sale at home and across the English-speaking world were souvenir plates, tablecloths, powder compacts, goblets, tea towels and entire dinner services. For the first time since the war, an array of decorated ceramics came from the Staffordshire potteries. Over 2 million coronation mugs were produced for distribution to schools. At the London County Council, intense debate centred on whether schoolchildren should be presented with a commemorative mug or a state-of-the-art propelling pencil in blue plastic. The mug won.

Much as it would have wished to exercise its authority, the committee soon gave up on the advertisers for whom virtually any product had a coronation affiliation. So it was that the 'Bendix automatic home washer' was promoted as the 'Queen of the Kitchen', while a manufacturer of prams claimed that they were 'fit for a princess'.

With horse-drawn coaches a rarity on the streets, there was a shortage of practical coachmen for the royal procession. An appeal for volunteers tapped into the still common occupation of brewer's drayman, though it is doubtful that those practised in driving heavy draught horses were qualified for processional duties. An application from a veteran of the Greene King Brewery in Bury St Edmunds was politely rejected.

A detail that attracted wide publicity had to do with the recipe for the oil used to anoint the monarch. Traditionally, it was a mix of orange, cinnamon, roses, musk and aubergine, though why those particular ingredients were deemed necessary was never explained. This, in any case, was academic since the remaining stocks had been destroyed in the Blitz. A story was allowed to circulate of a retired chemist who, improbably, had a copy of the recipe. The likelihood is that ordinary olive oil served the purpose.

There were those of the Earl Marshal's circle who could be thoroughly irritating, with demands for preferential seating and a clear view of the proceedings. Having turned Longleat into a profitable business by opening his stately home to the public, the 6th Marquess of Bath demonstrated his talent for publicity by seeking permission to travel to the Abbey in his family coach-and-six. The Earl Marshal told him there would be nowhere for him to park.

As the coronation drew near, the media indulged in an orgy of royal gossip set against a historical backdrop. When the precise significance of the

Sword, the Sceptre and the Orb had been exhausted and there was nothing more to say about the thirty-eight earlier coronations since the Norman Conquest, a note of desperation entered the daily commentary. The *Sunday Times* deserved some sort of prize for the revelation that St Edward's crown was roughly equal to the weight of *Debrett's Peerage* while the Imperial State crown was heavier than *Who's Who*.

Rehearsals of one part or another of the service were held daily from 14 May. James Lees-Milne who, as Secretary of the National Trust, had all the right connections and was not inhibited from exploiting them, was rewarded with three seats at a dress rehearsal when the Duchess of Norfolk stood in for the Queen:

> We were in our seats by 8 a.m. They were in the first range built over the entrance to the north transept. Thus we looked across to Poets' Corner and over the theatre in the middle of which was set the Queen's throne on steps. The seats are hung with sky-blue damask hangings embroidered with crowns and insignia. The floor is covered with golden yellow carpet, plain. I could just see King Edward's chair on my left but not the throne of state or the altar. A magnificent spectacle.[16]

While Lees-Milne had unkind words for some of the participants (his usher, George Howard of Castle Howard, later Lord Henderskelfe, was 'very bedraggled' and 'an uncouth creature'), he had high praise for the dowager Duchess of Devonshire 'in red velvet, wearing an enormous diamond tiara and small coronet, a heavy train of infinite length and long white gloves'.

The Queen attended two full-scale rehearsals to watch the Duchess of Norfolk go through the paces under the direction of her husband, the Earl Marshal. In her private quarters in Buckingham Palace, Elizabeth practised her role 'attached to sheets tied together to mimic her thirteen-foot train'.[17] A frequent labour she had to endure was to get used to wearing the Imperial State crown, weighing in like *Who's Who* at 2.5lb. Keeping it in place while saying her lines and thinking ahead to her next move needed all her concentration.

For the press, no detail was too inconsequential. Breathlessly reported was the shortage of postilions' boots for the outriders and that the silk for the coronation dress came from Lady Hart Dyke's silk farm in Kent. Close attention was given to Norman Hartnell's white satin creation. Decorated with floral emblems of eleven Commonwealth countries, it was to become the centrepiece for an exhibition that was to tour Canada, Australia and New Zealand.

Two days before the coronation, the *Sunday Empire News* informed its readers, 'Her Majesty is not one of the light breakfasters. She likes to follow her fruit juice with a substantial dish of bacon and eggs.'

Four months had been spent on new make-up for the Queen. The beauticians had eventually settled for a peach-tinted foundation and a special lipstick to tone with the purple robe of state.

Noël Coward was among those who came to be heartily sick of London's makeover. The city, he noted in his diary, has 'become increasingly hellish, swarms of people and a perpetual misery of traffic congestion. The streets are chaos ... It will be a comfort when it is all over.'[18] 'I've nothing against the Queen,' protested a shopper. 'I'm just absolutely sick of seeing her face on everything from tinned peas upwards.'

Commenting on London's street decorations, including 1,000 waterproof and dirt-proof roses, 5ft across, provided by the Regent Street Association, the architectural historian John Summerson wrote:

> We shall not be sorry to see the end of decorated London ... this litter of strung bits, bearable only as the days mount to *the* moment, intolerable thereafter. Tom-toms cannot din louder than the pelmets so unrhythmically hung in some of our streets.[19]

Equally aggravating for the cultural elite was the repetition of popular songs with a coronation theme. At the top of the hit parade was the Welsh crooner, Donald Peers, whose soft-centred signature song, 'In a Shady Nook by a Babbling Brook', had taken him to stardom in variety and on the radio. For the coronation, he rendered 'In a Golden Coach':

> In a golden coach
> There's a heart of gold
> That belongs to you and me.
> And one day in June
> When the flowers are in bloom
> That day will make history.

Two hundred thousand copies of the sheet music were sold. Other musical attempts to cash in on the celebrations ranged from the 'Coronation Waltz' and the 'Windsor Waltz', for the middle-aged, to 'Coronation Rag' and 'Britannia Rag' for the generation that was more energetically disposed.

To enliven the party spirit and against the advice of the Minister of Food, Churchill ordered sugar rationing to be relaxed and eggs to be taken off rationing, allowing for a choice of cakes and pastries not seen in twenty years. Homemade toffee apples were all the rage. But for all young people, the concession that earned the biggest cheer was the end of sweet rationing. Shopkeepers were besieged by schoolchildren arguing how to get the best value for their pocket money. But the bureaucratic fear of a run on supplies that would empty the shops did not materialise.

The competitive element entered into the plans of towns and villages to make the coronation memorable. Since meat rationing was still in force (it was not finally abolished until June 1954), permission from the Ministry of Food had to be sought for barbecues when it was proposed to roast a whole pig or, in some ambitious communities, a whole ox. For the latter, permission was limited to those places where it could be shown that ox roasting had been part of an earlier coronation. Seventy-two applications were approved.

The dish of the year was coronation chicken. It consisted of cold chicken breasts with a curried mayonnaise and whipped cream dressing and an apricot topping. The inspiration came from Constance Spry, best known for her floral arrangements, and her business partner, the chef Rosemary Hume. Having been commissioned to arrange the coronation flowers at Westminster Abbey and along the procession route, the two ladies, joint principals of the Cordon Bleu School in Mayfair, were asked to cater for the banquet for foreign dignitaries in Westminster Hall.

Though simple to prepare, coronation chicken was made exotic by the rarity of fresh curry spices, not to mention whipped cream, in austerity Britain. That the dish soon entered the culinary mainstream was thanks to intensive farming producing cheap chicken meat. Labour costs were minimal; it needed only one man to prepare up to 15,000 chickens for slaughter. The cost of the meal was further reduced by ersatz mayonnaise and the addition of more readily available spices. If the results did not always meet the highest standards of cuisine, coronation chicken was ideal for television addicts who preferred to eat off their laps rather than miss any of the action. To supplement the meal, television celebrity chef Marguerite Patten told viewers how to prepare melon cocktails and salmon mousse.

Whatever the limited palatability of these dishes, they were superior to much of what was on offer in the average kitchen. As Christopher Morley reminisced, 'Chop cabbage and smoke haddock and steam kipper, Invoke the sausage with the vellum skin, That ought to be provided with a zipper.'[20]

However trivial some of the coronation coverage may have been, it came as welcome relief to other news that filled the front pages in the year up to the coronation. In the morning rush hour on 8 October 1952, the overnight express from Perth crashed into the rear of a local passenger train standing at Harrow and Wealdstone Station. There were one hundred and twelve fatalities, including the driver and fireman of the Perth Express, who were thus unable to explain why they had passed a cautionary colour light signal and two semaphore signals at danger. This rail disaster, Britain's worst ever, led to the installation of the automatic warning system on all main lines.

Then in late January and early February, a night-time combination of a spring tide and gale-force winds caused disastrous flooding along the North Sea coast of Britain, the Netherlands and Belgium. Of the 2,551 deaths, 307 were in Lincolnshire, Norfolk, Suffolk and Essex, with another nineteen in Scotland. Memories are of houses built on vulnerable land being swept away and of a night out on a roof waiting for rescue. This followed soon after a more localised coastal tragedy in the village of Lynmouth in north Devon, when thirty-four lives were lost in an avalanche of flood water that swept down on the village.

For those who lived in built-up areas, the winter fogs, with air so foul it could be tasted, brought death and depression. The Great Smog of the winter of 1952–53 closed central London while enveloping a 50-mile belt over the capital and its suburbs. The few buses that were still on the move had their conductors walking in front to point the way. The elderly and those suffering from bronchitis and asthma were told to stay indoors. The healthier specimens who ventured out were liable to get themselves lost trying to find their way about an otherwise familiar neighbourhood. The demand for face masks soon outran supply.

The death rate from the Great Smog was put at 12,000, with 150,000 needing hospital treatment. Yet there was no attempt to stop people smoking in public places. Under pressure from the coal lobby and its economic partners, the gas and electricity industries, the government was slow to act. In the time-honoured way of delaying a decision in the hope that the problem would somehow go away, an investigation was set up under the direction of a civil engineer, Sir Hugh Beaver, Chairman of the Committee on Power Station Construction.

Reporting in 1954, the recommendations of the Beaver Committee led to the creation of 'smoke control areas' in towns and cities where only smokeless fuels could be burned. But this only after a political fight to force the government to restrict domestic coal burning. The Clean Air Act did not come into force until 1956.

Out in the countryside, the familiar sight was of emaciated corpses of rabbits killed by myxomatosis, a highly contagious virus spread deliberately to reduce the damage caused by rabbits to arable crops. Public sympathy for the cuddly bunny made it a criminal offence to encourage the virus, but after the National Farmers' Union put pressure on the government, the disease was allowed to run its course until it had all but wiped out the rabbit population. However, nature was not so easily frustrated. A breed of wild rabbit resistant to the virus soon came to occupy the fields.

Among other pre-coronation events of note, the London trams finally gave way to diesel buses on 6 July 1952. The route of the last journey from central London to the New Cross depot took three hours longer than usual, progress being held up by cheering crowds along the way. Shortly before the finale, my father, a steam train and tram fanatic, took me to London to share his nostalgia. I was 13. We caught a tram in Kingsway to take us to the Elephant and Castle. When the conductor came to the upper deck to collect our fares, Dad waxed lyrical on the charms of a life on rail, ending with a heartfelt sympathy for the conductor: 'This must be a sad day for you.' The response was unexpected: 'You wouldn't talk like that if you had to walk up and down these f★★★★★★ stairs every five minutes.' Dad was silent for the rest of the journey.

Just a month before the coronation, the headlines were of a disaster that might, if the truth had come out earlier, have seriously dented the celebratory mood. In May 1953, the world's first jet-propelled airliner, the De Havilland Comet, Britain's pride and joy, proved not to be the miracle of aeromantic dreams. A BOAC flight from Calcutta, caught in violent storms, crashed with the loss of forty-three passengers and crew. Marked off as a freak accident, the tragedy dropped off the front pages to make way for more cheerful news. It was not until after the coronation that two more air disasters led to the withdrawal of the Comet's certificate of airworthiness. Metal fatigue was diagnosed. A redesigned Comet was launched in 1958.

After all the planning and preparation, what was needed to raise the coronation above all previous royal festivals was a national morale booster to launch the country into the new Elizabethan age. Hopes had been pinned on John Cobb, three times holder of the land-speed record, who was set on breaking the water-speed record in *Crusader*, his jet-propelled speedboat. In September 1952, on Loch Ness, he was touching 200mph when *Crusader* flipped. Cobb died, and with him any immediate likelihood of another daredevil taking up the challenge.

The spotlight shifted to the latest bid to conquer Everest. The ninth attempt to scale the world's highest mountain was led by Colonel John Hunt, an experienced climber who brought military precision to the operation. As the *Times* special correspondent accompanying the expedition, Jan Morris (writing as James) was impressed with this 'earnest and serious man, a leader of genuine inspiration, a superb organizer and a person of deep religious feeling'.[21]

With the refusal of the Nepalese authorities to allow powerful radio transmitters so near their northern frontiers, Morris had the problem of sending news back to the newspaper, preferably without rivals spoiling the exclusive. Morris settled for using runners to carry coded messages to Kathmandu, where they could be radioed to London. By mid-May, the runners were covering the 180-mile trek over rough country at impressive speed. The fastest, who did it in six days, earned the 'fabulous sum' of £20.

On 27 May, after one failed attempt, a second assault was made by New Zealander Edmund Hillary and Sherpa Tenzing Norgay. They reached the summit at 11.30 a.m. on 28 May 1953. Before descending they took photographs and, at Hunt's request, buried a small cross in the snow. Morris was among those waiting for the heroes' return at Base Camp:

> Hillary brandished his ice-axe in weary triumph; Tenzing slipped suddenly sideways, recovered and shot us a brilliant white smile; and they were among us, back from the summit, with men pumping their hands and embracing them, laughing, smiling, crying, taking photographs, laughing again, crying again, till the noise and delight of it all rang down the Cwm and set the Sherpas, following us up the hill, laughing in anticipation.[22]

To achieve maximum impact, the news was held back in London until the morning of the coronation when Sidney Holland, New Zealand's Prime Minister, declared that Hillary had put 'the British and New Zealand on top of the world'. Later that year, the release of feature-length documentary *The Conquest of Everest*, scripted by the Northern Irish poet and playwright Louis MacNeice and narrated by Welsh actor Meredith Edwards, introduced a British rather than a purely English dimension that was likely to appeal to recent migrants. All was now set for the party of a lifetime.

# 6

# OVER THE AIR

The BBC was quick to put in a bid to televise the entire coronation. It was a bold move. The relationship between the royal family and the broadcasters had long been edgy. As early as 1922, the suggestion was made to the Palace that the King's Christmas broadcast should be relayed over the airwaves. But in those early days of radio, George V was suspicious of a medium that could magnify, but not correct, errors of presentation. He rejected the idea.

Ten years later, when broadcasting had proved its worth, he was more amenable. His voice, 'strong, emphatic, vibrant, with undertones of sentiment, devoid of all condescension, artifice or pose', reached some 20 million listeners across Britain and the Empire.[1] It helped that he could call on the services of professional writers from Rudyard Kipling to the romantic historian Arthur Bryant to give his speeches the polish that was quite beyond his own capabilities. The strong Christian stance taken in the Christmas messages of 1934 and 1935 was the result of having Gordon Cosmo Lang, Archbishop of Canterbury, as his speech writer.

The 1932 Christmas message was transmitted worldwide. As recently appointed Director General of the BBC, John Reith judged the broadcast to be 'most impressive and excellent' and 'the most spectacular success in BBC history thus far'. He recorded in his autobiography:

The King had been heard all over the world with surprising clarity; only in New Zealand were parts of the speech inaudible owing to the atmospherics. It was sensationally starred in foreign countries; the *New*

*York Times* in large type: 'Distant lands Thrill to His "God Bless You"'; two thousand leading articles were counted in Broadcasting House.[2]

George V continued to make a live broadcast every Christmas Day until his death in 1936. But it was not yet a fixture. As a prime minister notoriously short on imagination, Neville Chamberlain could see no point in continuing the annual observance when, in his view, it was impossible to produce something new and interesting to say every year. Reith fought back successfully, noting in his diary, 'How pathetic, almost unbelievable. How typical of the attitude of politicians.'[3]

But if, broadly speaking, radio was acceptable in royal circles, the hazards of television were much more of a challenge. The first programme of the world's first high-definition television service was called *Here's Looking at You*. It was transmitted from Alexandra Palace on 26 August 1936. The official opening of BBC television followed in November. Live programmes, from 9.00 to 11.00 every evening, were interspersed with Disney cartoons and cinema newsreels. Outside broadcasts covered Prime Minister Chamberlain's return from Munich, test matches and the cup final. One hundred and forty-five live plays were produced in 1938. But with the closure of the television service for the duration of the war, there was much catching up to do.

Television had a powerful rival in the cinema newsreels. Part of every cinema programme from early in the century when Pathé News was launched, the newsreels found favour with the establishment by virtue of their restraint. Nothing controversial was allowed to intrude on providing innocent entertainment for the masses. Self-censorship highlighted all that was positive and cheerful, though solemn occasions such as royal funerals were respectfully recorded.

For those in the spotlight, the fear of misrepresentation by moving pictures was not altogether unfounded. Of wretched memory was the film reconstruction of Edward VII's coronation by Charles Urban, a pioneer of cinematography. Spotting the chance for a quick profit, he got together with Georges Méliès to produce a fake newsreel of the event. This he did by sending photographs of the Abbey interior and costume designs to Paris, where Méliès engaged a washhouse attendant to play Edward and a music-hall singer his Queen for a six-minute version of the ceremony.[4] It was a great success, though not with the royals.

For true representation, cinema audiences were mesmerised by images of the funeral of Edward VII. The cameras were out again the following year for the coronation procession of George V and for all subsequent turning points in the royal saga, albeit with limited access. Jealous of a potential contender for the coverage of royal events, the cinema newsreels lobbied to hold back the BBC. The Archbishop of Canterbury gave them his blessing.

There was never any question of allowing television cameras into the Abbey for the coronation of George VI, though it was the first to be filmed. A forty-man camera crew, who had to wear dinner jackets, were in the Abbey to give a flavour of the proceedings to cinema audiences. The risk to royal dignity was minimal. Even a shot of Queen Mary wiping a tear was edited out. John Reith accepted the put-down, settling instead for radio coverage but without a voiceover.

However, the royal procession was televised. The BBC's Director of Television, Gerald Cock, placed his cameras on the central plinth of Apsley Gate where he could get a clear close-up view of the procession without interruption. He then went to the Palace to ask the King if he would smile into the camera when his carriage passed. 'The King agreed and wrote on a slip of paper that he kept inside the coach. "Look right outside the window at Hyde Park Corner and smile".'[5] Freddie Grisewood, a familiar voice of the BBC, provided the commentary. The press was ecstatic. 'The coronation marched into English homes yesterday,' enthused the *Telegraph*. Reith was well satisfied:

> There had been occasional difficulties with the Earl Marshal or his office, but this was to be expected; there were certainly no precedents for them to consult. He gave the engineers a fright on the afternoon of May 10 by saying they must all be out of the Abbey by 4pm next day; not even a night watchman could be left. The idea of leaving unguarded all the complicated and delicate gear upon which so much would depend on May 12 [coronation day] was intolerable. I had to come in on that myself.[6]

The only other worry for Reith was the King's coronation broadcast:

> The King had rehearsed his speech on a closed circuit in the Palace; he had taken immense trouble over this broadcast; in the playbacks was studying to get the best speed, inflexion, tone.

The BBC was, of course, taking no risks. A gramophone record of the speech as delivered during the final rehearsal was ready as a standby in case anything went wrong.[7]

In the event, all was well – not so with the commentary for the Coronation Spithead Review, the largest assembly of warships since the Coronation Review of 1911. Reporting for radio live from the battleship HMS *Nelson*, Thomas Woodrooffe had overindulged with former naval colleagues before taking up the microphone. Within seconds it was clear that he was sloshed out of his mind. After several slurred references to the fleet being 'lit up', as indeed he was, the sound faded. Remarkably for such a staid organisation, Woodrooffe got away with a mild reprovement and a week's suspension. The BBC said he was 'tired and emotional'.

By the late 1930s the potential of television was widely recognised. 'As an invention it is tremendous,' noted Harold Nicolson, 'and may alter the whole basis of democracy.'[8] But with the war, the media revolution was put on hold. Failing to recognise a morale-boosting provider of essential information, the Chamberlain government, in an act of towering stupidity, closed down the service.

It was six years before it was relaunched and then only for a few hundred thousand viewers in the London area. With radio as the dominant medium, the upstart generated little enthusiasm in the higher reaches of the BBC. In 1946, the former war correspondent Robert Barr, who had moved from radio to television, ran into a senior sound producer at Broadcasting House. '"Good Lord, I thought you were dead." "No, I'm not," said Barr. "Ah yes, gone to television; same thing really."'[9]

It was up to the King to decide on the vexed question of how the wedding of Elizabeth and Philip should be presented to the country. The central question was how far television was to be allowed to intrude into the Abbey. Rejected out of hand was the filming of the wedding ceremony, judged to be a 'private and religious' matter, though in this context 'privacy' was surely a hostage to fortune.

Having created a film unit to accompany the royal family on the South African tour, the BBC felt sufficiently confident to bid for as much coverage of the wedding as propriety would allow. But, yet again, this put television in competition with the cinema newsreels, who refused any co-operation with their dreaded rival. In the end, the King was persuaded to allow for filming and live television coverage of the return procession up the nave after the service.

Around a million viewers tuned in. But it was radio, with thirty-two microphones deployed in the Abbey, that claimed the lion's share of public attention.

The television coverage of the funeral service of George VI was limited to a few minutes, though the impact of the world coverage was out of all proportion to the time allocated. The funeral procession attracted an audience of 4.5 million, the largest yet. The event made for exceptional television. 'The black-veiled new queen, the lilies on the coffin quivering in the breeze, the birds flying above Windsor Castle's Round Tower as the flag was lowered, all showed up in beautiful chiaroscuro.'[10]

The advance of television began to accelerate in 1950 when Alexandra Palace was supported by a second transmitter, this at Sutton Coldfield. A year later, a new transmitter at Holme Moss allowed viewers in Manchester and the West Riding to catch glimpses of the Festival of Britain and to share with Midlands and London viewers a play 'specially written' by Terence Rattigan called *The Final Test*, including filmed sequences at the Oval. For the first time, a general election featured political broadcasts with wooden-top party stalwarts putting their case to the viewing public.

With the opening of transmitters at Wenvoe and Kirk O'Shotts in 1952, 80 per cent of the population came within technical reach – the highest proportion in the world – and the number of licence holders rose to 2 million. It was estimated that up to 5 million viewers watched the first direct transmission from Paris showing the 14 July celebrations.

But with the variable quality of the screen images, not to mention the substandard content on television, radio still had the edge. Looking back from his vantage point in the 1970s, Douglas Bridson, Assistant Head of Radio Features from 1950, reflected, 'The excessive timidity of the BBC Higher Command in the early post-war years is truly ludicrous to remember ... But the fact remains, its role as the BBC saw it, was to reflect the most respectably orthodox opinion as it already existed.'[11]

Condescension was buttressed by apprehension. After his initial excitement at television as a force for change, Harold Nicolson confessed to his diary the fear that it would 'abolish newspapers, cinemas, the stage and reading'. Others from the cultural top drawer, like T.S. Eliot, warned of television as a 'menace to community living and to child development'.

No attempt was made by the government to challenge this view. Not to be trusted to know their own best interests, the people had to be protected from content that the pundits considered to be malign.

After the departure of Sir William Haley to edit *The Times*, the search for a director general with a safe pair of hands settled on Major General Sir Ian Jacob, former Assistant Secretary to the War Cabinet, who was on friendly terms with Churchill. Prior to his appointment, he had been in charge of the Overseas Service where, much to Churchill's liking, the objective was to promote a favourable view of Britain across the world.

That Jacob was a shoe-in to the top job was largely in recognition of his administrative talents. But to say that he was conservative in his tastes is to put it mildly: 'He distrusted intellectuals and carefully shunned controversy.'[12] Moreover, he was said to 'possess to the full the unbelievable self-confidence, arrogance and righteousness which so characterised the BBC after the war'.[13]

While Jacob professed a liking for opera and ballet, he was indifferent to drama and allergic to light entertainment. The image he presented to staff was of the only employee to enter Broadcasting House wearing a bowler hat, the symbol of dyed-in-the-wool conservatism.

The break with convention that somehow managed to escape the blacklist was radio's *Goon Show*. With Spike Milligan as the presiding genius, the Goons sent up all that middle-class culture held most dear, such as the 'Ascent of Mount Everest' (from the inside) and 'Through the Sound Barrier in a Wardrobe'. Milligan used Cockney slang to introduce words that would have caused apoplexy had the stuffed shirts known what he was talking about. A fond memory of schooldays is of the spoof peasant revolt against the wicked 'Idleburgers'. Did no one in the higher reaches say the word out loud?

More suited to mainstream acceptability was *Mrs Dale's Diary*, the daily events in the life of a doctor's wife who was always worried about her hard-working husband, Jim. Launched as a radio serial drama on 5 January 1948, this saga of suburban routine continued on its monotonous way until April 1969. In 1951, *The Archers* started on their interminable journey.

For television, closely monitored restraint remained the order of the day. What passed for news was a recording of the nine o'clock bulletin on radio, repeated on television, in sound only, at the end of the evening. Twice a week, *Television Newsreel* presented a quarter of an hour of pre-recorded snippets of sporting events and other hardy perennials such as the monarch handing out Maundy Money or the Olney Pancake Race. It was not until July 1954 that the BBC embarked on an evening news programme with a newsreader providing the links. Here was the opportunity for the BBC to set itself apart from the standard fare served up by the cinema newsreels, but the obsession with 'objectivity' mitigated against any serious scrutiny of politics or politicians.

As BBC news took its lead from the daily press, so too did drama follow the diktats of live theatre. For the *Play of the Week*, there was even a ten-minute interval when the screen went blank and a bell sounded to recall viewers. Despite the Goons, comedy was heavily censored. Anyone who attempted humour had a 'red for danger' attached to their lapel. It was the governing rule of the Variety Programme Policy Guide that no offence should be given 'to any part of the diversified audience'. Writers were told that 'music hall, stage and to a lesser degree, screen standards, are not suitable to broadcasting'.

If the guardians of morality were slow to catch on to Goonisms, they were quick to detect double meanings when none were intended. A dance number played by Geraldo's orchestra, which had the line 'Why don't we do this more often, just as we're doing tonight', had to be changed to 'just as we're doing today'. Other well-known songs that had to be modified included 'Let's Put Out the Lights and Go to Bed'. The revised version changed this to 'Let's Put Out the Lights and Go to Sleep'.

Advertising was anathema to the BBC. The censor's twitch was pronounced whenever there was a risk of a commercial brand occupying air time:

> Nobody on-air was allowed to Hoover a carpet, they were obliged to vacuum clean it. We were similarly forbidden to make use of certain brand names which, heretofore, we had not even realised were brand names: Cellophane, Linoleum, Vaseline, Escalator, Menthol, Aspro – though you could get away with aspirin ... On BBC TV, they were equally punctilious about permitting brand names to appear in shot. If a particular product was essential to a scene, it was the duty of the prop man to disfigure its logo with a felt pen so that the name was no longer apparent. Hence, a treasured sitcom moment: a breakfast-table scene in which the foreground was occupied by a cereal box bearing the label, 'Ellogg's Orn Lakes'.[14]

But even with the blanket rule against anything unseemly, royalty remained suspicious of the invasive power of television. Would the coronation prove to be the exception to royal inhibitions?

From the point of view of the BBC, the coronation had the qualities Jacob and his senior colleagues most desired: a major event that promised to be hugely popular while meeting all the requirements of propriety. Perversely, the Establishment was slow to appreciate the opportunity. When formal application was made to the Coronation Committee to televise the entire event, the reaction was hostile. With the exception of Sir George Bellew, Garter Principal King of Arms, who was second only to Fisher in planning the coronation service, the Queen's advisers were as one in warning of 'an intolerable strain on the Queen and on everyone else' and that 'no mistake could ever be rectified'.[15] If there was to be television coverage, it had to be restricted to the procession on entry as it moved eastwards towards the organ screen, and later westwards as it moved out. Bellew could see how royalty might benefit from allowing the public to feel part of the coronation, but for now he was a lonely voice.[16] Churchill was at his most pompous when he told the House of Commons, 'It would be unfitting that the whole ceremony, not only in its secular but also in its religious and spiritual aspects should be presented as if it were a theatrical performance.'

Predictably, Fisher was resolutely opposed to anything that threatened the religious solemnity of the occasion. In his mind, television was associated with the 'low entertainment' that he deplored in any context. He was not joking when he told journalists that 'the world would have been a happier place had television never been discovered'. The argument that broadcasting equipment would interfere with sight lines and that high-voltage light, particularly when it was focused on the Queen, would be distracting begged the question as to why, then, were newsreel crews to be allowed in the Abbey?

Arguing the case for the BBC was George Barnes, who had moved from Controller of the Third Programme (Radio 3) to become Director of BBC Television. His appointment caused ructions among the TV veterans who had assumed that the job would go to one of them. With the coronation in view, doubtless it was his persuasive personality that gave Barnes the edge. One of his former colleagues said, 'Barnes was a tall sandy-haired charmingly diffident man who was much liked by all who worked with him.

His humour was as dry as a good martini, and he even had the ability to see the funny side of himself.'[17]

Jacob was supportive, though he was not the forceful advocate of coronation coverage portrayed by his admirers. He was content to let Barnes make the running. Where the Director General was critical to the future, was in his promoting his Ten Year Plan for bringing 95 per cent of the population within range of the television service.

In his dealings with the Palace, Barnes presented the friendly and sympathetic face of the BBC. It helped that the popular press gave him full backing. When the *Daily Express* found that four out of five of its readers favoured televising the coronation, it made front-page news. To restrict the cameras was a 'monumental piece of misjudgement', boomed Cassandra, star columnist of the *Daily Mirror*. Riding a tide of public opinion, Barnes took the offensive, making clear, for example, that the latest technology had reduced the level of light required and that any untoward incident could be edited out of the live transmission by a sharp-eyed producer in his control box in the Abbey.

What was the Duke of Edinburgh's share in the debate? As a modernist he might have been expected to favour an initiative that would enable the monarch to reach out to her people. If he held back it was because he had little choice but to side with the Queen, who voiced her fears of being exposed, at this most important moment of her life, to the close scrutiny of the all-seeing cameras. Doubtless he engaged in gentle persuasion.

The furore created by the press did not pass unnoticed in Downing Street. Acutely sensitive to editorial opinion, Churchill shifted ground. Having declared on 7 July that a ban would remain in force, by early October it became clear that he had had a change of heart. After a round-table meeting with the Archbishop, Sir Alan Lascelles and Sir Harold Emmerson, Permanent Secretary to the Ministry of Works, Fisher wrote in his diary, 'From the first word it was quite obvious that [Churchill] had made up his mind that everything should be televised except, possibly, the Consecration and the Communion.'[18]

The House of Commons was told of the decision on 28 October, with Churchill emphasising that the cameras would in no way detract from 'the utmost moral seriousness' of the occasion. Details of the television coverage were announced on 8 December. As Fisher had anticipated, there were to be no pictures of the anointing ceremony or of the Queen receiving Communion. Only four cameras were to be allowed in the Abbey.

In trumpeting a victory, the press gave the impression that it had been the Queen who had responded to public demand. It would have been more accurate to say that she had given close attention to those of her circle who were converts to the cause, notably Viscount Swinton, a pre-war air minister and currently Chancellor of the Duchy of Lancaster, who was on close terms with Churchill. The Queen was assured that all would be done to allay her concerns. Cameras would be allowed beyond the organ screen so long as there were 'no close-ups'.

The rule was made for breaking. 'We used every trick in the book because people deserved to see the Coronation,' recalled Peter Dimmock, then head of the BBC's fledgling Outside Broadcasts division:

> There was a rule that no camera could be closer than 30 feet from the Queen. I got a girl to walk down the aisle as though she was the Queen, but used a two-inch lens – the widest there was – and she looked a mile away. They [Buckingham Palace] were happy with that, but what they didn't know was that I was going to use a 12-inch lens that would give the best close-up of the Queen that there had ever been.[19]

Dimmock was also responsible for the famous shot of Prince Charles with the Queen Mother, looking down on Elizabeth at the moment when she was about to be crowned.

In October 1952, a long-awaited extension of television coverage was announced with two new transmitters at Pontop Pike in County Durham and at Glencairn in the hills overlooking Belfast. Both were opened on 1 May 1953, just in time for the coronation. Both were 'makeshift, austerity affairs', housed in pre-war outside-broadcast vans. On each hilltop, a skeleton staff of eight engineers lived in a wooden hut.[20]

Many who rented or bought televisions for the coronation had them installed in time for the FA Cup Final, the first football match to reach a mass TV audience.[21] The game had a thrilling second half. Blackpool was 1–3 down to Bolton with only twenty-two minutes left, yet managed to win 4–3, with two goals scored by the 38-year-old Stanley Matthews, one of the greatest players of the British game. Most of the 10 million viewers who followed his career in the press were seeing him in action for the first time. John Moynihan, later a football writer, watched the game on a set owned by his friend's father, an antique dealer in St John's Wood: 'Blackpool's winning goal in the dying moments saw the living room come to life as "men seized cushions and hugged them to their bellies" … The room was electric, the television screen swarming with Blackpool players hugging and embracing and we were hugging and embracing.'[22]

No better warm-up for the coronation could be imagined.

# 7

# A COUNTRY AT ODDS
# WITH ITSELF

Brought up in a controlled setting, what did Elizabeth know of the country of which she was now sovereign? She had no need to be told that Britain had much to be proud of. Ending the war as one of the victors, it enjoyed a booming economy with a line-up of blue chip companies that straddled the world.

In 1950, Britain accounted for a quarter of world trade in manufacturing, was the foremost shipbuilder and the leading European producer of coal, steel, cars and textiles. For the first and last time the United Kingdom was the world's largest car exporter. Incredible as it must now seem, Britain was the leading car exporter to the United States, where small family cars such as the Morris Minor found favour.[1] Companies such as Rolls-Royce, De Havilland, English Electric and Pye, the pioneer of radio and television equipment, were highly visible symbols of excellence. British exports were back to their pre-war volume by 1947. Three years later, they were two-thirds higher.

Yet everything about Britain seemed scruffy and down-at-heel. Looking back from 1997, novelist Doris Lessing recognised how difficult it was for her younger contemporaries to understand what a poor country Britain was after the war:

Few people had central heating: we were the laughing-stock in Europe because our attitude towards it, for somewhere in a corner of a puritanical national soul there is still a feeling that to be comfortable and warm is self-indulgent. We had gas or electric fires, fed by coins put into a meter. This meant that people returned from work into freezing rooms. Refrigerators were only just becoming common. I had a food safe on a wall and bought milk and meat as I needed them. Most floors had rugs or mats on stained or painted boards; wall-to-wall carpeting was still to become general. You could go into a house or flat full of good old solid furniture, but there was no heating, no refrigerator, the kitchen was still furnished by a china sink and wooden draining boards, and chilly floors shivered under beautiful rugs. A lot of furniture was still 'Utility', because of the war. During the war, Utility furniture and Utility clothes were all that could be bought new, and both seemed designed to prove just how ugly necessity had to be.

An average young person taken back to stand in a quite unremarkable home of then, the early and mid-fifties would be ... well, what? Embarrassed, probably. All too recent for comfort: the world of their grandparents, a threadbare, cold adequacy in everything.[2]

'England was so poor,' wrote Ted Hughes in one of his last poems. 'Was black paint cheaper? Why were English cars all black – to hide the filth? Or to stay respectable, like bowlers.' And ending, 'Our sole indigenous art-form – depressionist!'[3]

Returning to Britain after working in America, the theatre and film director Lindsay Anderson said:

Coming back to Britain is also, in many respects, like going back to the nursery. The outside world, the dangerous world, is shut away: its sounds are muffled. Cretonne curtains are drawn ... Nanny lights the fire, and sits herself down with a nice cup of tea and yesterday's *Daily Express*; but she keeps half an eye on us too, as we bring out our trophies from abroad, the books and pictures we have managed to get past the customs. Nanny has a pair of scissors handy, to cut out anything it wouldn't be right for children to see.[4]

It was one of the paradoxes of coronation year that while the economy was booming as never before, dinge and abject poverty was widespread. Up to a fifth of housing in London and other cities was classified as slums. For many households, running hot water was an unimaginable luxury. The outside loo with a chamber pot under the bed for night relief was standard, as too was the weekly ritual of the tin bath in the kitchen.

Food shortages were high on the list of discontents. In 1950, the weekly meat ration was down to 1 shilling's worth. The following year it fell to 8*d*. It was not until July 1954 that bacon, ham and beef finally came off points. Substitutes for conventional fare were promoted by a hard-pressed Ministry of Food. Shortly before Elizabeth's accession, housewives were urged to try ration-free 'rich, meaty Vienna steaks' costing only 2 shillings and sixpence. How could this be? It turned out to be canned whale meat with its oily, fishy taste.

Even less tempting was whale steak and kidney pudding, whale-steak casserole and curried whale steak. There was even a whale-meat advisory bureau in Mayfair's Upper Grosvenor Street. The sales campaign fell short of expectations. Four thousand tons of unwanted whale meat stored in Tyneside warehouses went into cat food. It was easier to pass off horse meat as the genuine article. A Soho horsemeat butcher had a daily queue of waiters from neighbouring restaurants.

Among the oddest recipes were haddock pudding, sausage croquettes and curried corned beef and vegetable pie, the latter suggested by Food Minister Maurice Webb to hard-pressed boarding house landladies in Weston-super-Mare who had demanded to know how they were supposed to keep their guests happy at table. The *Sunday Graphic* recommended beaver cooked with onions, presumably to disguise the taste.

What for most people was a colourless and dull life led to a social malaise that was reflected in the high street, where a take-it-or-leave-it attitude, with endless queues, made shopping a miserable experience. Even when a few 'luxuries' appeared on the home market, their availability depended on joining a long waiting list. An autumn 1951 issue of *Lilliput*, a monthly magazine, featured the 'chair of the future … light weight, rust-proof, hard wearing, constructed on sound engineering principles to bring you lasting pleasure down the years'. There was only one drawback. The model was for export only, though rejects 'with some flaws' were available on the first come, first served principle.

What had gone wrong? The answer was a combination of arrogance and complacency. The arrogance was part of the make-up of almost every British politician. With the defeat of Nazism, Britain, at least by its own estimation, was one of the three great superpowers. But keeping up with the United States and the Soviet Union came at a cost the country could ill afford.

The heaviest burden on the national income was the spiralling cost of defence. At five times its pre-war level, defence expenditure accounted for up to 8 per cent of gross national product, and 23 per cent of the entire national budget, more than any other country except the Soviet Union. Whether the money was spent efficiently was another question. For the moment, by keeping up appearances across the globe, Britain was a force to be reckoned with. British troops were stationed in West Germany, Austria, Italy, Libya, Malta, Cyprus, throughout the Middle East and over a patchwork of colonial outposts. Fears of Russian incursions into Western Europe meant keeping a large standing army in Germany. Though hard pressed to find the money, Britain backed American action against North Korean forces when they crossed the 38th Parallel in June 1950.

In October 1952, Britain became the third nuclear power after tests were successfully carried out at the Montebello Islands off Western Australia. The news was greeted ecstatically by sections of the press, who saw it as confirmation of Britain's might to sit at the top table. Until the Campaign for Nuclear Disarmament was founded in 1957, few questioned the strategic value of a weapon that could, for all practical purposes, only be used in concert with the United States. It was prestige that mattered, irrespective of the cost.

Prestige was also at stake in economic policy. It was an article of faith to maintain sterling at an artificially high exchange rate against the dollar. This required a massive build-up of gold and dollar reserves to support the pound and to safeguard sterling as the second world currency. As an inevitable consequence, exports were more expensive and thus uncompetitive, a burden on manufacturing studiously ignored by a government which refused to contemplate devaluation.

The net result was that the post-war years of austerity were far more austere than they needed to have been. And the result of that was a country in the doldrums with a general feeling that if life was hard, it was likely to get harder. Meanwhile, sit tight and hope for the best.

An insight into the British character in the lead-up to the coronation was provided by Geoffrey Gorer, who based his study on 14,000 responses from readers of the *Sunday People*, then the country's second-most popular weekend paper with a circulation of over 12 million.[5] The national profile that surfaced gave the average citizen as working class, a self-assessment based on family background and education, with schooling for the majority finishing at the age of 14 or under.

At base was an instinctive fear of breaking the mould. Young people should be seen and not heard, corporal punishment was justified at home and in school, 'knowing your place' was socially desirable and the voices of authority had to be respected. Those who rose above their class were viewed with suspicion, even hostility. 'Improving one's position is not without dangers in England,' noted Gorer.[6]

The police were held in high regard, at least by those who had no first-hand experience of the heavy hand of the law. 'An ideal model of behaviour and character' was one typical comment. A 38-year-old man in New Malden declared the police to be 'the first body of men of this kind in the world'.

When it came to personal relations, more than half of the respondents described themselves as 'exceptionally shy', counterbalanced by a majority who felt that 'people are not so narrow minded as they used to be', a hint of a less hidebound future and seen as no bad thing. Celibacy before marriage was axiomatic, while drink and infidelity were judged to be the major causes of marital breakdown.

Gorer concluded, 'There seems every reason to believe that the sexual morals of the English have changed very little in the present century.' To which a recent commentator adds, 'The social relationships and institutions of the society, the basic values and sentiments and styles of life of which they are a reflection, remained more or less intact.'[7]

Though disturbing on several counts, nowhere is there any mention in Gorer's survey of the British passion for tobacco. The startling figures were given by Chancellor Hugh Dalton in his 1947 Budget Speech to the House of Commons: 'We are now smoking one-third more than before the war, more than 250 million pounds weight a year; more than 100,000 tons of tobacco; more than 100,000 million cigarettes and 70 million ounces of pipe tobacco.'

When the health hazards became a talking point (the first study linking smoking with lung cancer was published in 1950), it was often assumed that the Treasury was reluctant to act in any way that would reduce the tax revenue from the sale of tobacco. But Dalton made a more telling counter-argument:

> About 80 per cent of our tobacco is imported from the United States and, to satisfy this insatiable demand, we are drawing heavily and improvidently on the dollars which we earn with our exports, as well as on the American line of credit. It is hardly to be believed, but the whole total of

our exports to the United States at this time barely exceeds, in value, our own consumption of American tobacco. The thing has become fantastic and must be stopped.[8]

He imposed a tax rise that increased the price of a packet of twenty cigarettes by about a third. But the public addiction was not so easily quashed. The sale of tobacco continued to rise throughout the fifties.

Britain was a country in thrall to old men, mostly of the middle and upper class, a generation who, having come through the war, found it hard to visualise anything better than a return to the 'good old days' which, of course, for most people were not good at all. Historians besotted with the welfare state – free education up to the age of 15, a free health service, subsistence pensions for the elderly and insurance against unemployment, all momentous achievements – are inclined to skip over the downside of a society in which any change was received with suspicion.

A businessman who imported an American automatic washing machine failed to attract investment for a British model. 'There's no call for it,' he was told. Another entrepreneur who headed a taskforce to drum up business in America was driven to distraction by the British disregard for market realities. 'Everything we sold was in black, dark blue or brown. On the West Coast where bright colours were the rule, a Lancashire suit or a Midlands car were too depressing for words.' An order for a fleet of London taxis was turned down because the manufacturer refused to put in a left-hand drive.

At home, next to 'It can't be done, Gov', the retort that ranked highest in the catalogue of lame excuses for inferior service was the unfailing clincher, 'That's not my job'. Fearful of a return to the unemployment of the 1930s, trade unions enforced strict demarcation while resisting mechanisation that might displace the human element.

When J.B. Priestley described his countrymen as the 'dullest adults in Europe', he was perhaps thinking of the English Sunday with its archaic laws enforced by the Lord's Day Observance Society. From his office in Fleet Street, the society's secretary boasted that he never cleaned his shoes on Sunday and would not permit his wife to iron a shirt. There was no question of allowing cinemas or theatres to open or for sports events to be held. When the society intervened, a Sunday ballet performance in aid of the restoration of Coventry Cathedral had to be cancelled. The Queen's Consort came in for censure when he was spotted out riding on the

Sabbath. In 1953, a bill to relax the rules on Sunday entertainment was defeated in the Commons by 281 votes to 57.

That Britain was in urgent need of a social revolution showed up most plainly in relations between the sexes. Having made an outstanding contribution to the war effort, women were expected to retreat back into the kitchen and the nursery, a bigotry that held sway even after a young woman was elevated to head of state.

The obstacles to women leading independent, full lives were many and various. Mortgages were denied to single women. Contraception was available only to married couples. It needed a man's counter-signature for a woman to rent a car or TV. Unequal pay for equal work was axiomatic.

Marriage was a bar to many occupations. The two British airlines, BOAC and BEA, required their hostesses to be single. Conditions of employment such as holiday entitlements and pensions were angled towards men. Most employers simply could not imagine a woman in a senior role.

On radio, a coronation year session of *Any Questions* was asked, 'Is it still a man's world?' The panellist rewarded with the loudest applause had this to say: 'I think that, generally speaking, quite seriously, in this country most of a woman's work is at home,' adding, 'Since we men earn most of the money, we deserve to escape from time to time from the terrific dominance of the home.' Everywhere there was encouragement for women to throw off the guise of masculine capability in deference to the traditional concept of feminine beauty (for the young) and maternal warmth (for the not so young).

In education, the lead came from John Newsom, Chief Education Officer for Hertfordshire. In a widely quoted report on the Education of Girls, Newsom, who was reckoned to be one of the more imaginative of his profession, argued that girls should be educated 'in terms of their main social function – which is to make for themselves, their children and their husbands a secure and suitable home and to be mothers'. For boys, 'the equivalent dominant is to earn enough to support their wives and families'.[9]

Sex was a taboo subject in schools, an embarrassment best to be avoided. In Brighton from 1946 to 1961, there was a total ban on sex education. In London, the subject could be on the curriculum as long as it was taught by someone not 'overly interested' in the subject, a condition that would have been a disqualification in any other area of study.

Homosexuality was seen as a threat to civilisation. Judges were lenient on police who, casual at best, tampered with evidence to secure a prosecution or entered premises without a search warrant. Agents provocateurs in public lavatories secured a string of convictions against well-known names. Dragged into court in 1952, the mathematical genius Alan Turing escaped prison by agreeing to oestrogen injections. Two years later, he took poison.

In coronation year, one of the best and best-known actors, the recently knighted Sir John Gielgud, was arrested at a public lavatory in Chelsea. The magistrate delivered harsh words ('This conduct is dangerous to other men ... and is a scourge in this neighbourhood') with a light sentence – a fine of £10 for a case of drunk and disorderly along with advice to Gielgud to consult a doctor. This produced a press backlash against such a benign punishment.

Censorship of the arts was all pervading. In force for nearly 100 years, the 1857 Obscene Publications Act allowed police and custom officials to enter private premises without a warrant in order to find, seize and destroy publications deemed to be 'of a nature to shock the common feelings of decency in any well-regulated mind'. In the early 1950s, few questioned these ground rules. Norman Mailer's debut novel *The Naked and the Dead*, now ranked as one of the 100 best novels of the twentieth century, was described by the *Sunday Times* as 'an extreme case of obscenity' using language 'incredibly foul and beastly'. The paper called for the novel to be withdrawn from sale.

It was one of the ironies of film censorship aimed at protecting young people that the A certificate, which ruled that under-16s must be accompanied by an adult, led to a form of soliciting outside cinemas ('Will you take me in, Mister?') and under-the-raincoat sex inside. In 1951, censorship was tightened with the introduction of the X certificate for movies deemed entirely unsuitable for under-16s.

The Board of Trade put pressure on cinema chains to reject *Chance of a Lifetime*, a Bernard Miles movie about a factory taken over and run successfully by the workers, on the grounds that it was communist propaganda.

The first sign that the public might not be entirely averse to reforming outmoded laws came with the 1948 Criminal Justice Act, which abolished hard labour, penal servitude and, against the advice of the Lord Chief Justice, flogging. A proposal to do away with the death penalty for an experimental five years was thrown out by the House of Lords. There followed a succession of notorious errors of judgement. In the month of the coronation, the trial and conviction of John Christie for the murder of four women including his wife put in doubt the conviction and execution of Timothy Evans in 1950, when Christie had appeared as a prosecution witness. Christie later confessed to the murder of Evans' wife and daughter. He was hanged on 15 July.

In 1952 a Somalian, Mahmood Mattan, described by his defence lawyer as 'a half-child of nature, a semi-civilised savage', was hanged in Cardiff for a murder he clearly had not committed – he had four witnesses providing an alibi, while four others had failed to identify Mattan in an identity parade. The key prosecution witness was paid to give evidence and in 1969 was jailed for life for trying to kill his daughter. That same year, 19-year-old Derek Bentley, who had a learning disability, was hanged for a murder committed by his underage partner-in-crime. A reprieve was rejected by the Home Secretary on the grounds that Bentley's fate 'must stand as an example to other gunmen', even though the condemned man had been armed with no more than a knuckleduster. Spurious reasons were given for the Speaker refusing to allow a Parliamentary debate, though it was clear that the chief consideration was to avoid bringing the judicial system into disrepute.

Between 1949 and 1960, 123 murderers were executed in Britain, 41 per cent of them under 26 years of age and around 50 per cent convicted of crimes of passion and/or crimes of a diseased mind with a psychiatric history of one kind or another. It was not until 1957 that the Homicide Act introduced diminished responsibility as a defence, while the death penalty for murder remained in place until 1965.

But despite its best efforts to keep a grip, the old order was not entirely secure. The catalyst for change was inherent in an economy that favoured young people with secure employment and bulkier pay packets. A new social and economic group, known simply as teenagers, began to flex its muscle. The novelist Colin McInnes caught the mood:

> The kids discovered that, for the first time, they had money, which hitherto had always been denied them at the best time in life to use it, namely, when you're young and strong. We had loot to spend, at last, and our world was to be our world, the one *we* wanted …[10]

What they did not want was the staid, drab world of their elders.

If they looked anywhere for inspiration it was to the United States which, by 1953, accounted for half the world's manufacturing output and 40 per cent of the world's income. It seemed that God's own country had it all – supermarkets, shopping malls, fast-food chains, residential air conditioning, freezers, dishwashers, detergents, ballpoint pens, hi-fi, tape recorders, long-playing records, polaroid cameras, four-lane highways and power steering. And they all worked. In Britain when, on rare occasions, marvels of domesticity did appear, they invariably broke down at the second push of a button.

The symbol of rebellion was the teenage desire to look different. In contrast to their pre-war predecessors, they did not aspire to be smaller versions of their parents. Jeans and T-shirts came into vogue. The biggest part of the teenage budget was spent on clothes – striped jerseys, winkle-picker shoes, bootlace ties and black leather jackets for boys; full skirts and shirts over jeans for girls.

Coffee bars were the places to meet. The unstated qualification for entry was to be young, or at least to look under 21:

> Teenagers favoured the unconventional, the noisy, unorganized and informal. At jazz clubs youngsters could wear what they liked without anyone staring; the juke box blared its harsh, noisy symphony while the kids slouched over its glossy, glittering top, looking aggressive.[11]

A youth subculture, deeply worrying for elders, came to prominence. Adopting an Edwardian style of tapered trousers, long jackets and fancy waistcoats, the Teddy Boys created a sartorial sensation that set them far apart from the grey, everyday wear of their parents. The contrast was all the greater for the distinctly un-Edwardian greased-up hair with the sides combed back to make what was appropriately called a 'duck's arse'. To older eyes, the Teddy Boys looked threatening, and some were.

But the rebellion from the bottom up did nothing for social reform, at least not for the present. Among the more idealistic of the latest generation, hopes that a stirring of youthful energy combined with the accession of a young Queen would lead to greater things were soon disappointed. As the modest Gillian Freeman discovered, 'Struck by an unsuspected surge of patriotism [I] cut short my au pair days in Stockholm, sold my bicycle and hurried home by Svenska Lloyd for the Coronation.' Freeman soon found that what she called the 'social impurities' had unexpected staying power:

> Bird's Eye had learned to freeze fresh fruit, and Utility Furniture had come off points in time for the Coronation, but it was going to take more than a decade to get rid of hanging. As for the Queen — well, we saw her enjoying a barbecue on television the other evening. And the concept of World Government I upheld so fervently in 1952 is as leaden as a dried-egg omelette.[12]

Presented as the opening of a door to a new age, the coronation could equally be seen as confirmation of the staying power of the old order.

# WELCOME HOME!

### Evening Standard 'plane greets the 400 sons of Empire

'Welcome Home!': the front page of the *Evening Standard* on the day that the *Empire Windrush* arrived in Britain in 1948, bringing 500 Jamaicans. Not everyone was to be so welcoming. (John Frost Newspapers/Alamy Stock Photo)

The 1951 Festival of Britain was a pick-me-up for a nation that still vividly remembered the Second World War. (Chronicle/Alamy Stock Photo)

In early 1953, gale-force winds and a spring tide led to disastrous flooding in parts of the UK, Belgium and the Netherlands; out of a European death toll of 2,551, the UK accounted for 307. It is still noted as one of the worst natural disasters in the UK. (Keystone Press/Alamy Stock Photo)

Elizabeth and her children meeting Prime Minister Winston Churchill, 10 February 1953. Churchill was besotted with Elizabeth and held weekly meetings with her.

Queen Elizabeth II, Queen of the Realm and of all her other Realms and Territories, Head of the Commonwealth, Defender of the Faith, 2 June 1953. (Keystone Press/ Alamy Stock Photo)

The newly crowned Queen and her consort. (Library and Archives Canada/K-0000047)

Sherpa Tenzing Norgay at the summit of Mount Everest on 29 May 1953, photo taken by Edmund Hillary. The news of the achievement was held back until the morning of the coronation for maximum impact. (Keystone Press/ Alamy Stock Photo)

Elizabeth and Philip started their 1953–54 Commonwealth tour in Bermuda; they were only there for twenty-four hours, but the Queen managed to find the time to meet Elizabeth, Philippa and Margaret, triplets born on the day of her coronation. (AP/Shutterstock)

Elizabeth and Philip greeted by children in Kingston, Jamaica. Jamaica was less than ten years away from independence at the time of the Commonwealth tour. Though the visit started tensely, a sense of fun soon took over. (World History Archive/Alamy Stock Photo)

Elizabeth receiving flowers from Mele Siu'ilikutapu, the granddaughter of Queen Sālote of Tonga (centre). Siu'ilikutapu would go on to be the first female parliamentarian in Tonga. (PA Images/Alamy Stock Photo)

General view immediately following the Unveiling of the Memorial by Her Majesty Queen Elizabeth the Second.

Elizabeth unveiling the Australian–American memorial in Canberra. (P.M. Hamilton, National Library of Australia, nla.obj-150807078)

Elizabeth leaving St Michael and All Angels Church in Colombo, Ceylon (now Sri Lanka). (Keystone Archives/Heritage Images/Alamy)

Elizabeth and Philip inspect servicemen in Gibraltar, the last stop of the tour. (World History Archive/Alamy Stock Photo)

HMY *Britannia* going to meet Elizabeth from Gibraltar at the end of the Commonwealth tour, May 1954.

John Osborne – seen here directing rehearsals for *The World of Paul Slicky* in 1959 – was one of the originators of the 'kitchen sink' art movement and a leading figure in the 'angry young men' literary group, the term coined in press for his first play, *Look Back in Anger*. He also has the dubious honour of being one of the last playwrights to have a work censored by the Lord Chamberlain. (Pictorial Press Ltd/Alamy Stock Photo)

The 1960 *Lady Chatterley's Lover* trial was a watershed moment in British society. First published in Europe in 1928, only censored copies of the book were available in the UK. But when the 1959 Obscene Publications Act was passed, with its provision for literary merit, Penguin seized the chance to publish the book in its entirety. They won the subsequent court case: the book sold 3 million copies. (PA Images/Alamy)

Princess Margaret and Group Captain Peter Townsend at Ascot, 6 June 1956. Margaret's relationship with Townsend – a divorced commoner some fifteen years older than her – was hugely controversial, even though many of her male ancestors had kept mistresses. (Keystone Press Agency/Keystone USA via ZUMAPRESS.com/Alamy)

# 8

# ORB AND SCEPTRE

The voice of royal protocol spent coronation eve on his boat moored on the Thames. Richard Dimbleby was picked up at 5.15 a.m. by a police launch to deliver him to the Abbey by 5.30. He was to stay in place for the next nine hours.

The soundproof commentators' box in the Abbey was a miniature two-storey house built between the two central arches of the upper gallery, immediately behind the High Altar. Dimbleby had half of the top floor to himself while the other half was occupied by two French commentators, one serving French radio and television, the other, radio for French-speaking Canada. On the ground floor were the commentators for BBC Radio (John Snagge and Howard Marshall), with a dividing wall between them and the senior television cameraman, D.R.G. Montague. 'It was rather like a wooden cell,' recalled Montague, 'with the roof too low for me to stand up straight, but equipped with a box seat and an electric fan.'

Dimbleby said:

I used to enter with a sort of Groucho Marx straddle and make for the box seat where I could straighten up sitting down – a paradox this, but true. From this seat I evolved numerous permutations of kneeling and sitting positions from which to make necessary adjustments and operational manoeuvres to the camera. My sole contact with the outside world once the door was shut was through my camera microphone and headphones – a sort of umbilical cord keeping me in contact with the … television control room in some other claustrophobic corner of the Abbey.[1]

Transmission was via five major control rooms, one of which was in the Abbey in the Head Verger's office.

By the time all the BBC team were in position, the least distinguished ticket holders were taking their seats. Outside, the spectators had already settled in. A film of the procession route taken three days before the event showed crowds already camping out to guarantee a front view. The litter in the streets is a reminder of what was then a peculiarly British shortcoming, though the absence of litter bins – a convenience the organisers might reasonably have been expected to provide – exacerbated the problem. On coronation eve in Trafalgar Square:

> People are lying and sitting on the pavement all round the square, right across the pavements. They look like pictures of war-time refugees, or like tube shelter people; they form a sea of bodies, heads over-lapping on to other people's legs. No space at all between one body and another. It is raining, steadily but lightly. Some have formed tents on the edge of the pavement using metal street railings from which they have hung coats, mackintoshes, newspapers, blankets. On one of these is a pencilled notice HOUSE TO LET – written across this, SOLD OUT. There is constantly a noise of an ambulance bell, and ambulances pass up and down every few minutes. This is the only traffic on the roads which anyway have people all over them so that a way has to be cleared every time for the ambulances to go through.[2]

In the Mall, the latest news was broadcast from loudspeakers attached to trees. There was clapping when the announcer referred to the large crowds who had spent the night out of doors, some of them appearing 'to be sleeping as soundly as if they were in their own beds'. The BBC's Barry Edgar talked to some of them, including a Swiss mountain guide and a family who had sailed all the way from Australia in a ketch.[3]

As the Abbey began to fill it took on the appearance of an upper-class enclave. While all 600 members of the House of Lords and their wives were invited, they were joined by only a handful of backbench MPs. It was almost as if a title of some sort was a prerequisite for admission – that and an affiliation with the Tory Party. Of the seventeen members of the royal household in attendance, seven described themselves as Conservative politicians while the rest were indubitably of right-wing persuasion.

At around 7.30, the first cars and carriages began to arrive at the Abbey. From his grandstand seat in the flower-decked Parliament Square, Geoffrey Grigson watched the peers and their ladies show off their finery: 'The cars decant them like burgundy. They trail their heavy scarlet behind them on the blue carpet.'[4]

The collective pomp was indeed impressive, more than enough to disguise the minor authorised economies such as the use of rabbit skin instead of ermine as trimming for the robes. Against heavy, intermittent rain, Boy Scouts held aloft green umbrellas to protect their seniors.

Grigson was feeling the cold. A welcome sight was a tea man with a container strapped to him, shouting, 'Luvverly Coronation tea, all hot, all boiling!' Thus warmed, Grigson took in the wider scene:

> Immediately, opposite my seat (which is in the rain, beyond the roof, alas, just above the road, and not fifty yards from the annexe) are the twin western towers of the Abbey. A little to the right hang the Royal Arms, enormous under a blue canopy, and under the flagstaff on which the Royal Standard will fly. Beneath flagstaff and canopy, shut fast, are the white doors, each with an EIIR in gold, by which at last the Queen will enter. Peers, princes, sultans, prime ministers will come, but these white doors will remain shut until the arrival of the Princes and Princesses of the Blood Royal.

Despite the elements, Grigson was impressed by the efforts made to accommodate the spectators:

> How skilfully, the stands have been angled across Parliament Square, how well they are shaped, and how well they are coloured! Long strips of clear yellow diminish to the corner wheeling round towards the Victoria Embankment. Above the yellow stretch the blue copings of stand after stand. Above the blue are the green trees, growing into, and through, the roof of the stands. Above the trees stretch the towers, from Big Ben's tower to the towers of the Abbey – the towers and all the grey pinnacles. On top of all, alas and alas, this grey, vapid low sky of unfriendly cloudage.[5]

Dignitaries unknown to the public, like Gold-Stick-in-Waiting and the Queen's Bargemaster, were identified by well-briefed commentators, to be greeted by loud cheers from the onlookers. Inside the Abbey, perched on a seat with no back, Harold Holt managed to keep his sense of humour:

> The oddest incident in the whole ceremony was the appearance just before the Queen's procession arrived and after the other royal processions had moved through, of two aproned maids – one pushing a hand-operated carpet sweeper around the Throne area, the other doing her bit of cleaning, broom in hand. 'They must be sweeping up the diamonds,' someone said.[6]

In anticipation of a long day, eyewitnesses were advised to take sandwiches and flasks of tea or coffee. Peers were fortunate in being able to secrete refreshment into pockets sewn inside their robes. Peeresses found that coronets made handy receptacles.

It was inevitable that with so many in a confined space, the number of toilets would prove inadequate. Peers and peeresses had their own lavatories while the rest had to queue for Ladies or Gentlemen. 'I thought this was carrying the class distinction a bit far,' noted Harold Holt. As the morning wore on, the lines of those needing urgent relief grew ever longer. 'A very French arrangement,' an elderly peeress was heard to mutter.

Journalists in the Abbey were given dispensation to share the lavatories assigned to the nobility. 'But visiting the "PEERS" was no ordinary matter,' said a BBC man. 'One could not just nip smartly away and come back at leisure. There were very strict security precautions and arrangements.'

> You had to wait outside the door of your own cubicle, and in good time (if you were lucky and traffic was light) a uniformed official would arrive to escort you there and back. I shall remember Richard waiting with patience and apprehension outside his cubicle, trying to catch the eye of this uniformed flunkey, just as one would hail a bus, and proceeding under escort to the 'PEERS' and eventually back again. This solemn ritual was carried out with all the dignity worthy of the occasion.[7]

For the youngest on parade it was quite a struggle. The future actor Jeremy Clyde was page to his grandfather, the 7th Duke of Wellington: 'There was quite a lot of survival technique involved because we weren't allowed to have a pee so there was no drinking the night before because it was a long day.'

There were, however, welcome distractions: 'All the pages had swords and if you give a 12-year-old a sword and another 12-year-old a sword it was a case of "have at you my liege" so all these pages were eyeing each other up and turning into Errol Flynn.'

The excitement of the crowds rose several notches when the morning newspapers went on sale proclaiming the triumph of the Everest expedition. The *Daily Express* had the best of it, with the inspired banner 'All This and Everest Too'. It was said that the young journalist who thought of the headline was never given any credit. In the back-stabbing tradition of the popular press, his superior suggested it to his superior as his own inspiration, who then did the same when talking to the editor.[8]

More predictable was the *Daily Mail* headline, 'The Crowning Glory', followed by the overegging first line 'Mount Everest has been conquered by Britain'. If nations were to be invoked it would have been more accurate to give the credit to New Zealand and Nepal. With little to go on as to Edmund Hillary's background, great play was made of the fact that he kept bees.

One participant in the coronation service had better reason than most for appreciating the achievement of Hillary and Tenzing. Twenty years earlier, the Scottish nobleman Squadron Leader Sir Douglas Douglas-Hamilton, then better known as Lord Clydesdale, had been chief pilot for the first flight over Everest. Described as 'one of the few last great spectacular flights remaining to be done', Clydesdale was praised by the expedition for 'his courage and foresight in taking part in what many then considered a visionary undertaking'.[9] Photographs of the summit helped in the planning of the Hunt expedition. In 1953, as the 14th Duke of Hamilton and Lord Steward of the Household, the intrepid aviator could justifiably share in the pride of the mountaineers.[10] And not just for his aeronautical exploits was the Duke of Hamilton celebrated. He was the only peer, the *Daily Herald* reported breathlessly, 'who has broken his nose five times'.

Nine processions converged on the Abbey to deliver the Lord Mayor, the Prime Minister, the royal family and their overseas guests. Last of all came the Queen's procession. Leaving Buckingham Palace at 10.15 in the heavyweight State Coach, drawn by eight Windsor Greys in trappings of crimson and gold, the Queen made a slow progress to the Abbey by way of the Mall, Northumberland Avenue and Victoria Embankment.

Lions and unicorns perched on arches along the Mall, seahorses rode around the Admiralty parapet and golden sovereigns were strung from the Treasury façade. Everywhere there were banks of tropical flowers and banners flying from buildings and lampposts. Twenty BBC cameras captured the Queen leaving Buckingham Palace to pass along the Victoria Embankment on the way to the Abbey.

The Trinidadian calypso singer, Young Tiger, rhapsodised:

Her Majesty looked really divine
In her crimson robe furred with ermine
The Duke of Edinburgh, dignified and neat
Sat beside her as Admiral of the Fleet.

Four more BBC cameras filmed the Queen's arrival at the Abbey then followed the procession as it moved from the West Door up the nave to organ screen and chancel. The procession was led by the Abbey Beadle followed by the chaplains and prebendaries. Then came the Dean of Westminster, preceded by his verger. A dash of colour was provided by the officers of the various orders of knighthood, heralds and standard-bearers. Equally resplendent were the officers of state: the Lord Chamberlain, Lord President and Lord Steward. The Cross of York and the Cross of Canterbury heralded the Primates.

Next in line were the bearers of St Edward's Staff and the Sceptre with Cross, followed by three sword bearers. The Lord Mayor of London, the Earl Marshal and the Lord High Constable of England moved along with the Sword of State between them.

A study of those who accompanied the Queen reveals some unexpected office holders. As Gentleman Usher of the Purple Rod, carrying the Purple Rod of the Order of the British Empire, was Sir Ernest Gowers, best known as the author of *Plain Words*, a bestselling scourge on clotted bureaucratic writing. Carrying the Union Standard was Captain John Dymoke, thirty-fourth holder of the Manor of Scrivelsby, who had inherited the office of King's Champion. He was spared the duty of his predecessors to ride into Westminster Hall at the coronation banquet to challenge all comers who might dispute the monarch's right to be acknowledged.

With the entry of the Queen came the Bishops of Durham and Bath and Wells along with Gentlemen-at-Arms. To carry her train, 21ft of heavy embroidered crimson velvet, the Queen had six maids of honour, all young and attractive daughters of the aristocracy. Baroness Glenconner or, as she then was, Lady Ann Coke, daughter of the 5th Earl of Leicester, had to hurry back from America where she had been promoting a line of pottery and getting over a failed love affair. She returned, she tells us, with a full order book.

Kitted out by Norman Hartnell in tight dresses and caked in heavy make-up to combat the strong lights, the maids were understandably nervous about getting through the entire service without feeling wobbly. Each had a phial of smelling salts tucked away in a glove; not the best place, as it turned out for Lady Rosemary Spencer-Churchill, daughter of the 10th Duke of Marlborough, whose phial was crushed when she shook hands with Archbishop Fisher. A powerful whiff of ammonia was released.

The Earl Marshal 'always looked angry' but was said to be goodhearted, while the Archbishop came over as pompous and officious until, after the ceremony, he handed round a hip flask of brandy for those who needed fortifying. The Queen was strikingly self-possessed, greeting her maids with a cheerful, 'Ready girls?' as they paused at the Abbey doors.

When it was all over, Lady Rosemary had to rush back to Blenheim to be with her mother, the Duchess, who was hosting an outdoor party where they roasted an ox for the villagers of Woodstock. Lady Rosemary's coronation dress was soon to go on show at Blenheim until, as she says, 'it started to deteriorate' – a bone of contention with her brother.[11]

From his seat near the pipes of the great organ and peering 'somewhat precariously' over the edge of the balcony, Cecil Beaton gave close attention to the Queen as she moved to the Chair of State:

> Her cheeks are sugar pink, her hair tightly curled around the Victorian diadem of precious stones perched straight on her brow ... she is still a young girl with a demeanour of simplicity and humility. Perhaps her mother has taught her never to use a superfluous gesture ... This girlish figure has enormous dignity; she belongs in this scene of almost Byzantine magnificence.[12]

Across the country, radio listeners and television viewers joined the Abbey service with the singing of the opening verses of Psalm 122. This was followed by the Recognition, as the Archbishop presented the Queen to a gathering of the people represented by boys from Westminster School, shouting, 'Vivat! Vivat!' as she turned to the four points of the compass and the trumpets blew, 'as the solitary figure bows humbly at each shattering volley'.[13]

The Coronation Oath had Elizabeth promising to govern her peoples of the United Kingdom of Great Britain and Northern Ireland and other direct dependencies and nations of the Commonwealth:

> ... according to their laws and customs ... [to] cause law and justice, in mercy, to be executed in all your judgements ... [and to maintain] the laws of God and the true profession of the Gospel, maintain the Protestant Reformed Religion established by law and maintain and preserve inviolably the settlement of the Church of England, and the doctrine, worship, discipline and government thereof, as by law established in England.

Elizabeth was presented with the Bible by the Moderator of the General Assembly of the Church of Scotland, a modest step towards the ecumenical service that must surely feature in any future coronation.

In and out of the Abbey the spectators had to use their imagination for the anointing with holy oil, which took place behind a canopy with the Queen seated on King Edward's chair – a replica, as commentators pointed out, made for the coronation of Charles II after most of the artefacts of royal regalia had been destroyed by Cromwell. In a break with tradition, there was no sermon to follow, a concession for which those on hard seats were truly grateful.

The climax of the ceremony was the crowning with St Edward's Crown, another copy dating from Charles II. As the Archbishop 'reverently put it upon the Queen's head', all present shouted, 'God save the Queen!' As seen in TV close-ups, her head, weighed down by a crown, gave her the appearance, said one observer, of a 'Byzantine icon'.

Crowds in Oxford Street broke into 'Land of Hope and Glory'. As the man on the spot, *The Times'* roving reporter 'found himself possessed of an uncontrollable grin'.

In paying homage, the Princes and peers knelt before the sovereign to give their first name and title. Except for Philip, who gave his name only, this because he was paying homage as the Queen's husband, not simply as a royal. Then the trumpets sounded, and the guns fired at the Tower of London.

Music played a big part in the coronation. Under the overall direction of Sir William McKie, the Australian organist and Master of the Choristers at Westminster Abbey, nine new pieces were commissioned including a revised 'Crown Imperial March' by William Walton, originally composed for Edward VIII's coronation, and, especially for 1953, 'Orb and Sceptre'. This came in for hostile criticism as substandard 'pomp and circumstance style' or, more politely, as a 'homage to Elgar'. But for a public keen on hummable tunes, 'Orb and Sceptre' remains a favourite for listeners of Classic FM. A contribution from Benjamin Britten fell victim to a severe bout of flu.

For the first time, the congregation was called upon to join in the singing. The hymn 'All People That on Earth do Dwell', arranged by Vaughan Williams, created a volume of sound that could be heard outside the Abbey.

There were a few blips in the service, though the only mistake spotted by the eagle-eyed was when the Queen forgot her carefully rehearsed curtsy during her processional entry. And Elizabeth Longford noticed the Queen having trouble trying to drag the heavy gold metal fringe of her dress across the Abbey carpet: '"Get me started", she whispered to the Archbishop, and with a holy pull she was off.' It was some time later that Longford realised 'the carpet had been laid, eccentrically enough, with the pile facing backwards'.[14]

Ambulance crews reported no serious casualties. One herald fainted during the final rehearsal and one page was taken ill. Harold Holt feared for the Duke of Kent, who 'gradually went a horrible green … but he stuck it through'. Likewise, 'the Lord Chancellor, weighted down with robes, wig and coronet, rocked ominously on his feet several times but remained perpendicular to the end'.[15]

The coronation, or rather the television exposure, was the making of Michael Ramsey, the unruffled avuncular Bishop of Durham who, following tradition, stood at the right hand of the Queen throughout the service. Said Dimbleby:

I am sure that millions of people watching their television screens must have seen the continuous glances which he gave the Queen, almost as though he were saying: 'Don't worry, my dear … it is going beautifully.'

It reminded me exactly of a father nursing his daughter through a trying ordeal.[16]

A familiar and popular figure, thanks to the coronation, Ramsey was marked as the obvious successor to Fisher at Canterbury. 'Never did the Church of England dominate the public stage more majestically' than at the coronation.[17]

For Richard Dimbleby, the highlight of the day was:

When the Duke of Cornwall first appeared by the side of his grandmother, the Queen Mother, in the Royal Box. We had been waiting for this, of course, and for an awful moment I thought that he was in a position in which our cameras could not see him.

His presence in the Abbey for the Coronation of his mother had been so widely publicised beforehand that we never would have been forgiven for not showing him to the millions of those looking in on television. You may imagine my relief when I heard the voice of Peter Dimmock, the television producer at the Abbey, saying in my headphones: 'I have got a lovely shot of Charles – mention him as soon as you like'.

With long-distance hindsight, one of the rarely mentioned oddities of the Abbey service was the juxtaposition of the 14-year-old Andrew Parker Bowles, page to the Lord High Chancellor, and the 4-year-old Charles, neither yet aware that they were to have a wife in common.

And the low point for Dimbleby?

It seemed to me amazing that even on this occasion we could not break ourselves of one of our worst national habits. Tiers and tiers of stalls on which the peers had been sitting were covered with sandwich wrappings, sandwiches, morning newspapers, fruit peel, sweets and even a few empty miniature bottles.[18]

However, perhaps the sight of noble peers departing the Abbey with their rubbish bags might have tarnished the dignity of the occasion. That other countries were better able to cope with discarded newspapers and packaging was suggested by a *Punch* cartoon showing a variety of signs in multiple languages except for the injunction, 'No Litter'. That was in English only.

Of the many schoolchildren who wrote an account of their coronation day, Mary McLay wins points for a lucid exposition:

On coronation day I watched the television. We invited fourteen people which included five children. We watched the procession and service in the morning, the five-mile procession in the afternoon and the summary of the coronation and the fire-works at night.

We were given a box of chocolates with a picture of the Queen on the lid and a tin of toffees with a picture of the Queen on horse-back on the side. My sister and I have a coronation mug each and the handle is in the shape of a lion wearing a crown.

My mother made a very special dinner for us which included a salad with scotch eggs and shrimp patties which everybody enjoyed.

It was very late at night when I got into bed and everybody told daddy and mummy how much they had enjoyed it and how very pleased they were to have been able to come.

There was praise for the BBC in delivering coronation footage to overseas viewers. In an operation dubbed Pony Express, tele-recordings were taken by helicopter from Alexandra Palace to Heathrow where three Canberra jets (still known as 'bombers') were ready to carry the images across the Atlantic to television stations in Ottawa, Toronto and Montreal. Not to be outdone, Columbia Broadcasting fitted out a chartered Stratocruiser with an editing suite so that film with commentary by Ed Murrow was ready for transmission eight minutes after the plane landed in Boston.

More ambitious yet was the National Broadcasting Company (NBC). About to take delivery of a British Canberra bomber, the Venezuelan Air Force agreed to stop off in the United States to deliver the coronation film. Unfortunately, the Canberra developed engine trouble and had to turn back two hours after taking off. NBC had to settle for a link to the nearest transmission point in Canada – a smart move, as it turned out, since the Canadian Broadcasting Corporation was first to go on air.

The only censure on the American coverage – one that raised Dimbleby's ire – was an advertising break which featured a mock interview with a chimpanzee known as J. Fred Muggs. The story was much exaggerated. As the BBC's chief correspondent in the States, Leonard Miall was able to set the record straight by telling his masters that it was, in fact, the live radio commentaries of Howard Marshall and John Snagge that were interrupted and then only because the shortwave reception faltered. Dimbleby's reputation was unscathed. (Ironically, the inaccurate version of the Fred Muggs episode was later used by the defenders of the BBC against the threatened inroads from independent television. Heaven forfend that such vulgarity should be allowed to sully British TV screens.)

To a succession of BBC triumphs must be added that of the *Radio Times*, which sold over 9 million copies in the week of the coronation, the largest sale ever for a weekly journal.

For cinema distribution, two films were made of the coronation, both in colour, for release six days after the event. *A Queen is Crowned* was scripted by Christopher Fry with a commentary by Laurence Olivier. On the evening of the coronation, Archbishop Fisher and the Duke of Norfolk were in the Pathé studio to view the footage. They demanded two cuts, those of the Queen and Duke of Edinburgh receiving the Sacrament and two close-ups of the Queen and Queen Mother which they judged too long. Released on 8 June, a mere six days after the actual event, the movies were dubbed in nine languages and shown in fifty-four countries. *A Queen is Crowned* became Britain's top box-office draw of the year and even did well in America. It was the high point of cinema's love affair with the monarchy.

Whatever her early reservations, the Queen was happy with her television performance. Later in the year, when she visited the BBC Lime Grove studios, George Barnes was elevated to Sir George.

After an interval following the coronation service, the royal family took up their positions for the return procession. As a television observer, a reporter for the *Manchester Guardian* commented:

The assembling took place in such a heavy downpour that the television screen resembled Hollywood's idea of an English rainstorm. Things suddenly became domestic and untidy. We saw sheltering royalty on its way into clarences and such elegantly named vehicles. We saw Sir Winston Churchill, all smiling now, though before he had looked massively pugnacious and gloomy, decked with his Garter hat and looking ferociously old English as he apparently had to remove it either to acknowledge the cheers or to get into the clarence. And at Grosvenor Gate was it not Sir Winston who was acknowledging the cheers out of the window of that little vehicle? Even the commentator so far forgot the usual muted style as to refer to his get-up as the 'new finery'.[19]

Others, less respectful, thought the medieval costume required by the Order of the Garter made the overweight Churchill on unsteady feet look like a dissipated Cardinal Wolsey. But he played to the crowds, waving and making the 'V' sign.

The progress to Buckingham Palace covered just over 5 miles and took nearly two hours. The State Coach drove down Whitehall to Trafalgar Square, then via Cockspur Street, Pall Mall, St James's Street and Piccadilly to Hyde Park Corner. From there, the procession made its way by the East Carriage Drive parallel with Park Lane to Marble Arch, then down Oxford Street and Regent Street to Piccadilly Circus. Then, the drive continued to the Haymarket, Cockspur Street and Trafalgar Square, to pass once more under Admiralty Arch and so to Buckingham Palace down the Mall.

By common consent, the outstanding decoration, if somewhat over-elaborate, was the floral screen covering the façade of the Dorchester Hotel. Designed by stage designer Oliver Messel, his creation gave the impression of a theatre curtain about to rise on a lavish opera. The processional route was lined with some 20,000 sailors, soldiers and airmen supported by a heavy police presence that included 5,000 constables brought in from the provinces.

James Lee-Milne and his wife, Alvilde, watched the procession from Brooks', the gentleman's club in St James's Street. They had some difficulty in getting there:

> There was a queue at South Kensington station but we eventually got into a train, jammed like sardines. At Green Park station got out and in our finery had to walk up the escalator which for some reason wasn't working … [At] Brooks's there was a vast concourse of members and friends. Hardly a seat to sit on. It was bitterly cold with the windows all out and steps up to balconies erected against the façade. We were perished and sat before a fire in the morning-room wearing overcoats.[20]

As the procession started the rain fell more heavily. Spectators marvelled at the discipline of troops able to march in perfect formation though soaked to the skin: 'There is a long pause while the Guardsmen wait in front of us and the rain pours down on their bearskins. This is due to the horse-artillery being unable to get their guns up the slippery slope of St James's Street.'[21]

> [Somehow,] the forty-seven bands in the procession and in the streets played in time, and the long cavalcade remained in step. The procession took nearly an hour to pass any given point. Every kind of uniform was seen, from the kilts of the Scottish regiments to the battledress of the Home Guard and the green tunics and skirts of the WRAC. The route, six miles long, was lined by the scarlet of the Guards, the Army in blues and khaki, and the Navy and Royal Air Force in their familiar uniforms.[22]

Over fifty countries of the Commonwealth and Empire took part in the procession. If there were any complaints from television viewers it was that 'not enough pictures of those thousands who had braved the weather and fatigue to watch the scene for themselves, and not enough close pictures of those who were taking part in the procession'.[23]

Of the 20 million or so television viewers who tuned in to the service for at least half an hour, the majority shared the screen with family or neighbourhood groups or watched the ceremony on large screens in cinemas, church and town halls, and factories. Every seat was taken in the Odeon, Leicester Square, and in the dance halls of Butlin's holiday camps in Filey, Skegness and Clacton. The 3,000 viewers who gathered in the Royal Festival Hall were each provided with a packed lunch.

Home viewing had its complications:

> Like many people, we had a new TV bought especially for the coronation – a Pye 12" with a purple screen in a huge bakelite cabinet that weighed a ton. It took about an hour for the valves to warm up, and then my dad had to spend another ten minutes 'tuning' it. When eventually we had a good picture, mum went and called in the neighbours and the kettle never stopped boiling.[24]

The *Daily Herald* doctor advised that the set should be on the floor, resting on books for 'the best way to strain your eyes and get a first class headache is by looking upwards'.

A star of the day was the Queen of Tonga, a large beaming lady riding in an open carriage, oblivious to the rain pouring down on her and her companion, the rather more diminutive Sultan of Kelantan. 'Who's that?' someone asked Noël Coward. 'Her lunch,' said the Master. It was a good story, but emphatically denied by Coward who complained that he had always wanted to visit Tonga but was now liable to have stones thrown at him if he stepped on to the island.

With the return of the royal party to the Palace, it was time for the official photographs orchestrated by Cecil Beaton. Having successfully negotiated the crowds outside the Palace, he was directed to the tradesman's entrance to be shown up to the Green Drawing Room. From the balcony of the inner courtyard, he watched the arrival of the carriages:

Every window framed the faces of Palace servants, and a group of them raised a tremendous cheer as the Queen Mother came back, waving and smiling as fresh as a field flower. Then, to the sound of distant roars, drawn by eight grey horses the bronze gold State Coach, with its Cipriano paintings and dark-strawberry padded silk, bowled through the central arch and back to home. The Queen looked back over her shoulder and appeared somewhat dazed and exhausted.

Not long after, girlish voices were heard at the end of the Picture Gallery. 'Oh hullo! Did you watch it? When did you get home?' From the mirror-doors of the Green Drawing Room I spied the Queen with her ladies, her excited children; the family asking questions, jokes, smiles, laughter, the high-pitched voices of the Queen and Princess Margaret heard above the others. The Duchess of Gloucester was leaning forward from the hips with almost perilous intent. The Duke of Norfolk, his duties successfully carried out, lolled behind one of the mirrored-glass doors.[25]

Beaton had his work cut out, with advice on all sides on how to do his job and Charles and Anne 'buzzing about in the wildest excitement'. When at last he managed to get the Queen to stand against a 'blow-up' Abbey background, he took a rapid succession of pictures. 'The queen looked extremely minute under her robes and Crown, her nose and hands chilled, and her eyes tired. "Yes," in reply to my question, "the Crown does get rather heavy." She had been wearing it for nearly three hours.'[26]

After a break in the proceedings when the family returned to watch the RAF flypast from the balcony, Beaton could relax. He felt himself lucky to be designated official photographer. It was against the wishes of Philip, who had lobbied for his friend, the society photographer known as Baron who had taken the photographs of the wedding of Philip and Elizabeth. The advantage for Beaton was having the Queen Mother on his side. Philip was overruled, a familiar pattern in the battle of royal wills.

At 9.00 p.m., as Big Ben struck the hour, 'all the BBC's transmitters joined together once more to bring to listeners, throughout the world, the voice of the Queen herself, broadcasting from Buckingham Palace to set the seal on this great Coronation Day'.[27] An hour later, Lord Rowallan, the Chief Scout, put a match to the bonfire in Hyde Park and set the beacons ablaze. Across the country up to 2,000 beacons were lit.

It had been a day of civic pride. Plymouth staged a pageant on the Hoe, depicting events in the city's history, including Drake's game of bowls before the Armada; Bristol re-enacted the voyage of John Cabot down the Avon; at Sandwich, Kent, Good Queen Bess offered sanctuary to French and Dutch refugees; Birmingham laid out a Garden for the Blind; fifty-two flags of the Dominions flew from the ramparts of Cardiff Castle, matching the decorated flower baskets in the main streets and the ceremonial arches leading to the civic centre; Manchester organised an exhibition of early Elizabethans at the art gallery and gave gifts to some 110,000 children; Liverpool held archery competitions and concerts, and lit up the ships on the Mersey; Blackpool lit a 50ft bonfire on the beach; and great Highland balls were held in Inverness, Glasgow and Edinburgh.

The celebrations were helped along by a coronation beer, stronger than any on sale since the previous coronation and a welcome change after the weak wartime brews. A butcher in Camden Town reverentially displayed a crown roast of lamb in red, white and blue.

Wherever there was a British presence abroad, glasses were raised to the new reign. Troops in the Korean war zone fired salvoes of shells containing red, white and blue smoke before sitting down to feast on ice cream provided by their American allies.

At home, street parties were all the rage, though the weather was liable to be disheartening. Bryn Jones of Lichfield recalls 'a dull, wet day'. He was served spam sandwiches, jelly and ice cream in a local grain merchant's warehouse. For J. Jacques of Guildford:

> My mother put a maypole up in the garden for the coronation and we twined red, white and blue crepe paper round it. Then it rained and the

colours all ran. We went up to London in my grandmother's car to see the decorations for the coronation, but all I remember (I was three) was breaking down on the Edgware Road.

Many of the happiest memories are from the north of the country, where the elements were kinder. Dorothy Greaves was an 8-year-old in Blackpool:

Our next door neighbours had a tiny Bush television and everyone around crammed into their living room to watch the Coronation. We had a street party and all our mums made food and we had tables down the length of the road. We were all dressed in white dresses with red, white & blue sashes and we all had union jack flags.[28]

A contributor to the Birmingham History Forum remembers:

Going round with my big sister collecting donations for the event, then my big brother rigging the PA system. (I recall him jumping down a ladder to see off some bloke throwing insults at his assistant, Hughie, for being a Northern Ireland Catholic.) Our school, Foundry Road Juniors, had commemorative gardens built and a commemorative plaque built into the wall. Us all being crammed into someone's front room to watch the event on their new 12"TV and then onto a bus to tour the other local celebrations. My brother getting drunk to ease the injury he sustained in the tug o' war. Mr Berry who ran a lucrative business breeding racing pigeons presented every kid in the street with a commemorative china cup and saucer. Yes, despite the rain it was a great day; my only disappointment was David Cheshier getting a double-barrelled pop gun as one of his presents when I didn't. The adults carried on long after we were tucked up in bed and buses had to be diverted the following day due to a hole being burnt into the road where they'd made a bonfire out of the advertising hoardings they'd torn down from the railway bank.

Houses up and down the land sported window displays with Union Jack tea towels or pictures of the Queen cut from newspapers and fixed to boards or trays. On many a village green, colourfully dressed maypole dancers demonstrated what few of them were prepared to admit was a pagan fertility ritual.

At Caston in Norfolk, the Petal and Purl lady knitters had spent six months and 1,000 balls of wool creating a life-sized model of the Queen in her coronation robes. So successful was the display in raising money for community projects, they went on to produce another sixty woollen figures recording village life.

In one of the few serious studies of local celebrations, Maurice Broady investigated forty-five parties in Birkenhead, each catering for between 30 and 140 children. Clearly defined neighbourhood boundaries marked out small, close-knit communities. It was tempting to see in this, the nation writ small, that these units together made for a wider unity, a country with shared loyalties under one flag and one Queen. Broady himself was disinclined to extrapolate, but others were quick to build a national edifice on shaky foundations.[29]

Local newspapers thrived on community squabbles. In Barnsley, members of the Co-operative Society protested against the portrait of their president on their souvenir tea caddy when they expected to see the image of the Queen. The parishioners of a Northumberland village took umbrage against their vicar who forbade the use of the church hall for a beauty competition. There were protests in the borough of Stepney, one of London's poorest, when the council decided not to decorate the streets but instead to send children for a day out at the seaside.

Said the Chairman of Stockton's celebrations, 'If someone offered me the Crown Jewels on condition I faced the questions at the next Coronation Celebration Committee I would refuse out of hand.' When the rain fell, a church hall or Scout hut came in handy. On Roman Road in East London covered market stalls were lined up to provide cover.

Despite extra rations, the treats handed out to children often fell short of expectations. Contempt for dry, curly sandwiches ('Just like British Rail') was excusable, but some parental demands were excessive. 'I never allowed my child margarine even in war,' wailed a mother who expected butter to be served. But perhaps in her relatively prosperous locality, that was the norm.[30]

Children of radical parents on the Isle of Man were encouraged to smash their coronation mugs as a protest against British sovereignty over the island. But their demonstrations lost out to the publicity given to the Manx youngsters, chosen at random from secondary schools, to sit in the Abbey alongside their Lieutenant Governor.

Another visitor to London who was surprised to be there was the 7-year-old Mancunian Chris Thomas, who shared the essay prize won by his mother on the theme 'Why I would like my child to see the coronation'. The family had 50-guinea seats on a balcony overlooking Regent Street.

A Suffolk teenager had a particular reason incidental to the coronation for remembering his trip to London:

I stood with friends high up on wooden stands at the Trafalgar Square end of the Mall to watch the royal procession. Next to me was an American with the most elaborate, expensive looking camera I had ever seen. He set it up to take a shot of the Queen's coach. At the critical moment he was pushed from behind, pitched forward and dropped the camera on the pavement below. In the same minute I saw the Queen, I learned a whole new vocabulary.

The coronation was not to everybody's fancy. The writer Frances Partridge, for one, was not enamoured:

The Coronation has come roaring towards us like a lorry heard approaching up a steep incline, and now, thank God, has roared away again. There has been an almost maniac note of mass hysteria about it all – culminating in the high-pitched screams of false excitement of the BBC commentators. We walked to the village in the afternoon to see how Ham's Coronation was going. It might have been a hundred years ago. Outside the school some of the children were dancing round a decorated maypole, while opposite them sat the village old folk doubled up on kitchen chairs and perfectly silent. All the ages between had gone off to somewhere livelier, I suppose. The little girls wore pink paper roses in their hair, and when the dance was over they lined up and sang *Land of Hope and Glory*. Ramshackle sports began in a rough field next door, organised by the 'Italian prisoner from Mr Hudson's'. No other representative of the 'gentry' being present, I was appalled to be asked to give away the prizes, and beat a hasty retreat.

The last item of this great day was a firework display at the Romillys's – very pretty as they burst over the water and dropped into it … I suppose it has meant fun for a great many people, though I allowed myself to be momentarily overcome by dislike for the mumbo-jumbo of the service, with its 'holy oil' and the rest, as well as the noisy way the English always pat themselves on the back and say how well the monarchy 'works'. It's just harmless, that's all. Burgo [her teenage son] of course is violently against it.[31]

Head teachers, particularly of independent and grammar schools, went into overdrive. Granting a five-day exeat in honour of the coronation, the head of Oundle in Northamptonshire had the school start the day with an assembly rendering of Zadok the Priest:

> The central act of the Coronation none of us saw, but we all knew that once again our Commonwealth and Empire, invested in the person of its Queen, was being consecrated to God. Our Chapel is but a small bough of the Church, yet it is like a pillar to support the School, and fills it with the strength of the Christ's Church Militant. Through the year our many visiting preachers continually remind us of this witness, and this term more than ever the Chapel has been the very centre of the School.
>
> Those who saw the Coronation processions saw a pageant of tradition, service and privilege, triumphant once more in a world where they are harder tried than iron on the anvil. Moreover, they are the metal of which all public schools are made, a continual inspiration and guard.
>
> May she defend our laws …
>
> God save the Queen.

Schoolchildren wrote glowingly about the coronation and what it meant to them. But these affirmations should be treated with scepticism. In his book about royalty's relationship with the media, Edward Owens takes as gospel the contents of over 200 school essays, a fair percentage of which came from a grammar school in Bury St Edmunds.[32] I can confirm their origin since I, aged 14, was one of the contributors, and I can tell Professor Owens that, with one or two exceptions, we wrote what we knew our teachers wanted to read. I did not record my real plus points – the end of sweet rationing, the ascent of Everest and the prospect of a day's holiday. Few of us were enamoured with the idea of monarchy or the ritual of the coronation. We left that to our elders.

For its television coverage, the BBC was given full marks for technical expertise, though there were critics who faulted the quality of the images.

For those viewing at home, the more serious grouse was of television screens that were liable to flicker or mist over at critical moments.

In retrospect, the obsequious delivery of BBC commentators was shamelessly overdone, with Dimbleby oozing piety, his vowels as rounded as his waistline and setting the tone. That said, the coronation put Dimbleby firmly in place as the automatic choice for commentator on all state occasions. It was not just his delivery that won approval. Said Sir Anthony Wagner, who succeeded Sir George Bellew as Garter Principal King of Arms:

> His preparations were immensely thorough. He came before rehearsals and to rehearsals, studied papers, asked questions, and was content with nothing less than a complete grasp of what would happen and why. And in his final performance the clear exposition of complexity, the vivid and sometimes humorous description, and the solemnity of history were blended in just the right proportions.[33]

Whatever we might now think of Dimbleby's style, there can be no denying his skills as an improviser. A week after the coronation the cameras were on hand for the Queen Mother's visit to the Royal School of Needlework Exhibition at St James's Palace. Never the best of timekeepers, she watched the start of the programme while preparing to set out from Clarence House. So taken was she with Dimbleby's commentary on the history of the school that she stayed to hear more, not realising that while waiting for her arrival Dimbleby was desperately filling in time. He kept going for twenty unscheduled minutes.

The BBC was not alone in its overblown deference. Press coverage of the coronation was almost baroque in its emotional intensity. On observing the royal procession entering the western door of the Abbey, the *Times* reporter felt:

> ... as though granted an artist's vision of life at one of its most exquisitely figurative moments. [As for the Queen] ... dignity went hand-in-hand with modesty, simplicity, gravity with a charm which shone like crystal within all that glitter and ecclesiastical effulgence.

The 'sublime' ceremonial was no less than a 'dedication of the State to God's service through the prayers and benedictions of the Church'.[34]

Churchill was equally extravagant with his expectation that the new reign would witness a 'golden age of art and letters' and a 'brightening salvation of the human scene'. On the eve of the coronation, he described Elizabeth as 'a lady whom we respect because she is our Queen, and whom we love because she is herself'. But it was Archbishop Fisher who topped them all when he declared that with the coronation, 'this country and Commonwealth were not far from the Kingdom of Heaven'.

As the *Annual Register* put it, this was indeed 'a religion of royalism'.

# 9

# HANDS ACROSS THE SEA

On the day after the coronation, the *Manchester Guardian* carried a cartoon by David Low, famous for his attacks on the rise of Fascism in the 1930s and the appeasers who held power until 1940. Low's take on the coronation was to show an overstuffed family who were comatose after seven hours of gorging on royal pomp. Of the 500 and more letters of protest, the large majority were hostile, in many cases hysterically so. One man was so consumed with anger and shame that he had to cut out the offending image before taking the paper home for his wife and two daughters.

A *Guardian* editorial put up a feeble 'on the one hand, on the other hand' defence of Low, who had only recently moved to the paper after twenty-six years on the *Evening Standard*. The New Zealand-born cartoonist, 'who expresses his own independent views', was excused for having been brought up in the 'more irreverent atmosphere of a young nation'. (He was 62, and had left New Zealand as a teenager.) The newspaper claimed his right to warn that 'unless we are careful, an affair like the coronation, in which rank and station seem to be elevated, can minister to snobbery, adding the country was protected by our healthy sense of democracy'.

> To warn us to take life seriously after our period of emotion hardly seems to be an offence, though perhaps he should have remembered that this time, thanks to the great technical achievement of the B.B.C., the emotion was really deeply shared throughout the whole country, and therefore takes longer to fade away. It was more than any earlier coronation, a relatively sober and serious celebration.[1]

This carefully measured response to what, after all, was less an attack on the Queen than on her more susceptible subjects, reveals just how little traction there was for anyone daring to challenge the inherent goodness of the first family.

The press portrayed the Queen as a dutiful wife and mother (while neglecting to point out that the children spent more time with their nurse than with their parents). Though inclined to be strait-laced on public occasions, this was put down to natural modesty and so counted in her favour, as did her love of healthy pursuits like riding and country walks. Said to possess a sharp humour and a sense of fun, she nevertheless deferred to the old guard among her advisers who kept Buckingham Palace under protective wraps. Her instincts were severely conservative.

As for her handsome, ex-naval officer husband, his occasional indiscretions were excused, even welcomed, as refreshing candour. The royal couple was seen as ideally representative of what was still essentially a backward-looking society.

Albeit of modest circulation, an article in *Sociological Review* was widely quoted as testimony to the coronation as 'an act of national communion'. The argument was all the more forceful for its two unlikely advocates: Edward Shils, a Professor of Sociology at the University of Chicago, and Michael Young, a Labour Party activist who had drafted the party's 1945 election manifesto. The two academics saw the coronation as an expression of all that was best in British society, confirming 'a degree of moral consensus such as few large societies have ever manifested':

> The Coronation Service itself is a series of ritual affirmations of the moral values necessary to a well-governed and good society. The key to the Coronation Service is the Queen's promise to abide by the moral standards of society.

Here was a Britain united as never before on the essential values such as justice, dignity of the individual and respect for legitimate authority.[2] It was a splendid vision affirmed by the Queen, who said of her coronation, 'It is not a symbol of a power and splendour that are gone, but a declaration of our hopes for the future.'

This was to sidestep the contradiction at the heart of the coronation that was to bedevil Britain for generations to come. The street parties, town and village celebrations and the crowds out on the streets of London spoke of a reconciliation between the old values and traditions and a new spirit of progressive dynamism. But there could be no reconciliation between opposites, only, at best, an uneasy accommodation. And even that was not to last.

It was Michael Young who was among the first to recognise that far from healing, social divisions were widening by the year. In 1958 he published *The Rise of the Meritocracy*, in which he saw a future where intelligence and merit, as divined by examinations and by having the 'right' sort of education, would become the determining factors in life chances. As much a warning as a prophecy, the book pointed to the creation of a deeply resentful underclass, judged to have no merit – the forerunners of today's populists. It was not long before it became abundantly clear that everything the Queen stood for – the Christian family at the heart of society, social stability with common ideals held together by mutual respect – was under mortal threat.

For the week following the coronation, London was one big traffic jam. Coachloads of day visitors streamed in from all parts of the country to see the street decorations and the illuminations. It cost half a crown to tread the Queen's way in the Abbey and there were thousands who were happy to pay the price.

Events crowded in. One Wednesday afternoon, the Queen drove through London's East End where hundreds of thousands packed the roads to greet the motorcade. When the royal couple stopped at the London Hospital, the police had trouble controlling the crowd. 'I nearly touched her – I nearly touched her!' screamed a woman. The *London Advertiser* reported on 5 June, 'The Queen, looking charming in a simple powder-blue fitted coat and matching scalloped cloche hat, smiled and waved a gloved hand again and again to the accolades of the people.' *A Queen is Crowned* and *Elizabeth is Queen* were showing at all the main cinemas, though the Essoldo in Bethnal Green Road gave priority to the X-rated *Cosh Boy* with Joan Collins, while the Regal in Bow Road offered Johnny Weissmuller in *Tarzan Triumphs*.

As Churchill's Private Secretary, Jock Colville was constantly in attendance on the Prime Minister for an exhausting round of saturnalia:

On Friday, June 5th, we went, again in full dress uniform, to the Foreign Secretary's banquet to the Queen, given by Sir W. Churchill in the absence through illness of Anthony Eden. It was at Lancaster House, just restored to its ancient glories at phenomenal expense, and while the tables were bright with the Duke of Wellington's famous 'Ambassador's' Service of gilt plate, the walls and the rooms were decorated by Constance Spry with flowers. Over 150 people sat down to dinner. Meg was between Prince Jean of Luxembourg and the Sheikh of Kuwait (the richest man in the world, but apparently a very grumpy magnate) and I between the representative of San Marino (in a magnificent uniform) and the soberly clad Icelander. W.S.C. was in his full dress of Lord Warden of the Cinque Ports, the Duke of Edinburgh in naval full dress which had been temporarily revived for the Coronation, and almost everybody resplendent in seldom-seen uniforms and jewels. After it was over we drove down the illuminated Mall – an unforgettable sight – to a reception at Buckingham Palace where again unwonted brilliance reigned.[3]

Three hundred ships were at anchor for the Spithead Naval Review. With some 300 British and Commonwealth aircraft taking part in the flypast, it was Britain's biggest ever military display, never to be repeated.

Derby Day was on 6 June. Colville and his wife got to the racecourse in record time, 'driving behind Winston's car at breakneck speed on the wrong side of the Kingston by-pass'. The first jockey to be knighted, Gordon Richards, won the race, with the Queen's horse coming in second. If she was disappointed, she didn't show it.

The next day, the royal couple and guests were at Covent Garden for the gala performance of Benjamin Britten's new opera, *Gloriana*. 'Dull, without melody as usual with Mr B,' sniffed Noël Coward. Colville was yet more scathing. Having praised Oliver Messel's designs ('superb') and admired the audience ('well dressed at Covent Garden for a change'), he was bored by the music ('above our heads') and, worst of all, 'The episode depicted by the opera, Elizabeth's squalid romance with Essex was totally unsuited to the occasion,' thus revealing a not uncharacteristic fusion of snobbery with ignorance.[4]

On Saturday, 13 June, came the first warning that all would not continue to run smoothly in the royal progression. Lascelles drove to Chartwell to tell Churchill that Princess Margaret had declared her wish to marry the recently divorced Peter Townsend. 'A pretty kettle of fish,' noted Colville. Churchill's first reaction was to give every encouragement to young love. As he was soon to discover, it was not so simple.

Frequent sightings of the Queen and Duke, if only in the rear seat of a limousine driving from A to B, delighted tourists, not least those from overseas who were in Britain for the holiday of a lifetime. That, at least, was how the travel agents put it across. Mass tourism was still in the future. Britain had 38 million visitors in 2018, the corresponding figure for 1953 was just 1 million. But since most of those travellers were from North America, they represented a healthy boost to dollar earnings. Few had ever before stepped out of their country. Simply by crossing the Atlantic by air or sea was to embark on a great adventure.

The airlines offered speed. Even by propeller aircraft, the journey from New York to London was down to twelve hours. But the planes were noisy, unpressurised and turbulent, and flying was expensive. A 'bargain fare' on the transatlantic route was around £2,000 in today's money. It was not until 1958 that more people crossed the Atlantic by plane than by ship. The sea passage was not cheap. But with round-the-clock entertainment and, for those in any class above steerage, almost unlimited food and drink, the great passenger liners had a competitive edge. As the Cunard slogan had it, 'Getting there is half the fun.'

Visitors from Australia and New Zealand could expect to be at sea for a minimum of twenty-eight days while the fastest flying time, with refuelling stops, was close on forty-one hours. An essential preliminary was to get written clearance from the revenue department that no taxes were outstanding; 'Shipping companies are forbidden by law to issue steamer tickets until this certificate has been produced.' Acknowledging possible food shortages in the mother country, 'Each traveller is permitted to take 50lbs of groceries, which is carried free by the ship along with the passenger's other personal baggage'.

By plane or boat, arrival in Britain was a bit of a let-down. Airport reception at Heathrow, then known as Heath Row, was no more than a collection of huts and tents. The first modern terminal was not opened until 1955. As for Southampton, favoured by the transatlantic liners for the quick rail connection to London, the still highly visible signs of war weariness were a miserable contrast, say, to the departure from New York with the Statue of Liberty receding to the skyline. A new terminal for Cunard passengers had opened in 1950, but the less favoured had to make do with grime-encrusted sheds where autocratic customs officials took their time searching for contraband. In the House of Lords, Lord Lucas compared Southampton to 'the back door to a fifth rate, down and out country'.

For those on a tight budget (the majority had to settle for hire-purchase travel, a down payment and the rest in instalments), the feeling of disappointment was liable to persist. Part of the trouble was the assumption by the tourist trade that Americans were an easy catch. Easily identified by their lightweight outfits, the women with cheerfully patterned dresses, the men with technicolour ties and white or blue shoes, the illusion held that all Americans were stinking rich and could pay excessively for inferior service.

The chief complaints were of substandard accommodation. Ethel Muller from New Jersey did not hold back in her castigation of the Great Northern Hotel at King's Cross, one of the chain of British Rail hotels. Though her room was large, the furniture was scruffy and old-fashioned. No soap or face towel was provided. A single bathroom for the entire corridor was some distance away from her room:

> I start out down the silent corridor. Under a lighted glass sign reading 'BATHROOM' I enter a cavern that is just exactly what the sign says. A monstrous room with shiny tile walls, it has four great booths, each containing a bathtub – nothing more! ... I find a door without a number on it which indicates what lies behind is not a bedroom. Yes! There are two small apologetic letters in black painted high on the frame 'W.C.' ... I am confronted by a raised dais upon which are two booths ... all elegance has departed. Choose either one, neither is in repair. The seats are viciously grooved ... Turning to leave, I am perplexed by the dismal and unclean towel hanging by one corner from a nail driven into the middle of the door.[5]

As editor of the famous *Blue Guides* to worldwide destinations, L. Russell Muirhead did his best to defend the indefensible, claiming 'there are few English hotels without some honest merit':

> Visitors from overseas should remember that the hotel industry and its management are very strictly controlled in England, and, while this may perhaps too often be used as an excuse for deficiencies, it is frequently the genuine reason for the apparent difficulty of providing full comfort at all hours of the day and night.

Muirhead's top tip for obtaining half-decent service was 'not to expect too much nor to appear to know too much'. The breathtaking assumption that it was the customer who had to make the running was endorsed by other travel writers. 'Good humour goes a long way, and a genuinely pleasant smile is worth many a sixpence.'

The wealthiest stayed at the Connaught, Claridge's, the Dorchester, Berkeley, Grosvenor House and the Savoy. No new hotels had been built post-war, though some in the higher grade like the Cumberland and Strand Palace had been adapted to American taste. The first of London's new luxury hotels, the Westbury, just off Bond Street, was not opened until 1955. It was built by an American syndicate.

Car hire companies went all out to attract tourist custom. Victor Britain, 'the car hire specialist', offered the latest self-drive or chauffeur-driven limousines starting at $2.80 a day, 'gasoline, oil and insurance' included. An added if dubious attraction was a free Gastronomic Guide to 'all the famous eating houses in London'. The cost increased sharply when a car was hired for more than a week – up to $7 a day with petrol extra. An enterprising traveller on an extended stay found a way of holding down the expense of motoring:

> Diligent search turned up a reliable firm that would sell us a brand-new car on a re-purchase arrangement. That is, we would buy the car outright, but at the end of four months the firm would take it back at a predetermined price. Thus we would be out only by the depreciation.[6]

A small car was recommended for Britain's narrower and winding roads, in country and town:

> After a few wildly careering rides by taxi we had looked forward with dread to operating our own car in the London labyrinth. But it is not so bad after all. True, there is plenty of turning and twisting to be done, because London abhors a straight line. But traffic signs are plain and all important crossings are light-controlled.[7]

Of fascination for tourists was the English pub, particularly when it matched a preconceived image of low beams, hanging horse brasses and sawdust on the floor. But even here, it was advisable not to be too pushy. Muirhead said,

'Order your drinks and consume it quietly; the habitués of the place will in due time engage you in conversation if you wish; they are as ready as anyone to enjoy the entertainment of conversing with a stranger when they are ready for it.' And on no account ask for chilled beer instead of the warm, tepid stuff. When an innocent tourist made what he thought was a modest request for some ice, the landlord reacted with the shock of one who was expected to offer free drinks.

An added frustration of pub life was the arbitrary setting of opening and closing times. As a rule, drinks could be sold over the bar from 11.30 in the morning to 3.00 p.m. and from 5.30 p.m. to 10.00 p.m. Local licensing committees could, and often did, alter the times but without extending the total number of drinking hours. In some country taverns, all-day drinking was permitted on market days. In parts of Wales there was no opening at all on Sundays. The landlords' calls for 'Last orders' and 'Time, gentlemen' to warn of the doors about to close, didn't allow for much leeway. There was a good chance that Constable Booby was somewhere in the vicinity, keen to make an easy addition to his charge sheet. Publicans who took a relaxed view of the rules were liable to lose their licences to trade. Often heard was the argument that if the tourist industry was to grow, pubs should be places where families, including children, could go and sit in comfort, but the culture of male boozing left little room for compromise.

The lowest standards of hospitality were set by the boarding and guest houses, many of them strung out along the coast. In downbeat mood, John Betjeman wrote of:

Our lodging-house, ten minutes from the shore.
Still unprepared to make a picnic lunch
Except by notice on the previous day.
Still nowhere for the children when it's wet
Except that smelly, overcrowded lounge.

And always it was, 'Don't this. Don't that.'[8]

Of the innumerable stories of boarding house blight, a favourite was of the Morecambe landlady who held on to the key to the bathroom. Asked why she kept the door locked, she claimed that if it was left open, thoughtless guests might want to take a bath every day.

For young travellers making a little go a long way, the cheapest accommodation was to be found at the YWCA, YMCA or at one of the Rowton Houses, a throwback to Victorian philanthropy for providing decent lodgings for working men. For a shilling a night you were allocated your own cubicle and allowed access to a shared bathroom and lavatory. A 'special', described as 'practically hotel accommodation with hot and cold running water and a built-in wardrobe', cost half a crown. There were six Rowton Houses in London. One of the biggest, later a conventional hotel, was in central Birmingham.

In a vain attempt to persuade hoteliers to raise their sights, the Board of Trade pledged a 90 per cent rebate on purchase tax where North American residency was above 20 per cent. This gave the humourist J.B. Morton ('Beechcomber' of the *Daily Express*) the pretext to introduce Mrs McGurgle, a draconian seaside landlady:

> Whenever a Government inspector is in the neighbourhood, her loyal patrons at once develop American accents. Even old Mrs. Tufter, who has lived on the top floor since the Flood, leans from her window to cry 'Yippee!' in a cracked voice, and the shyest commercial gentleman demands iced waddah with his breakfast …

Never one to take leave of a running joke, Morton had Mrs McGurgle introducing 'one or two continental touches into her establishment':

> It will no longer be called Marine House, but 'Casa McGurgle', or 'Hôtel McGurgle et de l'Univers'. She has already written to a Miss Kelvick, who used to sing 'Where My Caravan Has Rested', to her own accompaniment. It is thought that this lady might introduce a kind of cabaret or café chantant atmosphere into McGurgle's. The cabbage, she tells me, will be cooked in a new way, 'with a lot of sauce', and the breakfast kipper will appear on the menu as *Kipper maitre d'hôtel*.[9]

Apart from the weather, the least attractive feature of the British way of life was what passed for culinary skills. The fried breakfast – eggs, bacon, sausage and tomato – was generally reckoned to be the best meal of the day. The Sunday roast with Yorkshire pudding and potatoes ladled in fat had a traditional appeal but did little to compensate for the daily helpings of boiled vegetables and dry meat smothered in thick gravy followed by stomach-churning custard with skin on the top.

Visitors could not quite believe what we put before them and the manner in which it was served. Margaret Bean remembered:

> The slatternly waitress with a dirty dishcloth over her arm took our order, and an enormous helping was dumped on our plates. An order for wine caused consternation. 'Wine!' she said in horror and went away to confer with the news that nothing was available except British sherry or (I think) someone's Invalid Port. She was disappointed when we turned them down. Afterwards she wrote out the bill and stuck the pencil behind her ear, and we paid at the desk.[10]

For a quick snack the municipal dining rooms, a hangover from the war, had official blessing. 'They served good meat, terrible vegetables and nursery puddings,' recalled Doris Lessing.[11] Of stronger appeal were the ABC (Aerated Bread Company) restaurants and Lyons' tearooms and corner houses, often running spacious restaurants where table service was by uniformed waitresses known as 'Nippies'. A close rival to Lyons were the restaurants set up by Italian–British caterer Charles Forte. But economies of scale to keep down prices were liable to debase quality. Marks and Spencer gave the best value in sandwiches to eat at the counter or take away.

To many native-born Britons it came as a surprise that foreigners were aghast at what was praised and promoted as 'good plain cooking'. The French-born gastronomic writer André Simon put it down to lack of imagination. In *Wine and Food*, he concluded sadly, 'the housewife looks upon cooking as a chore and a bore; she prepares without any pleasure meals which are eaten without any pleasure, without any complaints if bad and without a word of praise if good.'

That said, in his popular guide to London, John Metcalf assured his readers:

> By and large, you will find the restaurants of London are pretty good. There's still, perhaps, a little too much of self-excusing being done on the grounds that life is difficult, and meat and butter and eggs and cream are hard to come by. The intelligent restaurateur prides himself on overcoming those difficulties.[12]

Except in smart restaurants where the menus were invariably in French, concessions to visitors who spoke a language other than English were rare. The common assumption that if English was spoken loudly enough anyone could understand it persisted, despite the absence of supporting evidence.

Having described English food as 'sodden, sour, shiny, sloppy, stale and saccharined', Raymond Postgate launched his counter-attack in 1951 with the first *Good Food Guide*, an annual repository of informed opinion on where to go for a good meal in pleasant surroundings. Tourists were well advised to keep a copy close by them.

A recurring moan of visitors, particularly Americans, was of the quality of the coffee. Nescafé Instant just about passed muster but there could be no excuse for Camp Coffee, derived from chicory essence. It came in a bottle identified by the image of an Indian Army officer being served by a Sikh mess waiter holding a tray with the bottle and a jug of hot water. The taste was bitter and nothing like real coffee. Relief came to those familiar with the Moka Coffee Bar in Soho's Frith Street. With a grand opening by Gina Lollobrigida at the start of the coronation year, the Moka espresso machine was capable of delivering a short, black espresso in fifteen seconds. Moka was soon selling over 1,000 cups of coffee every day.

Well aware of Britain's difficulties as a tourist destination, the government-sponsored British Travel and Holidays Association (BTHA), with offices in St James's, worked overtime to put a gloss on what was on offer. A veritable tidal wave of handy brochures 'on all aspects of British life' presented the country as history in aspic, an image that was rounded off by the medieval splendour of the coronation. A gaggle of travel writers took their lead from the BTHA.

A typical promoter of postcard Britain was Leonard Kendall. Here he is at his most lyrical:

One of the principal charms of England is that one never knows what is just round the corner. Each twist and bend of the lane or road reveals some new delight. A lovely thatched cottage, a quaint old half-timbered inn, a stately mansion or a charming little bridge or toll gate. One may encounter a strange and amusing old sign, or monument, or perhaps some stocks or a whipping post. Again, you might behold a gracious church, or the still beautiful ruins of some ancient abbey or priory, or maybe the mighty ramparts of some mediaeval castle, its weathered masonry and battlemented towers and turrets, its drawbridge and portcullis, conjuring up romantic visions of bygone days.[13]

If, for certain parts of the country, all this was just about believable, harder to take was Kendall's praise for our 'magnificent roads and splendidly organised transport'. Britain's first stretch of motorway, the 8-mile Preston bypass, was not opened until 1958 (it was closed again after a few weeks to repair frost damage), while the M1, the country's first full-length motorway, carried its first traffic the following year.

Kendall was not alone in headlining hostages to fortune. *Come Visit Britain in Royal Autumn* had the chutzpa to claim that 'Britain's temperate climate is gentle enough for comfortable year-round sight-seeing'. Equally shameless was the assurance contained in a BTHA booklet that 'no journey will prove uncomfortable is guaranteed by the finest railways ... in the world'. First-hand experience told a different story, with complaints of 'dirt', 'discomfort', 'filthy seats', 'filthy windows that hide the scenery' and 'hopeless rail connections'.

Britain as a bucolic paradise was challenged by the Anglophile American writer Drew Middleton:

> This picturesque, rural England has not been a true picture of the country for over a century. But the guidebooks and the British Travel Association still send tourists to its shrines, novelists still write charming dated pictures of its life, and on both sides of the Atlantic the movies and stage continue to present attractive but false pictures of 'Olde Worlde' England.[14]

Not surprisingly, no one in the tourist industry was interested in tempting fate by presenting an accurate picture of contemporary Britain.

If food and accommodation could be disappointing, those from faraway places had no complaints about entertainment, particularly in London where the coronation theatre season, middle class to its core, was in full swing. John Gielgud led a season of Restoration comedies while Robert Donat, the English movie actor most familiar to American audiences, appeared in a revival of *Murder in the Cathedral*.

*Dial M for Murder*, which started as an American television play, was judged to be the thriller of the year, but that was before the opening of

Agatha Christie's mystery, *The Mousetrap*. Starring husband and wife Richard Attenborough and Sheila Sim, the play was slotted in for a long run, though no one guessed that it would still be going strong seventy years later. A tenuous royal connection was provided by a revival of George Bernard Shaw's *The Apple Cart*, in which Noël Coward was at his superior best playing a king who upstages his quarrelsome politicians.

Derided by the critics, a more conventional take on royalty was offered by Anna Neagle as Queen Victoria in a lavish musical, *The Glorious Years*. As the young Turk of the drama critics, Kenneth Tynan led the charge. 'Miss Neagle,' he wrote:

Acts in a fashion so devoid of personality as to be practically incognito; second, she sings, shaking her voice at the audience like a tiny fist; and, third, she dances, in that non-committal, twirling style, once known as 'skirt-dancing', which was originally invented to explain the presence on the stage of genteel young women who could neither sing nor act.

As to the music, 'a series of production numbers seem to have been recovered from the wastepaper basket of a bankrupt impresario of the period'.[15] But as it turned out, the star of the show, much loved by moviegoers, was critic-proof.

Cashing in on the Elizabethan theme, a raft of Shakespeare productions commanded the box office. At the Old Vic, the Queen and her Consort saw a not very distinguished revival of *Henry VIII*. In fact, none of the attempts to give Shakespeare a contemporary significance really came off. One critic was driven to remark that, Shakespeare lover though he was, he was beginning to feel he had had enough. 'It would be idle to pretend that this was an outstanding year for the West End theatre,' declared *Theatre World*, adding that special coronation productions 'were not on the whole marked by originality'.[16]

Ironically, the number one Shakespearian production of the year was the American movie version of *Julius Caesar*, starring Marlon Brando as Mark Antony, James Mason as Brutus and John Gielgud as Cassius. A critical and financial success, the film thrashed its stage rivals.

The only outstanding new plays were Graham Greene's *The Living Room*, acclaimed as 'the finest debut of this generation', and *The River Line*, with its behind-the-lines wartime theme by Charles Morgan. Americans in town were made to feel at home with the imported musicals *Guys and Dolls* and *Porgy and Bess*.

The oddities of theatregoing had some appeal. Sylvia Gill, an east coast American, was 'intrigued by your very pleasant custom of a tea-tray on my lap during the intermission', though not all her compatriots were similarly charmed. Peter Roberts complained of:

> ... crockery clatterers who return their tea trays only in the darkness of the second act. Don't these trays cry out to be abolished anyway? Those so hungry that they cannot stir from their seats cannot possibly be satisfied with such meagre fare. Film audiences would never dream of taking tea between films. They go to see and enjoy the movie, free from that picnic approach to the theatre.[17]

For those who ventured out of London there was Shakespeare at Stratford and an abundance of festivals that overlapped with the coronation, including Aldeburgh, Bath and, new to the game, York and Norwich. Complementing Edinburgh, the welcome sign was put out for festival visitors to Perth, Inverness and Dumfries. The Belfast Arts Festival encompassed music, drama, opera and ballet as well as Irish folk dancing. The 5th International Musical Eisteddfod was held at Llangollen. No doubt catching up on family connections, the newly established Pitlochry Festival, with its tent-like theatre (now a state-of-the-art auditorium) in the heart of Perthshire, welcomed an influx of American tourists, one of whom described 'the theatre in the hills' as 'one of the highlights of our visit to Britain'.

For visitors who had witnessed the coronation and wanted a reminder of the experience once they had returned home, a speedy publishing venture gave them the opportunity to take away a book called *The Story of the Coronation* by Randolph S. Churchill, only son of Winston. Randolph was an alcoholic pest, notorious for his ill manners and boorish behaviour, who had mastered the skills of popular journalism. As one of the Gold Staff Officers or ushers in Westminster Abbey, he might have been expected to write a first-hand account of the ceremonials. Instead, with padding from an earlier generation of famous diarists, he threw together a hotchpotch of lists of regalia, royal vestments and orders of service spiced with his own acerbic comments on matters such as the role of the Duke of Edinburgh in the royal partnership. Embarrassed into writing an introduction, Sir George

Bellew, Garter Principal King of Arms, gave a masterful demonstration of damning with faint praise:

> Not everyone will agree with all the judgements and opinions expressed by Mr Randolph Churchill. His approach to some aspects of his subject is controversial, but this may be found refreshing. In any event one cannot but respect the application of research which the author has evidently devoted to his complicated task.[18]

The novelist Peter Vansittart was fond of telling of his encounter with Randolph ('I heard it first at a lunch party') at a country house weekend. Randolph was staying nearby:

> After dinner, latish, he wandered in, sufficiently drunk to imagine himself in some hotel, an illusion reinforced by the sight of us unknowns sipping our drinks. Brusquely he ordered a double brandy, which our hostess, handsome, talented and at this moment perplexed, swiftly supplied, while not recognising him. Matters seemed well. Churchill settled himself down like an ill-designed galleon on a yellow sandbag, until a woman, a painter of some merit, resumed the conversation. 'The Queen does perfectly well, even considering her salary.'
>
> The last word struck the gate-crasher like a pogo-stick. He staggered up, he swayed, pudgy, glistening, outraged, he drew breath, then bellowed, 'I will not have my monarch insulted', and banged her in one eye.
>
> All looked at her husband. Of considerable literary achievement, he was physically small. Eyes ranged the company, eventually accosting the youngest and tallest present. Myself. I had boasted at dinner of my physical fitness and was now, silently but emphatically, being invited to prove it. Churchill was showing signs of improving his feat, on the remaining eye, as though dissatisfied with his first attempt.
>
> I thought, I thought fast, snatching the brandy bottle and, dangling it before him like an amateur matador, drew him towards the door across the hall, past the front door, into the cold, cold night where I finally halted, yielding the bottle. He emptied it, spun unexpectedly patted my shoulder and, with considerable dignity, tipping me half a crown, shouldered his way through an imaginary multitude towards wherever he had come from: Mecca, Jerusalem or Downing Street.[19]

If Randolph was on fighting form, his father, despite the frailties of age, was even more so. Defying all expectations, he ignored hints to stand down as Prime Minister immediately after the coronation. He did not have to look for an excuse for hanging on. As heir apparent, Anthony Eden had suffered a botched gall bladder operation and was in no fit state to succeed. The bigger question was whether Churchill was strong enough to continue in office.

On 23 June, having seen Eden and his wife Clarissa (Churchill's niece) off from Heathrow for a crucial operation in Boston, Churchill returned to Downing Street to host a dinner for Alcide De Gasperi, premier of Italy. At the start all went well, with Churchill delivering a witty speech about the visit of an earlier Roman statesman, Julius Caesar. But at the end of the evening he was unable to get out of his chair. Those close to him assumed he was worse for drink but it was soon apparent that something more serious was happening. This was the stroke his doctor, Lord Moran, had foreseen. Moran thought it unlikely that his patient would survive the weekend but by the following day Churchill was sufficiently recovered to chair the Wednesday Cabinet meeting. The little he said was slurred, with his mouth drooping, his left side was paralysed, and he could walk only a few tottering steps. In the afternoon he left for Chartwell, where he began a slow recuperation.

Nothing of this appeared in the press. When the three major newspaper owners – the Lords Beaverbrook, Bracken and Camrose – were let in on the secret they were flattered into agreeing to clamp down on the sensational news. The official line was that the premier had been overworking and was resting at Chartwell. In little more than six weeks he was back in Downing Street preparing the leader's speech he was to make at the October party conference. Much to Eden's chagrin, there was no further talk of Churchill's retirement. Or, rather, there was plenty of talk among his colleagues, none of whom so far had the courage to tell him bluntly it was time to go.

When Churchill was convalescing at Chartwell, the Queen offered to visit. This was thought not to be a good idea. Churchill did not want to be seen in a poor light. 'Tell her we'll meet at the St Leger,' he said. Had she insisted, an interesting constitutional question would have arisen. Seeing Churchill looking frail and helpless and knowing Eden was still under doctor's orders, would she have felt bound to ask who was in charge?

In the event, the old warrior was sufficiently recovered by October to preside over the Tory Party Conference. The wild reception for his speech confirmed him as the undisputed leader as long as he wanted to hold on. A few days later, he was told he had won the Nobel Prize. He was disappointed to find the award was for literature not for peace.

# 10

# WORLD STAGE

The royal tour of Australia and New Zealand, broken off at the death of George VI, was resumed in November. Churchill saw it as a 'royal pilgrimage' that would cast a 'clear, calm, gay and benign light upon the whole human scene', though it was more like a triumphal progress, transcending, however briefly, race, religion, colour and political dogma.

Right from the start, a public relations success was almost guaranteed. Post-war Commonwealth ties with Britain were strongest in Australia and New Zealand. As Ben Chifley, Australia's Prime Minister, told Attlee in 1946, the three nations alone 'fully represent the British tradition'. It was a view widely endorsed by political commentators. The diplomat, journalist and adventurer Robert Bruce Lockhart said it all:

> To the old Dominions Britain exported not only men and money, but also ideals and the British way of life. These the sister-nations share. They have the same respect for the law, the rights of the individual and tolerance. They have more of less the same two-Party system of Government. They eat the same breakfast and play the same games. Contrary to all foreign prediction, this Anglomania is increasing instead of declining. Cricket, Rugby football and golf cement the Commonwealth.[1]

Sentiment was reinforced by trade. In coronation year, Britain took in three-quarters of New Zealand's exports and two-fifths of Australian exports. Of the imports into those countries, Britain accounted for over half. In addition to manufactured goods, Britain sent its people. In so far as immigrants were welcome, it was the mother country that was the major source. Between 1947 and 1952, over 360,000 British migrants landed in Australia, having paid a mere £10 for the sea passage. Known, inevitably, as the 'Ten Pound Poms', they enjoyed a standard of living that was way above anything they were used to.

On any weekday in London, rain or shine, queues of would-be emigrants were to be seen outside the Commonwealth High Commissions. In 1950 an international opinion poll found that 42 per cent of Britain's population and 58 per cent of those under the age of 30 would emigrate 'if free to do so', the highest proportion of the eight countries canvassed. Suffering the pains of austerity, one young ex-serviceman spoke for many when he told an interviewer, 'I wish I were anywhere but this goddamned country. There is nothing but queues and restrictions and forms and cold and no food.'

For Kathleen Upton, making do was in a tiny flat with 'wet bed linen draped across the kitchen' while trying to bring up a family, including a daughter suffering asthma, on the low wages brought home by her husband. The coronation, 'bleak, wet and utterly miserable' on the Sussex coast, was the last straw.

James Saxton was 15 when he and his family emigrated from Essex in 1951:

> The post-war world was a pretty dismal place to grow up in. A colourless, featureless world of 'make do and mend'. A world of 'Utility' this and 'Utility' that. A world of shabbily dressed, pinched faced mums, perpetually forced to queue for an illusive [*sic*] 'something'. A world of self-righteous politicians who kept making biting forceful speeches which all boiled down to we, the public at large, working hard and being fed less … A sense of futility permeated our lives. We, as a nation, had given our all and then some – so where was our reward?[2]

By the end of 1954, Australia had attracted close on a million post-war immigrants and their families, with the British equal in number to all other nationalities put together. It was a trend encouraged by the British Government. As Labour's Commonwealth Relations Secretary put it in 1950, 'The solidarity and increasing strength of the Commonwealth depends on the increasing migration of people from this country.'

'This is a British community and we want to keep it a British community,' declared Harold Holt who, as Australian Immigration Minister, beefed up the appeal of a new life in a land promising, according to the brochures, 'endless sunshine, blue skies and white, sandy beaches'.

Once settled in their new home, the Ten Pound Poms found that their allegiance was still as much to Britain as it was to Australia. Schoolchildren recited an oath of loyalty: 'I love my country and the British Empire. I salute her flag, the Union Jack.' 'God Save the Queen' was played at the end of every evening in the cinema and theatre and even at sporting events. Empire Day was celebrated as a sacred occasion and in many schools, particularly in South Australia, the country's history was taught almost as a footnote to the story of a glorious Empire.

In New Zealand, it was quite common for citizens to think of themselves as 'more British than the British', with traditions dating from the first settlers. There was much talk of New Zealand carrying the banner of the British race.

The royal six-month tour was to begin with flights to Bermuda and Jamaica where the royal party would board SS *Gothic*, a converted passenger cargo liner designated the royal yacht while the newly commissioned *Britannia* was still undergoing sea trials.

On 21 November, the Queen Mother hosted a farewell party for the young couple at Clarence House. Noël Coward was a guest, though he was expected to sing for his supper. Ever the performer, he made no complaint:

> It really was enchanting. I wisely took Norman [Hackford, his pianist], and sang well. Peter Ustinov did his 'impressions', brilliant but too long. There were only about thirty people present. Everyone looked lovely and I had long conversations with the Queen Mother whom, as usual, I adored. The Queen and Prince Philip didn't leave till after three and so I didn't get to bed until four.[3]

Two days later, the streets between Buckingham Palace and London Airport were thick with spectators out in the chill of a late autumn evening to witness the start of a long journey. As the car pulled out of the Palace forecourt, Charles and Anne were spotted at a window to wave off their parents. They would not see them again before the spring. Churchill, Attlee and Eden, along with the Queen Mother and Princess Margaret, were at the airport to bid their farewells.

The first stop-off point of the tour was Bermuda, a crown colony from 1684, 600 miles off the US mainland. Bermuda was yet to be a haven for offshore finance, but in 1953 the island, with its subtropical climate, thrived on American tourism. With a population that was over 60 per cent Black, it nonetheless passed without comment that the Queen's welcoming party, led by governor Sir Alexander Hood, was exclusively white.

Hood was an interesting character. A former Director General of Army Medical Services, he ended the war with a distinguished record as an innovator and as honorary physician to George VI, a distinction that may have had something to do with his appointment as Governor of Bermuda in 1949. By the time of the Queen's visit he had twice had his period of office extended. But in his private life, all was not well. With a marriage on the rocks, Hood was heading towards the divorce court, a disqualification for receiving the Queen.

In the event, no breath of scandal was allowed to taint the proceedings. Eighteen months later, Hood resigned without explanation. After his divorce in October 1955, he remarried the same day, continuing to live in Bermuda for the rest of his life.

In the twenty-four hours the Queen was in Bermuda, she and the Duke drove in an open carriage through the capital, Hamilton, where she met war veterans and recently born girl triplets, named appropriately Elizabeth, Philippa and Margaret, with each clasping a miniature Union Jack.

The white ruling minority judged the visit, the first by a reigning monarch, to be a huge success. 'We have had royal visitors before,' declared the *Royal Gazette*, Bermuda's premier newspaper:

> ... but never before has there been such rejoicing.
> And a day later, this ancient colony has had the proudest moment in its 344 years of history ... Our beautiful and gracious young Queen and her handsome Consort, who already had our deep loyalty and admiration have now won our hearts completely.[4]

But this was without reference to those who were excluded from the celebrations. Of the 1,000 guests at the garden party held at Government House, only sixty were Black, while later, at the state dinner, not a single

Black face was to be seen, except among those serving the meal. In London, the left-wing press led by the *Mirror* and the *Herald* rounded on Hood as the diehard defender of racial prejudice. Hood claimed naively that he had merely followed precedent. For the state dinner, the foremost thirty families had been invited. To which the *Herald* responded tartly, 'To blazes with the first families of Bermuda. Offend *them* for a change.' The row overshadowed what the *Royal Gazette* called 'our proudest moment', though the royal couple were held in no way to blame for what the *Mirror* claimed to be a 'mammoth blunder' by the Bermudian administration and an 'insult to the Commonwealth'.[5]

It was then on to Jamaica, where the Governor, Sir Hugh Foot, was an experienced colonial administrator and diplomat, the eldest son of a highly political family which included Michael Foot, journalist and Member of Parliament who, for three years from 1980, would be Labour Party leader. Hugh Foot was destined to be the last Governor of Cyprus.

Well on the way to independence, which was finally granted in 1962, Jamaica gave the Queen a multiracial welcome, though newsreel images of spectators at the airport show less enthusiasm than idle curiosity. The visit warmed up with a relaxed sense of fun. For example, when a Mr Kidd, 'with old world courtesy … placed his coat before the Queen for her to walk on', thus becoming 'the first of many Sir Walter Raleighs of the tour'.

In the House of Commons, Churchill picked up on the Elizabethan symbolism when, in typically effusive style, he sent good wishes to the royal couple as they boarded SS *Gothic* on the next stage of the tour:

> Her Majesty's ship *Gothic* is more spacious and travels faster than the *Golden Hind*, but it may well be that the journey the Queen is about to take will be no less auspicious and the treasure she brings back no less bright than when Drake first sailed on an English ship around the world.

Fiji and Tonga were next on the visiting list from 17–20 December. For BBC reporter Wynford Vaughan-Thomas, this was the highlight of the entire tour:

> Here are two groups of islands that fulfil all one's dreams of what a tropical Pacific paradise should be. In Fiji the memorable moment came when the Royal car was escorted by stalwart fuzzy-haired Fijian runners,

carrying burning torches, on its way to the Grand Pacific Hotel. By tradition Fijians are supposed to show respect for distinguished visitors by keeping silent, but on this occasion tradition was thrown to the winds or rather a new tradition was born. Cheers and songs echoed across the still waters of Suva Bay as the Queen and Duke came out on to the balcony ... Her Majesty was in one of those magnificent silvery white court dresses she wears so well, and with the deep blue of the Order of the Garter rivalling the velvety blue of the tropic night. She smiled and waved, the very embodiment of youthful grace and regal dignity. At that moment she was surely the Faerie Queene of every woman's dreams.[6]

The Tonga experience was made indelible by a magnificent feast. It was hosted by Queen Sālote, who had made such a joyful impression on the coronation procession. Wynford Vaughan-Thomas was among the throng to gorge on 'suckling pig by the yard and tropical fruits by the ton'.[7] In Tonga, it appeared that statesmanship was equated with eating on a grand scale. With Queen Elizabeth holding to her reputation as a light eater, it was left to Philip to uphold the gastronomic honour of the royal visitors.

There was a moment when the two Queens shared a memory of the coronation:

It came when Her Majesty was driving with Queen Sālote in an open carriage and the rain began to fall. The two Queens looked apprehensive. Then Queen Sālote produced a large umbrella. Her mind must have gone back to that rainy day in June when she had braved the London weather. The two Queens looked at each other and neither could restrain a smile of amusement.[8]

All but hidden by torrential rain, the *Gothic* docked in Auckland on 23 December:

The New Zealanders were understandably anxious that their welcome should be correct in every detail. The lucky ones who were to attend garden parties practised their curtsies, and there was a run in bookshops on guides to etiquette. But all those anxieties melted at the first sight of Her Majesty ... I shall never forget the excitement in the voice of my colleague, Don Donaldson of the New Zealand Broadcasting Service, as he described the Queen's stepping down the gangway on the quayside. He counted all the remaining steps she had to take. 'Four … three … two … one … she's in New Zealand!' He fairly shouted his triumph into the microphone and the whole of New Zealand caught his enthusiasm.[9]

With the Queen making known her wish to 'see and be seen', every school laid on free transport for young people to be given the chance to catch sight of the royals. The object of their affection appeared in forty-six towns and cities and attended 100 functions. The smaller centres were overwhelmed by the influx from outlying regions. Tirau, with a population of around 600, attracted a crowd of over 10,000. Three hundred and eighty thousand medallions were struck to be presented at school parties. Treated to community singalongs, the Queen could have been forgiven for feeling heartedly sick of hearing 'Land of Hope and Glory', 'Sussex, Sussex by the Sea' and 'There'll Always be an England'.

On processional routes, buildings deemed to be less than presentable were hidden behind screens while those that passed muster were decked with bunting and flowers. Cars flew Union Jacks and in the open country, sheep were to be seen with their wool dyed red, white and blue. Security was minimal. At Greymouth, the 11-year-old Pat Jamieson ran alongside the royal car for half a mile until Philip leaned out to tell her, 'If you run much further, you'll burst.'

Margaret Lomas was aged 6 when the Queen came to Whangarei. She was staying in what until recently had been the Commercial Hotel. In honour of the occasion, it was now the Grand:

> In the evening our family walked – about 20 minutes or so – to the hotel and with many others chanted, 'We want the Queen, we want the Queen'. This had no response (they were most probably having dinner), so the chant changed to 'We want the Duke, we want the Duke'. This seemed to work as they soon appeared on the balcony to the loud cheers of the crowd. I was sitting on my father's shoulders so had a great view. I remember they looked very happy, and there was a wonderful feeling in the crowd.

When the Queen arrived in Auckland, the young George Smith, though, by his own admission, not much of a royalist, had a ringside seat:

I was working along with my Mother and her old Aunts … who owned a small shoe store on Karangahape Rd, near Queen St. So we were able to put some chairs outside the store front on Karangahape Rd and stand on them well above the rest of the crowd and watch the motorcade drive along Karangahape Rd. I remember the Queen did not look quite real, as her facial makeup was quite stunning, and she showed not a blemish, but all her youthful vitality.

At Auckland's hospital, anticipating a much-needed comfort stop, the organisers provided:

… an appropriately stationed lavatory with a cushioned toilet seat covered in a Tartan cloth; most assuredly the correct pattern too. As it turned out, her Majesty did not seek the use of the facilities so once she had left the premises, all the young doctors and interns and other staff at the hospital, had some fun having their pictures taken while sitting on the tartan padded Royal Throne.

Aged 18, Caroline Woon was one of a 'marching team' waiting to demonstrate the art of creating patterns of fluid humanity:

While we were waiting, my Scots friend, also about 18, sat and explained to me why she as a Scot would not, could not, feel excited about Elizabeth as she was not, in reality, *HER* Queen let alone Queen Elizabeth II as true Scots had never even recognised the first Elizabeth … Finally, Elizabeth arrived and I, looking at her with curiosity, saw her look back at us as Philip said … and you could see what he was saying … 'Who are they?' and her reply that we were 'marching teams'. Unheard of in Britain and at that time unique to NZ. I can only think that that conversation between them had the effect of unleashing some sort of latent emotion because my Scots chum emitted what can only be described as a throaty roar of patriotism, wonderful in its intensity and then charged like a wounded bull out of our designated area, trying to barge like an All Black through another block of people in front to get even closer. I ran after her, half concerned that she was going to commit regicide and half envious of such a loud voice compared to my squeaks. I caught up with her and we bounced up and down then, puffing and yelling, the only way to catch another glimpse. The noise was deafening, the sun hot and our queen moved regally on. The moment had passed. Excited discussion of our first glimpse of Royals in the flesh, history being made and didn't we get up close? And did you hear what she said, she recognised that we were marching teams and wasn't she beautiful, much more beautiful in the flesh and we might be able to get another look at her if we break ranks (as if we hadn't already) and run across to the back where she hasn't been yet. All of this from my Scots friend!!

Overall, there were few signs of dissent. The communist Mayor of Brummel boycotted a reception and a resident of Whanganui attracted attention when he refused to leave a shop to watch the royal couple pass by: 'I'm not getting up for those Pommie buggers.' But hostility did not extend beyond individual protests.

In Wellington, the Queen opened New Zealand's Parliament in its centennial year wearing her coronation gown and seated on a replica of the throne in Westminster Abbey. Having given her blessing to the foundation stone for the Anglican cathedral and laid a wreath at the Cenotaph, the British High Commissioner, Sir Geoffrey Scoones, eulogised the visit as a symbol of imperial unity, adding, possibly with more emphasis than he intended, 'at least among countries of fundamentally British stock'.

New Zealand's fairy-tale story was interjected with grief. On the day after the Queen's arrival, the Tangiwai railway bridge was swept away in a torrent of ice, boulders and volcanic ash, taking with it the Wellington-to-Auckland night express. One hundred and fifty-one died in the freezing river. After referring to the tragedy in her Christmas message, the Queen visited two of the survivors.

The rest of her worldwide broadcast from Auckland focused on the Commonwealth, which 'bears no resemblance to empires of the past. It is an entirely new conception built on the highest qualities of the spirit of man; friendships, loyalty and the desire for freedom and peace.' To that perception of an 'equal partnership of nations and races', the Queen pledged to give her 'heart and soul every day of my life'. She ended on the hope that her visit had 'demonstrated that the Crown is a human link between all the peoples who owe allegiance to me – an alliance of mutual love and respect, and never of compulsion'.

In the heady atmosphere of mutual admiration, this flight of fancy of 'all friends together' with one friend, by virtue of age and tradition, senior to the others, was happily endorsed. That a different view might be taken elsewhere in the Commonwealth and Empire was not allowed to spoil the magic of the moment.

The idyllic vision of a bright future for a British-led family of nations was carried through to the final stage of the tour. Under a fierce February sun, the Queen and Duke set off on a two-month traverse of Australia which took in fifty-seven towns and cities. The cheerleader was Prime Minister Robert Menzies. An Anglophile, who described himself as 'British to the bootstraps' and a dedicated monarchist, Menzies was also a canny political operator who saw the royal tour as an opportunity to reinforce conservative values. His aim was to present to the outside world an image of Australia as a united society confident of a bright future.

Press coverage followed the British pattern of emphasising the virtues of 'hearth, home and service'. The *Australian Women's Weekly* said that the Queen and 'her handsome husband and her two children make her a figure who stands not only as the head of the British Commonwealth but as the example of that happy family life which is the foundation of a nation'. Male ascendency, which many sturdy Australians accepted as a gift from God, was tempered by the awareness that the Duke had to walk two paces behind his wife. Nonetheless, the Queen was said to rely on his manly presence:

> It must be a great relief for Her Majesty, who, of necessity, often finds herself in factories and establishments, the mechanics of which hold little of feminine interest, to know that the sharp, masculine mind of the Duke will soon be involved to the enormous delight of the person showing them through, in the examination of some complicated process.[10]

It helped that the Queen had been 'brought up to the everyday values of country life … in the common sense philosophy of farm and stockyard'.[11] The concept of the nation as one big united family was harped on by Menzies:

> This is a great thing for Australia. It reduces the bitterness of political and industrial dispute, and creates a sense of community. We have occasionally forgotten we are one people with no real class differences. We have all the elements of unity and shared experience. We go wrong only when we allow ourselves to be poisoned by the talk of class warfare

and of the privileged classes. There are not too many people with privileges in our country who have not earned them the hard way.[12]

From the land of promise, Menzies stretched out a hand to prospective migrants from the mother country, while the Queen did her bit in promoting Australia as a country that smiled on the newcomers:

> This country offers wonderful opportunities for men and women from the Old World, and to those in the United Kingdom who seek wider scope for their talents and resources Australia may well seem the promised land, for it is a spacious country with a healthy, vigorous people and vast natural resources. Only a pessimist would set bounds to its future.

In an eight-week stay, the royal couple made 207 car journeys and thirty-three air flights, keeping up to five engagements a day.[13] Events in the royal calendar ranged from life-saving demonstrations at Bondi Beach to addressing 107,000 schoolchildren at three open-air venues to opening a session of Parliament. Almost everywhere the reception was ecstatic.

Ron Penn, representing 'a grand country, inhabited by grand people', was part of the Honour Guard for the coronation pageant at the Sydney Showground. For this event, the Sea Cadets arranged themselves into the shape of a gigantic Union Jack flanked by 'ER'.[14]

The following day the *Sydney Morning Herald* declared the coronation and the royal visit to be a symbol of the 'supreme achievement of the British race'. Rhapsodies in verse took pride of place in the popular press. As the resident poet of *Women's Weekly*, Dorothy Drain extolled 'this English girl ... spanning a continent', courtesy of Quantas:

> From crowds to cheering crowds, and glimpse below
> Those wide and lonely wastes where once
> Came other English girls, braving a wilderness to bring
> Like hers, the soft beauty of an English spring.

Dame Edna Everage would have been proud of her.

But voices of opposition, though muted, were heard above the clamour. Among those who condemned 'sycophancy and the cultural cringe' as inappropriate to a 'new nation developing our own character', the

Reverend Calvert Barber of the Wesleyan Church in Canberra spoke for many ordinary Australians when he rejected 'the snobbery, the jingoism, the fawning, the gilded self-seeking which has seemed at times to associate the Throne with a particular party or class'.[15]

A glimpse of the not-too-distant future was provided by Kathleen Barrand who, as a 15-year-old in 1949, settled in Geelong, Victoria. She adopted without question her mother's British patriotism and devotion to the monarchy. Kathleen kept a diary of every moment of the Queen's visit to Geelong and took great pride in her collection of coronation mugs. However, recalling all this in later years, she noted that her daughter was openly republican.[16]

Care was taken to keep racial discrimination under cover. Aborigines were seen waving flags, cheering and giving flowers to the Queen, the very model of model citizens, but usually in groups separated from white Australians. Invited to Canberra to meet the Queen, a leading Aboriginal artist, Albert Namatjira, was refused hotel accommodation. Displays of Aboriginal culture emphasised the 'primitive, the strange and the ancient'.[17]

By contrast, Australia as a whole was portrayed as a sophisticated, advanced economy. And one where no risks, however slight, were to be taken with the safety and security of distinguished guests. When the arrival of the royal couple in Western Australia coincided with an outbreak of poliomyelitis, there was talk of cutting short the visit. Instead, the Queen and the Duke had to sleep and eat on board the *Gothic* with only occasional forays into the real world.

Despite this setback, for which Menzies came in for sharp criticism for being overcautious, the two months in Australia were judged a triumph. Of the total population of 9 million, around 75 per cent turned out to see the royal couple at least once.[18] Bubbling with exuberance, Churchill saw 'no limits [to] the reinforcement which this royal journey may have brought to the health, the wisdom, the sanity and the hopefulness of mankind'.

Churchill might have been less sanguine had he paid closer attention to reports filtering back from the Imperial outposts visited by the Queen and the Duke on the journey home. Communist unrest threatened the ten-day stopover in Ceylon, where the Anglophile ruling elite was keen to demonstrate its loyalty to Britain and to the Crown. Responding to the call for a full performance, the Queen opened both Houses of Parliament borne down by the weight of her coronation robes.

In Uganda, it was tribal differences that gave trouble. Shortly before the royal arrival, the Governor had exiled the Kabaka of Buganda, the largest of Uganda's kingdoms. His offence had been to demand succession from the Protectorate. When the Queen was in Entebbe and Kampala, both in Buganda, no successor to the deposed Kabaka had been elected. Nerves were stretched by the state of emergency in neighbouring Kenya, where the death toll from the savage Mau Mau uprising was mounting by the day.

It must have come as a relief to the Queen to be greeted by familiar and friendly faces in Malta. A dramatic reception was organised by Mountbatten, now promoted to Admiral with two jobs – Commander-in-Chief of the British Mediterranean Fleet and NATO Commander-in-Chief of Allied Forces in the region. Having left the *Gothic* in Tobruk, it was on the new royal yacht *Britannia* that the head of state approached the island:

> Mountbatten practised a spectacular manoeuvre to greet the royal couple … The Fleet advanced at twenty-five knots, twice the speed of *Britannia*, then turned inwards and swept past the Royal Yacht, sailing so close that some of the ships splashed *Britannia*'s decks. The exercise was perfectly safe provided that no mistake was made, but even a tiny deviation could have caused a disastrous accident. It never occurred to Mountbatten not to try the manoeuvre, and when one of the navigators later told him that he had aged years during the few moments the ship had taken to pass the yacht, he professed surprise. 'I had not appreciated how worried they had all been, as I wasn't in the least worried.' Certainly he achieved his object of impressing the royal party. 'At no time during this World Tour, either before or afterwards, had quite the same thing been seen,' wrote Conolly Abel-Smith, Captain of the Royal Yacht; 'the dash, timing and setting were things quite different and superior to other occasions. Her Majesty and the Duke of Edinburgh went out of their way to remark on the magnificent exhibition.'[19]

Prince Charles and Princess Anne were among the welcoming party. They had flown to Malta ten days earlier for a round of excursions organised by the Mountbattens:

The Prince of Wales's first recollection of his great-uncle is of a tall figure standing on the jetty at Valletta to greet them. Mountbatten, he remembered, was wonderful with children, always tipping them over or throwing them up into the air. He would tell them stories, usually about things he had done rather than fairy tales, and seemed always ready to make time to be with them. It was the beginning of a relationship which was to become progressively more important to both parties.[20]

The last leg of the tour took in Gibraltar, another trouble spot where security was stricter than it had been in the German war. Spain closed its consulate in Gibraltar at the beginning of May and closed the border for the two days of the Queen's visit.

With the Queen's return home, she was feted on all sides for bringing together Commonwealth and Empire as never before. Royal Navy warships and a flotilla of private craft escorted the *Britannia* up the Thames to a welcome of a forty-one-gun salute. Crowds roared their approval. Yet most people, if pressed, would have found it hard to give a coherent account of what the tour had really achieved or, indeed, what the Commonwealth and Empire really amounted to.

The figures were indeed impressive. On various counts, around 6 billion citizens in a landmass covering 15 million square miles were wrapped in the Union Jack. Empire Day, an annual celebration when schoolchildren were versed in the superiority of the Anglo-Saxon race and its civilising mission, was marked across the English-speaking world. But the fact remained that the Commonwealth and Empire were hard to define. A mixed collection of territories, acquired mostly by nefarious means, with varying degrees of loyalty to the mother country, had little in common.

The concept of unity in diversity was first given wide coverage by the Queen when, as Princess Elizabeth in 1947, she had made her broadcast from South Africa, acclaiming the evolution of 'our great imperial Commonwealth to which we all belong'. The doctrine was adopted enthusiastically by the media.

In the week before the coronation, the *New York Times* had praised the Commonwealth as a 'single association of nations, the greatest that the world has ever known', adding 'the members of the Commonwealth are not held together by the written word or the unsheathed sword but by common interests and aims, common ideals and traditions':

Aside from having a common governmental tradition, the nations of the Commonwealth also are linked by the similarity of their judicial systems, their community of economic interests, their joint concern for the military security of vast and important areas of the world, a certain degree of common citizenship and nationality, a process of continual consultation on mutual problems and – not least – their voluntary recognition of the British Crown as the symbol of their association.

The coronation released a groundswell of goodwill. 'The Crown may seem a fragile link,' wrote Robert Bruce Lockhart:

> ... but in human affairs the symbol means more than signed documents, and the silken cord holds better than the strongest chain. The Queen is Canada's Queen, Australia's Queen and Queen of the other sister-nations, and to Canadians, Australians and New Zealanders she is 'Our Queen', and the 'our' makes a world of difference.
>
> No foreigner and no British subject who saw the Coronation could fail to have realised the immense unity, fervour and loyalty of the sister-nations of the Commonwealth. Never in any period of the history of the English-speaking world has there been such devotion to the Crown as there is today.[21]

But it did not take much to open the cracks in a stage-managed façade. When the Queen toured Canada in 1959, fury descended on the head of Joyce Davidson, an otherwise inoffensive television host who, in an unguarded moment, commented, 'Like most Canadians I'm pretty indifferent to the visit of the Queen,' adding, 'We're a little annoyed at still being dependent.' The overreaction of politicians and press was prompted by sensitivities attached to the highlight of the trip, the joint opening by the Queen and President Eisenhower of the St Lawrence Seaway, an ocean-going link between the Atlantic and the Great Lakes that had taken more than a generation to get through the American Congress. The event was too important to be put at risk by careless talk. Davidson was suspended from her current affairs programme, eventually departing Canada to restart her career in New York. But she was not without support on her home ground. Though it passed without comment at the time, a Gallup poll showed that 48 per cent of Canadians were no more than modestly interested in the Queen's visit – hardly a ringing endorsement of royal patronage.

In Britain, idealism foundered on differences within the political class on the country's imperial role. On the far right of the Tory Party, a vocal minority looked back to an imaginary golden age when British rule went unchallenged. When, at the 1948 Conservative Conference, Bernard Braine thundered, 'We are an imperial power or we are nothing!' there were few in the audience who did not hear this as a declaration of white supremacy.

It was a mindset that found malign expression in the treatment of newcomers to Britain. The 1948 British Nationality Act which allowed unrestricted entry for all colonial and Commonwealth citizens, a basic principle of Empire unity, released a floodtide of latent racism. When the first post-war immigrants from Jamaica arrived on the *Empire Windrush*, they were welcomed in the press as 'five hundred pairs of willing hands'. The view was not widely shared. For the most part, the newcomers were treated abominably. Imperialism was all very well as long as the subject people knew their place, which, most certainly, was not in Britain. Openly racist pressure groups included the White Defence League and Oswald Mosley's Union Movement.

Representing the lunatic fringe in all its muddled thinking was the League of Empire Loyalists, founded in 1954 by a bevy of retired army officers with fantasies of making Britain great again. The league was anti-American, anti-colonial independence, antisemitic and a supporter of apartheid.

Even people who might otherwise have claimed to be broadminded were quick to show their displeasure when newcomers disturbed their complacency. It was standard practice for employers to impose a colour bar. It was not until 1967 that the Cowley car works accepted non-white workers. The publicly owned Bristol Omnibus Company employed only white drivers and conductors until forced to change by a boycott by Black Bristolians. In 1955, West Bromwich bus workers staged a one-day strike to protest the employment of a single Indian conductor. Some shops and pubs refused to serve any but white customers, while in newsagents' windows where flats and lodgings were advertised, 'Whites only' was a common condition of renting.

With the introduction of the 1948 Nationality Act, the post-war Labour Government had made a strong case for equality. Home Secretary James

Chuter Ede told the House of Commons, 'We believe wholeheartedly that the common citizenship of the United Kingdom and Colonies is an essential part of the development of the relationship between this Mother Country and the Colonies … the coloured races of the Empire … are the equals of people in this country.'

Not all his colleagues agreed. It was a widely held assumption that the Act would only apply to the white dominions, and when this proved to be a misapprehension, there was talk of diverting immigrant vessels to East Africa. The newcomers were not so easily put off:

> Between 1948 and 1962, over 250,000 West Indians arrived in Britain. They were British subjects clinging to suitcases and gaudy hats. They were coming to the Motherland and their minds were full of preconceived images of the Empire's most important city: Marble Arch, Buckingham Palace, Hyde Park Corner. The images were fixed in the collective imagination, and knowledge of these places suggested participation. A shared history, being able to recognise these buildings and locations and, most importantly, talk about them with the authority of an insider – would surely produce a happy encounter with Britain. These colonial migrants arrived in Britain holding on to their preconceptions as tightly as they held on to their luggage.[22]

Poignant delusions made the let-down all the greater. When it came to deciding the future of the colonies, Labour was ambivalent.

Having assumed a mandate to grant independence to India, nationalist aspirations elsewhere in the Empire were kept on hold. The colonies could expect to be granted independence but not yet. Labour's Deputy Leader, Herbert Morrison, found no dissent when he claimed that leaving the colonies to work out their own salvation would be like handing over 'a latch key, a bank account and a shotgun to a ten-year-old child'.[23]

Well-meaning efforts to strengthen imperial interdependence produced a catalogue of embarrassing failures, not to mention deep-rooted prejudice. Hopes of recruiting a military force in Africa to compensate for the loss of the Indian Army fell at the first hurdle, with the Chiefs of Staff deciding that 'the black infantryman was poor value for money since he took longer to train and could never attain the same level of operational efficiency as his white counterpart'.

There were Utopian visions of economic expansion. A giant poultry farm to be constructed in The Gambia promised 20 million eggs a year. 'Expect little for two or three years,' said Lord Trefgarne, Chairman of the Colonial Development Board. 'But by then we should be really under way, employing hundreds of thousands of young workers in the colonies.' It was not to be.

More ambitious by far was the scheme for clearing 2.5 million acres of Central Africa for the cultivation of groundnuts, a cheap and plentiful source of fat. The vision soon faded on misfortunes and misjudgements. There were not enough tractors and those that were at work broke their prongs on the sun-baked ground. A prolonged drought attacked the few groundnuts that were actually planted. Those that survived were dug up by baboons. While Britain was gearing up for the coronation the entire costly groundnut fiasco was written off with disillusion on both sides, the Africans feeling they had been exploited while their benefactors were confirmed in their opinion, in the words of the economist Lionel Robbins, that 'few black Africans of the Central African tribes have yet developed the qualities of leadership or the education and experience to act without control'. Reflecting the view of the white settlers, he added, 'The predominance of the white man ... must continue for at least another generation.'

This patronising assessment did not go down well with the subject peoples. The result was a series of 'emergencies', such as the Mau Mau rebellion in Kenya (1952–60) and guerrilla attacks in Aden (1963–67), when white settlers aided by the British military tried, usually unsuccessfully, to keep an uneasy peace.

Even in the dominions, unity with the mother country relied as much on sentiment as on practical politics. When, as part of the royal tour, Philip visited the Woomera rocket range, the press touted the 'unique role of South Australia in imperial defence' and stressed the interdependence of Australia and Britain in defending the free world. Missing from the equation was the critical role allotted to the United States.

The Anzus Pact, signed in 1950, put Australia and New Zealand under the US defence umbrella. Britain was not party to the treaty. Canada, meanwhile, looked to NATO for its protection, while all three dominions made clear their aversion to getting involved in Britain's quarrel with the colonies. At the Commonwealth Prime Ministers' Conference following the coronation, India, a non-aligned nation, caused consternation when Pandit Nehru pledged moral support for the Mau Mau uprising in Kenya.

The same confusion was evident in trade relations. The idea of a self-supporting Empire, bound by an interlocking system of trade, had been part of political discourse for over half a century. It foundered on the reluctance of Canada, Australia and New Zealand to enter a one-sided deal whereby they provided the raw materials for British manufacturing. The eventual compromise was imperial preference, a semi-protective arrangement whereby Britain gave favourable terms to import from the dominions and colonies. This worked, up to a point. Fifty per cent of British trade was with the Empire and Commonwealth. But this was a long way from an imperial economy. And the figure was dropping by the year as the terms of trade shifted in favour of the industrialised nations and against the primary producers. Moreover, for all the talk of fostering economic development in the colonies, most of the important projects were funded not by London but by the World Bank.

The illusions of imperial might kept their hold on Britain's political elite. 'The Empire is our life,' declared Anthony Eden. 'Without it we should be no more than an insignificant island off the coast of Europe.' Yet this was to ignore momentous events across the Channel, where the first steps towards unity were taken with the 1951 creation of the Coal and Steel Community. The brainchild of Robert Schuman, French Foreign Minister, the aim was to integrate the coal and steel industries of France, West Germany, Italy, Belgium, the Netherlands and Luxembourg to make another continental war 'not only unthinkable but materially impossible'.

Britain was invited to join but held aloof. The case against Europe was put with stupefying arrogance in a statement from the NEC of the Labour Party a month after the unveiling of the Schuman Plan:

> Britain is not just a small crowded island off the Western coast of Continental Europe. She is the nerve centre of a worldwide Commonwealth which extends into every continent. In every respect except distance we in Britain are closer to our kinsmen in Australia and New Zealand on the far side of the world than we are to Europe. We are closer in language and in origins, in social habits and institutions, in political outlook and in economic interest. The economies of

the Commonwealth countries are complementary to that of Britain to a degree which those of western Europe could never equal.[24]

The same reasoning dominated Tory thinking. When Eden entered Number Ten, he refused to take seriously the Messina Conference which led to the Treaty of Rome and the setting up of the European Economic Community. Said Eden, 'I feel in my bones that we are not European.'

'That's a funny place to have thinking,' responded Paul Henri Spaak, the Belgian Foreign Minister.

As a result of Eden's myopia, Britain threw away the best chance it ever had of leading Europe while the EEC, later the EU, developed along lines determined by the Franco-German alliance. Most of the problems Britain has had with Europe date from these early miscalculations.

The Queen rose above the fray. In her Christmas broadcast for 1954, she stuck to the brief she had adopted as heir apparent. There is 'nothing quite like the family gathering in familiar circumstances', she assured her listeners before launching into an effusive tribute to 'our Commonwealth hearth', which 'becomes more precious than ever by the contrast between its homely security and the storm which sometimes seems to be brewing outside, in the darkness of uncertainty and doubt that envelopes the whole world'.

The enduring qualities of Commonwealth and family were recurring themes in the Queen's annual message to her people. In 1955, looking forward to her visit to Nigeria the following year, she made the bold claim that a 'large part of the world looks to the Commonwealth for a lead'. With no mention of nationalist disruption and disorder across the Empire, the Queen held to the fantasy that Britain had discovered the secret of 'different nations ... living together in friendly brotherhood, pooling the resources of each for the benefit of all'. It was a noble vision with only a tenuous connection to the reality. At best, the Commonwealth was a comfort zone that did no harm – not unlike the monarchy.

# 11

# AFTER THE BALL

Many the heart that's aching
If you could read them all –
Many the hope that has vanished –
After the ball.

(Victorian song)

Even before the coronation with its full exposure to the viewing public at home, the royal family had come to be regarded as public property, an ever-interesting source of revelation, real or imagined. An early attempt to impose restraint on the media was an abject failure. In 1950, Marion Crawford (Crawfie), one-time governess to Princesses Elizabeth and Margaret, broke cover in the weekly *Woman's Own* with a series of insider's knowledge of life at the Palace. Subsequently published as a book, *The Little Princesses* was ghostwritten by an American journalist and serialised in the United States in *Ladies' Home Journal*.

The articles and the book were a sensation. Guided by her bank manager husband, who is assumed to have encouraged her literary efforts, Crawford made more than £75,000 in fees and royalties, while *Woman's Own* all but doubled its circulation. On such fragile foundations are fortunes made.

The Crawford affair caught the royal family on the hop. Jealous of their privacy and fearful of giving away confidences that might detract from the image of harmonious domesticity, the reaction to harmless tittle-tattle was brutally excessive. In the Palace circle, Crawford became a non-person, air-brushed from the lives of her once devoted charges.

Following up with a short biography of Princess Margaret, Crawford continued to write for *Woman's Own* on royal and society events. Her second career was cut short when she gave her readers a vivid description of a royal outing which never took place, a rail strike having led to its cancellation. When she died in 1977 her funeral was shunned by the royal family and no flowers were sent.

Inept public relations served merely to whet the public appetite for Palace gossip. Manning the barrier against inquisitive journalists was Commander Richard Colville, Press Secretary from 1947 to 1968, a 'clam like figure' whose undisguised contempt for all scribblers was returned in full measure. Colville, wrote Cecil Beaton, is 'ashen-faced and like the wicked uncle in a pantomime … deals so sternly with all of us who are in any way connected with the Press'.[1]

Taking the view that whatever he pronounced, even when less than truthful, should be accepted without question, Colville failed to see that this amounted to an open invitation to royal reporters to dig deeper. His officious incompetence helped to set the trend for ex-butlers, footmen and other functionaries in the royal household to supplement their modest incomes by revealing all.

Speculation on the role of the Queen's Consort featured regularly in the tabloids. Courtiers were fond of quoting Prince Albert, who believed that the husband of an English Queen 'should entirely sink his own individual existence in that of his wife'. This was not at all Philip's style. In any case, the constitution no longer required a consort able to give guidance on public business. He made his position clear when he told the press, 'I mean to make a success of the job. I am not going to be just a polite shadow behind the throne. I shall strike out in due course, in my own way.'

Intense interest was aroused when his name was associated with another news sensation of the early 1950s, the reported appearance in the night sky of unidentified flying objects, familiarly known as flying saucers, the supposed harbinger of an invasion from outer space. Despite the scepticism of the Astronomer Royal and fellow scientists, UFO sightings, however improbable, were taken seriously by otherwise level-headed pundits. Among those who were persuaded was Air Marshal Lord Dowding, Commander of RAF Fighter Command in the Battle of Britain, who believed that invisible and death-defying spirits were being spread across the world.

Subscribing to *Flying Saucer Review*, Philip took to sharing stories of extra-terrestrial visits with 'Uncle Dickie', who speculated, 'If they come over in a big way they may settle the capitalist–communist war.' Witnesses were summoned to the Palace to give their accounts of sightings. When a report came in that an extra-terrestrial being was lodging at a house in Ealing, an equerry was sent to investigate. He reported an encounter in which the stranger declared the Queen's Consort to be 'of great importance in future galactic harmony'.[2]

In fairness to the technically attuned Duke, science fiction, with its all too plausible glimpses into the future, was the hot talking point of the 1950s. In coronation year, the movie adaptation of the H.G. Wells classic *The War of the Worlds* was a box-office hit, while *The Kraken Wakes* by John Wyndham, a story of an alien invasion portended by fireballs falling into the sea, was one of the bestselling books of the decade. In the age of atomic power and with the realistic prospect of space travel, it was all too easy to jump from fiction to fact.

Philip soon moved on to more practical ways of occupying his time. Working with Kurt Hahn, the German educationist and head teacher at his old school, Gordonstoun, and with Lord Hunt, leader of the ascent on Everest, Philip put his name to the Duke of Edinburgh Award. Intended for boys aged 15 to 18, a similar programme for self-development activities was launched for girls two years later. Though now judged to be a success, initially the award did not meet with universal acclaim. David Eccles, Education Minister from 1959, was cuttingly dismissive. He told Philip, 'I hear you're trying to invent something like Hitler Youth.' The old suspicions died hard.

However worthy, the award was hardly a full-time job for Philip. While he soon found other interests, such as the protection of endangered wildlife, the frustration of the royal progress with fixed smiles and polite hand-shakes began to show. Rumours of his straying from the marital path were frequently in circulation. For all his efforts to establish a clearly defined independence, it was impossible for him to escape his primary role as an adjunct to the Queen. His frustration was palpable.

With his wicked habit of blunt speaking and his inability to bear fools gladly, Philip was a courtier's nightmare and a news editor's dream.

Designated the black sheep in the whiter than white Palace flock, he was known to be on fractious terms with the Queen Mother, who held doggedly to her place in her daughter's closed circle, referring to her late husband as the King in a way that suggested he was still in evidence, and expected to be consulted on all but the most trivial issues. Quoting friends at court, Cecil Beaton explained the Queen Mother's reluctance to move to Clarence House, 'for there won't be the number of servants she's accustomed to'.[3]

The close attention given to Philip's relations with his adopted family was as nothing compared to the speculation on the marital prospects for Princess Margaret, whose name was now openly attached to a divorcee. Outed by the *Sunday People*, Group Captain Peter Townsend was a former equerry to George VI and a much-decorated Battle of Britain pilot. As part of the royal household, he was in regular contact with Margaret, who came to lean on this older and charming man as an emotional support. Though sympathetic, Elizabeth held back from assenting to a burgeoning relationship.

Her advisers were quick to observe obstacles to this love match that were not those that would normally trouble ordinary families. The son of a colonial administrator, Townsend was most emphatically not royal, or even of aristocratic blood. Yet more pertinent was Townsend's marital status. As the innocent party in divorce proceedings, he assumed that once the formalities were over, he would be free to make a formal proposal to Margaret.

Such innocence was almost endearing. It came up against the Queen's basic philosophy of family life. Three months before her accession, she had staked her position at a Mothers' Union Rally in Central Hall. Her adoring audience was urged to fight against 'growing self-indulgence, of hardening materialism, of falling moral standards'. She went on, 'We can have no doubt that divorce and separation are responsible for some of the darkest evils in our society today.'

Given the scandals attached to her family history, this was pushing her luck. But as a young, married woman very much in love with her husband, there can be no doubt she meant what she said. That she risked falling into a trap of her own making must never have occurred to her until she faced the prospect of backtracking on all she held dear by condoning her sister's marriage to an unrepentant sinner.

Called the 'romance of the century', front-page stories underlined the parallels with the clash of the old and new morality that had brought about the abdication of Edward VIII. Inevitably, the Church of England was drawn into the affair, with Archbishop Fisher, known to be uncompromising on the indissolubility of marriage, in the line of attack for threatening to wreck the life of the young Princess. From the tabloid press came calls for the disestablishment of a Church so clearly out of sync with modern life.

Margaret was persuaded to put her romance on hold while the Queen was on tour of New Zealand and Australia and until she had passed the threshold of her 25th birthday. Meanwhile, Townsend was packed off to a non-job as Air Attaché in the Brussels Embassy. There was no word from the Palace, Colville taking the line that the royal right to privacy should preclude press comment. Much to his fury, this encouraged the newspapers to build up the story by consulting their readers. A *Daily Mirror* poll found that a substantial majority supported the royal romance. The moral questions that preoccupied the Archbishop were clearly irrelevant to the general public. 'Come on Margaret,' shouted the *Mirror*, two days before Margaret's 25th birthday, 'Please make up your mind.' By the winter of 1955, the *Manchester Guardian* was reporting that 'nothing much else but Princess Margaret's affairs is being talked about in this country'.

What were known by the tabloids as 'the stuffed shirts' had their say via Sir William Haley, former Governor General of the BBC and now editor of *The Times*. For Haley, the questions raised were neither ecclesiastical nor constitutional. Rather, the critical issue turned on the concept of royalty as representing the model family, the ideal for all the Queen's subjects at home and across the Empire and Commonwealth:

> If the marriage which is now being discussed comes to pass, it is inevitable that this reflection becomes distorted. The Princess will be entering into a union which vast numbers of her sister's people, all sincerely anxious for her lifelong happiness, cannot in conscience regard as a marriage.

Really? As Ben Pimlott pointed out, this took no account of the kings, including the first king of the twentieth century, who had consorted with mistresses. And what of those Christians who regarded the marriage of a divorced person as legitimate? Or of the Queen's subjects in Ceylon, Africa and elsewhere who were not Christian. Were their views to be ignored?[4]

Haley skirted the question. For the whole society of the Commonwealth, the royal family existed as 'the symbol and guarantee of the unity of the British peoples. If one of the Family's members became a cause of division, the salt has lost its savour. There is no escape from the logic of this situation.' If Margaret refused to give way, 'the price should be, not just the loss of her constitutional rights but a full withdrawal from royal public functions into private life'.

Archbishop Fisher was fully in accord, though he resisted media pressure to declare himself openly. This was not surprising, given his tendency to tie himself into doctrinal knots over the remarriage of divorced persons. Said the Archbishop, whatever the circumstances of a marriage breakdown, any subsequent relationship is clearly adulterous, deserving of reprobation, while adding, paradoxically, that the end to a marriage 'often comes as a blessing to both parties and the children'.

Praising Margaret as a 'conscientious and regular churchgoer', he spoke of frequent sessions with her when, presumably, he felt free to offer advice, stressing his belief in marriage as a lifelong commitment and that 'any weakening of this resolve would lead to an increase in the number of marriage breakdowns'.[5] Asked on television to justify his position to a public that expected more than 'no comment' from the head of the Church, Fisher responded waspishly that he did not care 'two hoots what people might be saying' and much of it represented a 'popular wave of stupid emotionalism', language that predictably stoked the anger of his critics. Declaring, 'The time has come for plain speaking,' the *Mirror* roundly condemned 'this cruel plan' to persuade Margaret 'against her will' to break off the relationship.[6] The *News Chronicle* led the way in demanding that the Church should re-examine its stance on the whole question of divorce and remarriage.

Until recently it was assumed that the Queen kept aloof, 'neither alienating her sister nor seeking to force her hand', as Pimlott has it.[7] But it now emerges that it was the Queen who came closest to providing a solution that might have satisfied all except the hardliners. Her take was made easier by Churchill's retirement to make way for Anthony Eden, himself, as it happened, a remarried divorcee. Documents released into the public domain in 2004 reveal that the Queen and her Prime Minister drew up a proposal to amend the Royal Marriages Act in such a way as to allow Margaret to marry Peter Townsend and to keep her royal title and Civil

List allowance, on condition that she and her children dropped out of the line of succession.

How, then, did it all go wrong? Margaret must have known that she had to hand a perfectly reasonable let-out when, on 1 November, she put her name to a communiqué in which 'mindful of the Church's teaching that Christian marriage was indissoluble' and 'conscious of my duty to the Commonwealth', she resolved to put these considerations ahead of her private happiness.

It was a decision that left the impression of a Princess unwilling to surrender her material privileges for the sake of marital happiness. As a retired courtier told Pimlott, 'Princess Margaret was not prepared to give up her royal status. If she'd been willing to take herself out of the line of succession and the Civil List, they couldn't have prevented it.'[8]

But there must have been more to it than that. Aware that forthcoming legislative changes would smooth the way to her marriage to Townsend, why did she allow herself to become a victim of motheaten morality?

Fisher was seen widely as the villain of the piece. The maverick Tory MP, Robert Boothby, claimed that Margaret took the critical decision after a meeting with the Archbishop at Lambeth Palace where Fisher argued his case with frequent reference to books (presumably on Church doctrine) open on his desk. According to Boothby, the Princess asked for the books to be put away.

The story was emphatically denied by Fisher. He had no books with him, he said. 'I received her as I would anybody else in the quietness of my study … She did say straight away what her decision had been, and I received it, of course, with gratitude and thanksgiving to Almighty God. And that's all there was about that.' Lady Fisher supported her husband, claiming in a letter to the Dean of Westminster that Margaret came to Lambeth Palace to tell the Archbishop of the decision she had already made.[9]

But this does not put Fisher in the clear. While he may have held back from an unequivocal judgement, his well-established opinions, however irrational, put across by a strong personality, must have made an impression on Margaret, already battle-scarred from other encounters with the anti-Townsend lobby.

In 1958, Townsend married a much younger Belgian woman who bore a striking resemblance to Margaret. Two years later, Margaret married the society photographer Antony Armstrong-Jones; the service was conducted by Archbishop Fisher. The story did not end happily. Rapid deterioration in the relationship ended in divorce in 1978. By then, Margaret had become a social misfit, a waspish, hard-drinking embarrassment to her family and friends.

Though not obvious at the time, the furore over Margaret's love life marked a turning point in the relationship between royalty and the public, itself undergoing a transformation. A more tolerant, open-minded society was beginning to emerge. When the *Church Times* attacked Sir Anthony Eden for remarrying during the lifetime of his first wife, there was a storm of protest. It was not long before divorce was no longer seen as a bar to touching a regal hand, though divorcees were still forbidden entry to the Royal Enclosure at Ascot.

Reporting in 1956, a Royal Commission on marriage and divorce caused hilarity with the assertion, on no evidence, that divorce by consent would lead to social disaster, and that the 'community as a whole might be happier and more stable if it abolished divorce altogether'. There was little dissent from the view of a stern but not unreasonable critic who dismissed the commission's deliberation as 'the most impressive selection of unsupported clichés ever subsidised by the taxpayer'.[10]

In the second half of the 1950s, the apron strings of the nanny state, already frayed, began to disintegrate. More women were going out to work, up to 36 per cent for singles and near 26 per cent for marrieds. The Trade Union Congress pressed for equal pay for equal work, albeit to be introduced over a lengthy period. Women in the Civil Service were set to achieve equal pay in seven annual instalments. The BBC took the lead in granting maternity leave.

Cracks began to appear in the Anglican united front when a Lambeth Conference of Bishops came out in favour of birth control if only within marriage. But there was one significant addendum in the ruling: 'The procreation of children is not the only purpose of marriage ... Sexual intercourse is by no means the only language of earthly love but it is ... the most intimate and most revealing.'

After the sensational publication of the Kinsey Reports on male and female sexuality in America, it was only a matter of time before Britain followed. In 1956, Eustace Chesser's *The Sexual, Marital and Family Relationships of the English Woman* revealed that premarital sex was increasingly common with around 11 per cent of women and 22 per cent of men admitting to sex outside marriage. Chesser's methodology came under attack for its middle-class bias but his broad assertion of a crumbling fortress of convention was supported by other studies. And in focusing on female satisfaction, or lack of it (43 per cent had 'a lot', 31 per cent 'a fair amount' and 5 per cent 'none'), he brought into the open a topic that the old-style moral crusaders chose to avoid or found repugnant.

A more assertive younger generation was less inhibited and less inclined to pay unquestioning respect to any authority based on time-honoured convention. And that included the first family. The eruption of youth culture, noted at the coronation, continued unabated in the second half of the 1950s. The import from America of the wildly exuberant rock'n'roll took hold after Bill Haley and the Comets released 'Rock Around the Clock' in September 1956. Haley was an unlikely youth icon, being over 30 and inclined to stoutness, but the sound he created gave a spark and energy to pop music, clearing the way for such as Lonnie Donegan who, with washboard, tea-chest bass and a cheap Spanish guitar, started a 'skiffle' craze in coffee bars across the country.

That the lightweight guitar was an aid to physical expression, overtly sexual, was exploited by Tommy Steele, Britain's first teen superstar. Gyrating in his white suit, he set the style for a whole stable of ever younger performers. They found their American match in Elvis Presley. Girls warmed to his sleek locks, long sideboards, full lips and dark curling eyelashes, while boys adopted his hairstyle.

The stuffed shirts were outraged. Said the retired Old Bailey judge Sir Travers Christmas Humphreys, 'Boys and girls are like dogs. You must teach them quite young to obey.' He lived just long enough to find out how wrong he was.

Contrariwise, it was the BBC, tied tightly to convention, that was itself a major catalyst for change. The success of the television coverage of the coronation set up expectations of higher standards in screen news and entertainment. Viewers were no longer prepared to be palmed off with content and production values reminiscent of silent movies. Embarrassing now are memories of political interviews tied to advance notice of the questions and of variety shows in the music hall tradition. Most programmes, including drama, were confined to the four walls of the studio.

The spur for the BBC to aspire to further and faster growth was the dawning of independent television. As early as 1952, a government white paper had tentatively envisaged 'some element of competition' to the BBC. Attracted to the possibility of reaching out to a mass audience, sundry business interests put forward applications for licences. The old brigade of hereditary peers, the Church and the judiciary, with the supporting ranks of the moralistic minority shouting them on, was united in shrill opposition.

A House of Lords debate in November 1953 was the platform for grave warnings of vulgar American commercialism undermining British youth. 'For the sake of our children we should resist it,' declared the Archbishop of York. 'We should not,' said a veteran Labour peer, 'give the people what they want but rather seek to educate them and guide them in the same manner that the BBC has done for so long.' He was supported by Lord Reith, who warned of cataclysmic consequences if the BBC monopoly was broken. In his view, sponsored broadcasting was on a par with 'smallpox, bubonic plague and the Black Death'. But then, Reith believed that, at best, all television, even that under BBC control, was irredeemably trivial.

Ironically, it was left to the Marquess of Salisbury, whose family had been the guardian of the conservative conscience for over half a century, to pour scorn on the opponents of independent television, arguing that it was nonsense for 'we sexagenarians to impose the dead hand of age upon the youthful majority in favour of competition'. Commercial television made its debut in 1955 with an advert for Gibbs' toothpaste. This might well have been counted as a public service since up to half the population never cleaned their teeth.

Thanks to the independent sector, the BBC began to grow up. The first step was the cancellation of the *Toddlers' Truce*, the hour between six and seven, potentially a peak viewing time, when, in the interests of getting the children off to bed, television closed down. In its place came *Tonight*, an offbeat mix of studio debates and reports from out and about on whatever was quirky and new. It commanded an audience of around 8 million. *Panorama*, starting on 11 November 1953, rated up to 11 million viewers. This was the programme that caused most offence in Whitehall, where the illusion held that political controversy was reserved exclusively for the elite. Also quietly forgotten was the understanding between the Postmaster General and commercial television that when a royal occasion was featured, the screen would be cleared of advertising for two minutes before and after.

If the force of change had been driven exclusively by popular style and entertainment, convention might have continued to rule over the matters where Church and state feared moral contagion. But even the middle-class bastion supporting traditionalism showed signs of crumbling. The springboard was education.

The 1944 Education Act guaranteed free schooling up to the age of 15, and for the brightest, entry to college or university. To make best use of scarce resources (Britain in the 1950s spent a smaller proportion of national income on education than it did in the 1930s), children were divided at the age of 11 between those who, having passed an intelligence test, were destined for an academic grammar school and the rest, who were sent to secondary modern or technical schools.

While the validity of the 11 Plus was fiercely contested, the political motivation was clear enough. If Britain was to rebuild the economy it needed to tap into the reserves of talent in the lower middle and working classes. The 11 Plus was intended to winkle out the hidden potential. One measure of success was that by the mid-1950s, two-thirds of grammar parents had themselves not gone beyond elementary education. But the social consequences, less appealing to the Establishment, were soon to become apparent.

Grammar students from modest origins felt patronised by the old guard, who were forever urging respect for anachronisms and for those in authority. Educated teenagers reacted against the inanities of polite society, the narrow minds of shopkeepers and managers who had done well out of the war, and the plummy monologues of out-of-touch politicians.

The rumblings of discontent were loudest among those who were dragooned into the military. From 1947, all 18-year-old males (no females) were liable for conscription for twelve months, extended to eighteen months from 1949 and to two years from 1950. The numbers in uniform peaked in the year of the coronation – 113,611 in the army, 36,909 in the RAF and 3,544 in the navy. In all, 2.3 million men were called up. Postings ranged from colonial outposts and active service in Korea and Malaysia to the British Army of the Rhine, Britain's biggest single overseas commitment. Of those exempted from military service, the highest number, 16 per cent of the total intake, were deemed to be physically unfit. For a supposedly civilised country, it was a staggeringly high figure.

Those excluded by age were easily persuaded that what young people needed was the discipline and self-control that came with military training. And if they put their minds to it, they would come to enjoy the experience. As a breezy leaflet distributed by the Association of Boys' Clubs reassured conscripts, 'It's rather like going to the dentist; you dread it beforehand but after it's all over, you are jolly glad you went.'

No mention here of the hours of square bashing, the ludicrous dance routines of marching men; no mention of learning to use a bayonet, the most useless weapon in the modern armoury, by lunging at stuffed dummies screaming foul oaths; no mention of scrubbing bricks clean then painting them white; no mention of the hatred that built up against semi-literate sergeants and corporals and the pleasure they took in inflicting sadistic humiliations; no mention of an officer class composed largely of war veterans hanging on for a decent income, minimum work and, as one put it, the life of a gentleman.

In contrast to the RAF and the Royal Navy, where technology and advanced weaponry helped towards efficient man management, the army was complacently outdated. Equipment was of early Second World War, even First World War, vintage. Uniforms were ill fitting and cumbersome. It was rare to find any item of military hardware that actually worked to order. Whole transport units – supposedly on hand for emergencies – were consigned to 'mothballing', never again to be relieved of their coating of grease and webbing.

All this and more to the discredit of the military was revealed when, in 1956, Britain and France, in collusion with Israel, invaded Egypt. Ostensibly to protect the Suez Canal, a major conduit for oil to the West, it was to overthrow President Nasser, the leading exponent of Arab nationalism. The conflict was short and sharp. American pressure saw to that. On the plus side, a botched operation proved the need to modernise the army while pointing up the wasting of resources on National Service.

There were those who welcomed two years in uniform as an escape, however brief, from dead-end jobs in derelict communities. But for the rest, the sheer inanity of what they had to endure was only mitigated by cheap booze and fags (the military contribution to addiction) and by counting the days to release. For Jonathan Brown, hero of David Lodge's novel *Ginger You're Barmy*, the army was 'the last surviving relic of feudalism in English society', run by entrenched but inefficient upper ranks requiring 'unquestioning obedience from the serfs beneath'.

As a breeding ground for rebels, National Service achieved all that its advocates were trying to prevent. 'The young,' suggested J.B. Priestley, 'less addicted to self-deception than their elders began to feel dissatisfied and restless.' Among the most vocal were the literary types who were slotted, not always by their own choice, into a pigeonhole for 'angry young men'. Kingsley Amis was 32 when he published *Lucky Jim*; John Wain's debut *Hurry on Down* appeared when he was 28; and John Braine was 34 when *Room at the Top* hit the bestseller list. All three books portrayed a society under the heel of what the writer and broadcaster Kenneth Allsop called the 'polished fuddy-duddies cut to the old Whig and Tory pattern'.

If anyone deserved to be labelled as angry young man, it was John Osborne. An occasional actor and aspiring playwright, Osborne's first and most powerful assault on the society he despised was *Look Back in Anger*. After a chorus of rejections, the play was taken up by the newly formed English Stage Company, where the artistic director George Devine was looking for new work. He got more than he bargained for.

As the anti-hero, working-class Jimmy Porter, educated out of his environment, screams against philistine pretentions, the Old Boy network and commercial and professional chicanery dressed up as service to the community. 'Nobody thinks. Nobody cares. No beliefs, no convictions and no enthusiasms.'

Critical reaction was mixed. There were those who found the play 'exasperating', 'vulgar', 'self-pitying drivel'. But Osborne was singled out for praise in *The Observer*, where the critic Kenneth Tynan shared the playwright's aversion to the Establishment and its pious assumptions. Under the heading 'The Voice of the Young', Tynan declared Jimmy Porter 'with his flair for introspection, his gift for ribald parody, his excoriating candour, his contempt for "phoneyness" … and his desperate conviction that the time is out of joint … is the completest young pup in our literature since Hamlet, Prince of Denmark.'

The spirit of revolution ran through all of Osborne's work. He compelled attention by charging at the enemy, all guns blazing.

The social impact of plays, books and even rock'n'roll must not be exaggerated. The Establishment still had a tight hold on the country. This showed up most obviously in the much-publicised campaign against 'the curse of deviancy'. The number of trials for homosexual offences had remained almost level since 1951 but the impression given by the newspapers, notably the *News of the World* and the *Daily* and *Sunday Express*, was of a growing corruption of the male gender that threatened civilisation itself.

'Wherever I go,' said Mr Justice Stable in January 1955, 'I find the same ugly story. I don't know what is happening to this nation. The percentage of cases of this class which we have to try today is absolutely terrifying. If this evil is allowed to spread, it will corrupt the men of the nation.'[11]

In April 1954, *The Practitioner*, a medical journal, published a special number on homosexuality. Captain Athelstan Popkess, Chief Constable of Nottingham, was selected by his fellow chief constables to present their views: 'Homosexuality is beginning to eat into the very vitals like a cancer. The public would be horrified if they knew its extent. A reform of the law was to be resisted.'[12] *The Practitioner* weighed in with the claim that 'sexual vice' meant the 'slow death of the race' and recommended a 'natural and bracing climate' as the only certain cure.

But the voices of toleration were beginning to make themselves heard. The *New Statesman*, *The Observer* and the *Spectator* supported decriminalisation of homosexuality for adult males in private. A few politicians took up the cause of reform. Speaking in a House of Commons debate on homosexuality on 28 April 1954, the free-thinking and, as it later turned out, bisexual Robert Boothby made the perfectly rational point: 'To send confirmed adult homo-sexuals to prison for long sentences is not only dangerous but madness.' He quoted Dr Stanley Jones, writing in the *British Medical Journal*, 'It is as futile from the point of view of treatment as to hope to rehabilitate a chronic alco-holic by giving him occupational therapy in a brewery.'

Liberal opinion eventually forced the Home Office to set up a committee under Sir John Wolfenden to consider homosexuality and prostitution. Reporting in 1957, the committee urged a change in the law to permit consenting adult homosexuals freedom in private. On the second theme, prostitutes were to be banned from soliciting on the streets, suggesting that prostitution was acceptable as long as it was invisible. The government made no effort to implement the first recommendation, which was subsequently rejected by the House of Commons by a large majority. The second recommendation was accepted without much dissent. The Homosexual Law Reform Society was founded in 1958. Homosexuality was not decriminalised until 1967.

The moralists were out in force to protest the publication of Stanley Kauffman's novel, *The Philanderer*. An enlightened judge put logic before irrational emotion. 'Are we going to say in England that our contemporary literature is to be measured by what is suitable for a 14-year-old school-girl to read?' The answer, a resounding 'No', was noted by the Director of Public Prosecutions, who decided not to bring an action against Vladimir Nabokov's *Lolita*.

Censorship was lightened with the 1959 Obscene Publications Act, drafted to protect serious literature. What this meant in practice was tested in a case brought against the unexpurgated *Lady Chatterley's Lover*. In a grand farce played out in court, thirty-five expert witnesses were called. When the book was cleared it sold 3 million copies.

It was towards the end of his term of office that Lord Chief Justice Goddard, a sadist in ermine, condemned to death the last woman to be hanged in Britain. A 28-year-old mother of two, Ruth Ellis was found guilty of a crime of passion, the shooting of her abusive lover. There was to be no reprieve.

The result of what was generally thought to be a miscarriage of justice was a shift in public opinion against capital punishment. In February 1955, the House of Commons, on a free vote, declared that 'the death penalty for murder no longer accords with the needs or true interests of a civilised society'. The Homicide Act, to allow for 'diminished responsibility' as a legitimate defence, was a barely satisfactory compromise with the dogmatists but it did reduce the number of hangings to four a year.

That reform was long overdue and was endorsed by *The Times*, with the comment that a visiting criminal lawyer from almost anywhere else in Western Europe 'would confirm that in his own country capital punishment, corporal punishment and the punishment of adult homosexuals was regarded as beyond the pale as the thumbscrew and the rack'.

# 12

# THE AGE OF
# IRREVERENCE

Devoted as it was to an imaginary golden age when deference and respect were the prime values, the royal family could not ignore the groundswell of discontent with the existing order. While the universal attraction of the coronation was at first credited with building a favourable image of Britain at a turning point in its fortunes, it was becoming commonplace to hear the heretical suggestion that a display of feudal splendour was perhaps not quite how Britain wanted to be seen by the rest of the world.

Not that such matters greatly bothered the Palace. After serving four monarchs, Alan Lascelles, awarded a knighthood, returned as Private Secretary four months after the coronation. But his replacement, Sir Michael Adeane, was 'as averse as his predecessor to allow any departure from precedent'. Richard Colville, that 'clam like figure', was allowed to hang on as Press Secretary until 1968, when the Australian William Heseltine introduced a more relaxed regime.[1]

In a modest concession to changing times, in 1957 the Palace announced that the following year would see the end of the annual jamboree for launching wealthy debutantes on to the marriage market. The writer Fiona MacCarthy was one of the last of the favoured few:

The long procession of virgins – for the vast majority of upper-class girls of seventeen were virgins in 1958 – passed in front of a young queen who not so long before had been a virgin herself. She had married Prince Philip in 1947 when she was twenty-one. From her height on the dais the Queen surveyed these serried ranks of girlish innocence, earls' daughters, generals' daughters, a Lord Mayor of London's daughter, English roses from the shires, fresh-faced girls with the slight blankness of their class and inexperience. There was a softness and sweetness and also an inherited silliness of manner, a gasp in the voice, a giggle and a flutter, in these participants in what Jessica Mitford, in her book *Hons and Rebels*, described as 'the specific, upper-class version of the puberty rite'.[2]

Among those who mourned the passing of a time-honoured ritual was Marguerite Vacani. It was at Madame Vacani's School of Dancing in Knightsbridge that generations of debutantes had learned the faultless curtsey:

The curtsey was part of the mystique. It was a question of leg-lock: left knee locked behind the right knee, allowing a graceful slow descent with head erect, hands by your side. Avoidance of the wobble, definitely frowned upon, relied on exact placing of the knees and feet. … Other dancing schools might purport to teach the curtsey. But as far as the deb world went there was no substitute. Madame Vacani, as she styled herself, a squeaky voiced, effusive, highly powdered tiny lady, had made herself the high priestess of the cult. She had something of the manner of a genteel sergeant major as she trained prospective debutantes. 'Now darlings, throw out your little chests and burst your little dresses.' Once learned never forgotten, like bicycling or skiing.[3]

Another who felt the loss was 'Jennifer', the *Tatler*'s social diarist, the indispensable source of dates for dances and other events where the debs could be inspected by eligible suitors.

But elsewhere the ritual display went unlamented. 'Since the last war,' noted the *Court Circular*, 'Society in the sense in which it was known even in 1939 has almost died.' To which *The Times* added cryptically, 'National regret at the change will not be widely felt.'

With the disappearance of the debs came an increase in the number of Palace garden parties for mid-ranking worthies, along with an annual five Palace lunches for those in the public eye to allow the Queen to be in touch with 'the real people'. For her part, the Queen Mother, according to the *Evening News*, listened to the radio soap opera *Mrs Dale's Diary*: 'I try never to miss it because it is the only way of knowing what goes on in a middle class family.'[4]

There remained a wide gulf between what the royal family stood for and political actuality. The Queen's Christmas broadcast for 1957, the first on television, disowned those 'unthinking people who carelessly throw away ageless ideals as if they were old and outworn machinery'. She went on to defend the 'fundamental principles which guided the men and women who built the greatness of this country and Commonwealth'. Sixteen million viewers were told that by sticking to the old rules, 'together we can set an example to the world which will encourage upright people everywhere'. Leaving aside the astonishing assertion that there were laudable fundamental principles underlying Britain's rise to world dominance, unless hunger for power and money was counted in, the message smacked of complacency that must have puzzled or offended many of those who were watching.

A vocal minority argued that the monarchy had to accelerate into the modern age if it was to survive. In the House of Commons, the thorn in the royal flesh was Emrys Hughes, Labour Member of Parliament for South Ayrshire. A popular figure, his attacks were dogged but never full-blooded, which was probably why they were not taken too seriously. Hughes was at his best in the Commons debate on the adjustments to the Civil List following Elizabeth's accession, when twenty-five MPs supported him in calling for a scaled-down monarchy on the Scandinavian and Dutch model. He proposed a 50 per cent cut in the Queen's allowance and a similar reduction for the Duke of Edinburgh. Proclaiming himself a republican, 'like President Eisenhower', he described the Civil List as 'the largest wage claim in the country', and in a dig at the Tory loyalists, he suggested they might extend their close scrutiny of the accounts of the nationalised industries to making economies in 'our oldest nationalised industry'.

The case for an increased Civil List to take account of the Queen's added responsibilities was put by the Chancellor of the Exchequer. Rab Butler was a patrician with a social conscience. The architect of the 1944 Education Act which extended free education for all children up to the age of 15, Butler's marriage into the Courtauld textile fortune gave him a large private income and access to high society. His Gloucestershire estate, Gatcombe Park, was later sold to the Queen as a home for Princess Anne. In Butler, the Queen had a sympathetic paymaster. In his speech to the Commons, he insisted that the royal household 'has had to undertake some striking economies in its own internal management', it was 'run on the most economical basis' and 'adequate measures are in place to monitor a continuous and continuing review of expenditure'.[5]

But this was to take a lot on trust. For a start, no one outside the royal circle of financial advisers, and maybe not even them, had any clear idea of the size of the Queen's private fortune. Estimates ranged, in today's money, from £220 million to a modest £140 million. The figures could be no more than inspired guesses since there was no telling the value of the Queen's collection of furniture, paintings and jewellery, the latter one of the world's finest. The official brush-off for inquisitive journalists was to point out that the Civil List had to balance against revenue from Crown land which went to the Treasury.

But this begged the question as to whether these extensive properties really 'belonged' to the Queen in the sense that Mr and Mrs Bloggs owned 21 Acacia Avenue. Were they not part of the national heritage? Of a certainty, the Queen would have got short shrift if, for example, she had decided to sell off Carlton House Terrace, part of the Crown Estate, not to mention the royal art collection, said to be held in trust for the nation, though rarely, if ever, seen by the public until the opening of the Queen's Gallery in 1962 allowed for selected items to be displayed.

Taxation was another contentious issue. It was known that the royal family escaped death duties but how much, if any, tax the Queen paid on her extensive land holdings and on revenues from her private investments remained and remains a mystery.

The case for reassessing the royal finances was set out by John Parker, a long-serving Labour MP and former General Secretary of the Fabian Society. Parker had no wish to abolish the monarchy, but he did want it to be modernised:

All revenues from the Duchy of Cornwall should go to the Treasury; palaces, whose upkeep was included in the Civil List, should be put under the Ministry of Works; it was absurd for the Palace of Westminster, for instance, to be partly in the care of the Ministry and partly of the Queen. The House should know what 'alms' were included in the Queen's vote – did the phrase mean that she still gave to the nationalised hospitals? Why must the Queen have thirty-five ceremonial horses; should there not be 'a pool' of horses, as there was a pool of ceremonial cars? Why should not junior royalty be allowed to earn their living like other people; and why shouldn't royal persons be paid salaries like other public servants?[6]

At Westminster, answers came there none. MPs who, in principle, favoured reform of the monarchy were disinclined to make it a priority. They had more than enough to occupy them without incurring the wrath of the patriots among their constituents. It was not until 1971 that a House of Commons Select Committee considered the future of the Civil List. A government led by Edward Heath was able to ensure a Tory majority on the committee which, to the relief of the Palace, defended the Queen's right to withhold details of her personal fortune and the material benefits from tax immunity. The Queen's Principal Private Secretary, Sir Michael Adeane, stressed:

> ... how unrelentingly she worked and how she could never look forward to retirement. She received 120 letters a day, and spent three hours reading Foreign Office telegrams, reports of parliamentary procedures, ministerial memoranda and Cabinet minutes. She was in ultimate charge of Buckingham Palace, Windsor Castle, Holyrood House, Sandringham and Balmoral. She travelled more extensively than any of her predecessors. Her volume of work had increased since her accession (the number of centenarians to whom telegrams had to be sent had increased from 225 per annum in 1952 to 1186 in 1970). Her visits to provincial towns, for instance, were stressful and exhausting: the strain of taking a lively interest in everything, saying a kind word here and asking a question there, always smiling and acknowledging cheers, when driving in her car; sometimes for hours, had to be experienced to be properly appreciated.[7]

In agreeing to a generous settlement for the Civil List, the House of Commons did provide for an ongoing review by a Board of Trustees who would report to Parliament every ten years. This could come back to haunt the royal family, should it ever fall out of public favour. While there was no such risk in the 1950s, there were signs of hostility to the excess of press coverage on the comings and goings of royalty and speculation on the lives and loves at the Palace. A minority, finding it all too much, were prepared to risk a counter-attack.

One of the first to put his head above the parapet was Malcolm Muggeridge. Describing himself as a 'knockabout journalist', Muggeridge was deputy editor of the *Daily Telegraph* when, in coronation year, he was offered the editorship of *Punch*, a once famous, mildly satirical weekly that was on the slide. The job for Muggeridge was to put some zest into the magazine to build circulation. This he did by courting controversy.

His first high-risk target was the visibly ailing Winston Churchill in the last phase of his premiership. A Leslie Illingworth cartoon showed the premier at his desk, jaw sagging, eyes sightless. The caption read, 'Man goeth forth to his work and to his labour until the evening.' Accompanying the cartoon was a Muggeridge article about a Byzantine leader called Bellorius. Nobody was in doubt as to who he really had in mind when he wrote, 'The spectacle of him thus clutching wearily at all the appurtenances and responsibilities of an authority he could no longer fully exercise was to his admirers infinitely sorrowful and to his enemies infinitely derisory.'

Muggeridge spoke nothing less than the truth. Up to the last, Churchill was looking for an excuse, however lame, to stay on in Downing Street. His last throw was to suggest that after years of grooming Anthony Eden as his successor, his Foreign Secretary of ten years was not up to the big job. Churchill's Private Secretary, John Colville, noted, 'a cold hatred of Eden',[8] while his opposite number on Eden's staff reported a disturbing conversation with Jan Portal who managed Churchill's diary:

> She now admits that the old boy, whom she loves dearly is getting senile and failing more and more each day ... Life is a misery to him; he half kills himself with work, cannot take in the papers he is given to read and can hardly get up the stairs to bed.[9]

Not a hint of this appeared in the newspapers. Whatever his disabilities, Churchill was immune to criticism. Was he not the greatest living Englishman, the saviour of his country? Though few would contest this, it was surely reasonable, argued Muggeridge, to suggest that he was long past his best. Apparently not. The staid readers of *Punch* were shocked beyond measure at what was regarded as a studied insult to all that was finest in the British character. Leading the attack was Randolph Churchill, who complained to Muggeridge that 'at least twenty of my friends ... have made it very plain how vile they think this action is'.[10] Muggeridge retorted his surprise that Randolph *had* twenty friends.

Dithering to the last, the 80-year-old Prime Minister finally departed Downing Street on 5 April 1955. Had he wanted, he could have sealed his illustrious career with a dukedom. He chose instead to remain simply Sir Winston. Maybe, surveying his troublesome family, he settled for damage limitation. The prospect of the dissolute Randolph parading aristocratic credentials was just too awful to contemplate.

Having taken a swipe at the central pillar of the Establishment, it was only a matter of time before Muggeridge wielded the cudgel against the monarchy. Not wishing to push his luck with *Punch*, he chose the left-leaning *New Statesman* for his latest assault. The article appeared in October 1955, just nine days before Princess Margaret cut her ties with Peter Townsend:

There are probably quite a lot of people – more than might be supposed – who, like myself, feel that another newspaper photograph of the royal family will be more than they can bear. Even Princess Anne, a doubtless estimable child, becomes abhorrent by repetition. Already she has that curious characteristic gesture of limply holding up her hand to acknowledge applause. The Queen Mother, Nanny Lightbody, Group Captain Townsend – the whole show is utterly out of hand.

He went on to ask:

… whether it wasn't time for the monarchy to engage professional public relations consultants, 'in place of the rather ludicrous courtiers who now function as such'. The royal family had to make a decision: do they want to be part of the mystique of the century of the common man or to be an institutional monarchy; to ride, as it were, in a glass coach or on bicycles; to provide the tabloids with a running serial or to live simply and unaffectedly among their subjects like the Dutch and Scandinavian royal families. What they cannot do is to have it both ways.[11]

While readers of the *New Statesman* were largely supportive, elsewhere in the media Muggeridge was reviled for his outrageous presumption. Spurred on by Lord Beaverbrook, the *Evening Standard* labelled Muggeridge as a traitor. Beaverbrook's anger was fuelled by the sure knowledge that

Muggeridge was pitching himself as much against the popular press as against the monarchy. It was in the mass-circulation newspapers that he found the most ludicrous manifestations of the royal soap opera. This from the *Daily Mirror*:

> There is an ornament standing in Mrs Lena Atkinson's prefab … it is the cup used by the Queen Mother when she popped into Mrs Atkinson's for tea yesterday. There is still the faintest trace of lipstick on the cup. 'I haven't washed it,' Mrs Atkinson told me. 'And I don't think I ever shall.'

And this from the *Sunday Pictorial*: 'Later a woman called from the river bank. "Thank you for the fly," she said. "It improved sport a lot." The woman was Queen Elizabeth, the Queen Mother. My friend was startled, but even so, standing in the river, she curtsied.'[12]

After five years at *Punch*, Muggeridge was shown the door after he published some satirical verses on the admission of Prince Charles to the prep school at Cheam in Surrey. It happened that Peter Agnew, whose family owned *Punch*, was also a Cheam governor. When Muggeridge tried to stop the removal of the offending piece there was a row that ended with his sacking, though, for public consumption, he was said to have resigned. But this did not require him to relinquish his role as chief royal critic.

While on a lecture tour of America, Muggeridge agreed to write on the royal family for the *Saturday Evening Post*. The result was a rambling piece in which he posed the question, 'Does England really need a Queen?' Contrary to the follow-up in the British press, at no point did Muggeridge call for the abolition of the monarchy. Rather, he conceded that 'a largely materialistic society like ours has a natural propensity to hero worship and the image of a royal family is in no bad way of satisfying it'.

However, he did take issue with the Queen's exclusively upper-class entourage, 'a circumstance which makes them quite exceptionally incompetent'. He also took a knock at the BBC, 'that supreme temple of contemporary orthodoxy', and at Richard Dimbleby, 'the high priest of this cult of royalty', described by Muggeridge as 'a large individual, with a luscious manner of speaking and a flow of eloquence which not even technical hitches can impede. He just goes on and on, in rich, full-throated ease.' Muggeridge concluded that 'without his ministrations the impact of the monarchy on the public would be appreciably less'. The worst he could find to say about royalty was that 'it is a generator of snobbishness and a focus of sycophancy – both unattractive sides of human nature'.

The timing was unfortunate. The *Post* held back on the article to allow for publication to coincide with the Queen's American tour. The tabloids were up in arms. The *Sunday Express* and the *People* gave over their front pages to denigrating Muggeridge. 'He has earned the contempt of all Britain,' opined the *Express*.

For the iconoclastic journalist there was a price to be paid. The *Sunday Dispatch*, having promoted him as 'the most provocative writer in Britain', decided to drop its plan to make him a regular columnist, while the BBC put a temporary ban on his television appearances. Sir Ian Jacob said later, 'I did not see why we should give a national platform to a man who had behaved as he had done.'[13]

Undeterred, it was not long before Muggeridge was back on mischievous form, this time to declare on an American TV chat show, 'The English are getting bored with their monarchy … the public realise the monarchy has become over-exposed. I think it is coming to an end.'

Muggeridge was asked, 'Would you miss the monarchy?'

He replied, 'Frankly, no.'

It was all carried off at a jokey level, the chat show host winding up by telling viewers, 'Gee, I hope they don't behead him. He's going back to Britain tonight.'

No sooner had the dust settled than Muggeridge was hit by another wave of hostile publicity occasioned by pressure on him to resign from his club. The haunt of actors, lawyers and writers, the prestigious Garrick Club belied its bohemian reputation when a pack of diehards, headed by Sir Lawrence Rivers Dunne, Chief Metropolitan Magistrate, decided that Muggeridge was guilty of ungentlemanly behaviour.

Rivers Dunne was the archetypal representative of an outmoded governing class. A great believer in self-control, moral duty and the firm enforcement of the law, he called for longer prison sentences and the reintroduction of birching for young offenders, while opposing the abolition of capital punishment. In the ideal world of Rivers Dunne, NHS expenditure on spectacles, false teeth and wigs would be diverted to fund sports clubs and playing fields to encourage urban youths to adopt manly pursuits. The rise in vice crime he blamed on the 'multitude of coloured men now entering the country'. It comes as no surprise that Rivers Dunne was obsessed by homosexuality, though he took heart from the decline in the 'old unholy traffic between soldiers of the Guards and Household Cavalry and perverts in the Royal Parks', which he credited to 'the ranks no longer wearing tight overalls off duty'. Well may it have been said by the royals, with friends like this who needs enemies?

Though Muggeridge had his free speech defenders at the Garrick, he did not put up much of a fight. Wearing the martyr's crown, he resigned from the club while protesting his inalienable right 'to say whatever I like about anything anywhere'. The pain was in attracting the malevolence of fanatical royalists who brought a whole new meaning to bigotry:

> His cottage at Robertsbridge [was] daubed with slogans by right-wing Empire Loyalists, a man spat at him when he was walking on the front at Brighton; a neighbouring landowner told him he could no longer walk across his fields. Even his eldest brother Douglas wrote a letter to the press disassociating himself publicly from Malcolm's views about the monarchy. … Most upsetting of all, perhaps, was a letter from an anonymous correspondent rejoicing in the recent death of the Muggeridges' youngest son Charles, killed while on a skiing holiday, in an avalanche near Chamonix in the Alps.[14]

Writing this in the last days of the Trump presidency with the American Right descending to mob tactics, it is easy to see a parallel. The anger felt by a large section of American society against those it deems to have robbed them of their assumed right to be of a chosen race was foretold in the British experience of the 1950s, when the once proud representatives of an acquired ethnic superiority lashed out at any suggestion that they might have had their day. To imply in any way that the Queen was less than perfect was to be ranged alongside the enemies of British ascendency, the reviled agents of a nation in decline. Common sense and rational argument had nothing to do with it.

As another critic of monarchy, the young Lord Altrincham was reviled as a class traitor, an even greater threat than Muggeridge to standards in public life. The son of a journalist and politician, the 2nd Lord Altrincham, or plain John Grigg, after he disclaimed the title in 1963, took over as owner and editor of the *National and English Review* on the death of his father in 1955. A Tory radical who supported the Anti-Apartheid Movement and was 'entirely opposed to hereditary seats in Parliament', Grigg championed the introduction of women priests into the Anglican Church. Though of small circulation, the *National and English Review* achieved notoriety for Grigg's plain speaking on sensitive issues.

In August 1957, under the heading 'The Monarchy Today', Grigg took it out on the Palace officials, the 'tweedy entourage' who were responsible for the Queen's speeches and her manner of delivery. 'Like her mother, she appears to be unable to string even a few sentences together without a written text – a defect which is particularly regrettable when she can be seen by her audience.' He went on, 'The personality conveyed by the utterances which are put into her mouth is that of a priggish schoolgirl, captain of the hockey team, a prefect and a recent candidate for Confirmation.' Grigg wanted a Court that was less dependent on the upper class and more representative of the Commonwealth.[15]

By no stretch of imagination was Grigg a republican. His offence, if any, was in saying in public what others were saying in private. A loyalist as devoted as Cecil Beaton echoed Grigg's call for a more relaxed head of state: 'I find it difficult to talk to her. The timing always seems jerky and inopportune ... As for her appearance, one would wish her to wear her hair less stiffly, or to choose dresses that would "do" more for her.'[16]

Beaton did not make his views widely known until his diaries were published in the early 1970s, when the royals were no longer regarded as beyond reproach. It was Grigg's misfortune that he jumped the gun, unleashing the fear and anger of those who dreaded the thin end of the wedge.

Two thousand letters landed on Grigg's doorstep. 'What right have you, you pompous prig of a peer, to criticise Her Majesty?' asked one of the milder correspondents. 'They say you are a known homosexual; we believe it,' wrote another.[17]

After an interview on television, Grigg was punched in the face by an incandescent Empire loyalist. In court, the defendant declared it was 'up to a decent Briton to show resentment at Grigg's scurrilous attack'. 'What I feared most was the overseas repercussions and publication in American newspapers. I thought our fortunes were at a low ebb and such things only made them more deplorable.' He was fined £1 and consoled by a few mild words from the magistrate.

Further comfort came from the Duke of Devonshire, who alluded to the case in his after-dinner speech to the Royal Society of St George.

'It is gratifying to think,' he said, 'how the lie has been given to those miserable men who try to cast aspersions on Her Majesty.' To which the Queen Mother's nephew, the Earl of Strathmore added, 'Lord Altrincham is a bounder, he should be shot.' With all the authority of one who, as he admitted, had not read the article, Archbishop Fisher joined in the condemnation.

Among Commonwealth leaders, Robert Menzies was predictably quick to defend the Queen:

> I think the Queen performs her duties in the Royal office with perfection ... If it is now to be said that she reads a speech I might say that many of the great statesmen in the world will have to face the same charge and had better be criticised for it.

Grigg gave his response in a front-page interview for the *Morning Herald*: 'Mr Menzies ... is typical of the very worst attitude towards the Crown. He simply blindly worships the Sovereign as someone above criticism ... puts her on a pedestal and genuflects.'

At home, a section of the tabloid press embarked on another round of sanctimony with the *Daily Mail* accusing Grigg of 'daring to put his infinitely tiny and temporary mind against the accumulated experience of centuries', while the *Daily Express* condemned a 'vulgar' and 'cruel' attack. Ingenuously, *The Times* stood by the Queen as one who could not look after herself. 'The Queen is not, and does not set out to be, other than a rather simple person' – a backhanded compliment if ever there was one.

Grigg was not without supporters. In a second television interview, when he was given police protection, he delivered a waspish comment on the number of holidays taken by the Queen. The next day, he was complimented by *Reynold's News* for 'saying out loud what many people are thinking'. There was praise too in the *New Statesman*, where Grigg was credited with breaking the hitherto unassailable Fleet Street law that 'the Queen is not only devoted, hardworking and young – but also a royal paragon of wit, wisdom and grace'.[18]

Grigg claimed that of the letters he received, three to one were in his favour. The *Daily Mirror*'s correspondents were four to one in his favour. Even the royalist *Daily Mail* discovered that 55 per cent agreed with his criticisms of the court.

Though Muggeridge and Grigg were forthright in their views, they managed to keep their side of the debate within the bounds of standard political discourse. However, when John Osborne entered the fray, all restraint was cast aside. As a radical dramatist, Osborne had a particular reason for disliking the royal household or, at least, that part of it that was the office of the Lord Chamberlain. Responsible for theatre censorship, this august figure had the last say on what could or could not be presented on stage.

It was one of the curiosities of the British constitution that protecting theatregoers from 'unpleasantness' was the responsibility of a senior courtier who also organised state visits, garden parties and other events under the broad heading of 'protocol'. Assisted by a team of retired Guards officers, the Lord Chamberlain's record of insularity was unremitting. Of unfond memory was the withdrawal of a 1938 Terence Rattigan play poking fun at Nazism because it upset the German Embassy. Other examples of cultural myopia included the judgement on Brendan Behan's *The Hostage* ('a filthy play with nothing to recommend it … a mere excuse for anti-British, anti-Catholic propaganda and a series of stupidly indecent songs') and Shelagh Delaney's *A Taste of Honey* ('I've read it and think it is revolting … it has no saving grace whatsoever').

Given that the Queen was supposed to stand above politics, it is surely surprising that she allowed herself to be associated with powers of censorship that were indisputably political. One of the functions of the Lord Chamberlain was to ensure that no public figure at home or abroad should be held to ridicule. This, of course, included the Queen and anyone with a royal title. It can be safely assumed that a vested interest was in play.

From 1952 to 1963, the Lord Chamberlain was the Earl of Scarborough, a former Tory MP, a retired major general and one-time Governor of Bombay who had written a history of the 11th Hussars. Scarborough wielded the blue pencil with all the enthusiasm of a diehard philistine. Of his time and that of his successor, Lord Cobbold, retired Governor of the Bank of England, drama critic Michael Billington wrote, 'It was as if the theatre was being censored by Disgusted of Tunbridge Wells.'

As a frequent victim of censorship, it is little wonder that Osborne was a vitriolic denunciator of the monarchy. When invited to contribute to a collection of fresh-thinking essays under the heading *Declaration*, he gave full vent to his bitterness. Osborne's latest biographer plays down the publication, arguing that Osborne's essay 'received considerable unmerited attention'.[19] It is odd that he should take this view of an outstanding polemic, worthy to be ranked high in the literature of protest:

I can't go on laughing at the idiocies of the people who rule our lives. We have been laughing at their gay little madnesses, my dear, at their point-to-points, at the postural slump of the well-off and mentally under-privileged, at their stooping shoulders and strained accents, at their waffling cant, for too long. They are no longer funny, because they are not merely dangerous, they are murderous. I don't think I want to make people laugh at them any more, because they are stupid, insensitive, unim-aginative beyond hope, uncreative and murderous.

As for royalty:

My objection to the royal symbol is that it is dead; it is the gold filling in a mouthful of decay. While the cross symbol represented *values*, the crown simply represents a *substitute* for values. When the Roman crowds gather outside St. Peter's, they are taking part in a moral *system*, however detest-able it may be. When the mobs rush forward in the Mall they are taking part in the last circus of a civilisation that has lost faith in itself, and sold itself for a splendid triviality, for the 'beauty of the ceremonial' and the 'essential spirituality of the rite'. We may not create any beauty or exercise much spirituality, but by God! we've got the finest ceremonial and rites in the world! Even the Americans haven't got that.

Osborne had few defenders; he had gone too far. A lone voice was that of James Cameron writing in the *News Chronicle*: 'Give 'em hell!' he cried. 'If John Osborne can make his customers feel, good luck to him, because if they feel enough it may stimulate their curiosity and when they start inves-tigating the roots of their dilemma they will in all probability be angrier than he.'[20]

But there was not much support from those Osborne might have counted as his allies. A launch of *Declaration* at the Royal Court was can-celled, partly for fear of upsetting Lord Harewood, the Queen's cousin, who was on the board of the English Stage Company. The party was 'hastily switched to a crumbling, recherché bohemian retreat'[21] in Chelsea where the guests included Aneurin Bevan, Michael Foot and the American actor

Rod Steiger. The publicity did wonders for *Declaration*; it sold 25,000 copies in three months. The Theatres Act, abolishing censorship of the stage, was not passed until 1968.

One of the last plays to be banned by the Lord Chamberlain before he lost his censorship powers was John Osborne's *A Patriot for Me*. Examiner Charles Heriot reported on 30 August 1964, 'Though we have had plays on the subject [of homosexuality] which have received a licence, Mr Osborne's overweening conceit and blatant anti-authoritarianism causes him to write in a deliberately provocative way: He almost never misses a chance to be offensive.'

The play was refused a licence, but the Royal Court Theatre found a way round the ban by presenting the play under the umbrella of a theatre club. Viewing the club arrangement as a subterfuge, Lord Cobbold took the matter up with the Director of Public Prosecutions, Sir Norman Skelhorne, who felt a prosecution 'would stand a good chance' but concluded that it would be 'inexpedient'.

On 11 August, the Comptroller, Lieutenant Colonel Sir Eric Penn, went to the Royal Court to see the play and reported:

> The dialogue, acting and form of production (clothes, etc.) have all been devised to give homosexuals pleasure at seeing their way of life depicted on the stage. I found this not at all to my liking but in judging plays it is necessary to keep one's own feelings to one side.

He added, 'The only two people I knew in the theatre were the Lord Chancellor [Lord Gardiner] and his wife.'

So, what, if any, impact did the royal critics have on general opinion? Superficially, not much. Five years after Muggeridge, Grigg and Osborne had had their say, Kingsley Martin deduced that royalty remained sacrosanct:

> British monarchy is never criticised. This is a remarkable change. A century ago courage was necessary to question the literal truth of the first chapter of Genesis, to doubt the Virgin Birth, or discuss problems of sex. The throne on the other hand was frankly criticised in the press and on platforms. In the twentieth century anyone can question the divinity of Christ, but no one attributes faults to the royal family.[22]

In the late fifties, the republican cause was adopted by the Labour MP Willie Hamilton, who took the populist stance, describing the Queen as a 'clockwork doll', Princess Margaret 'a floozy' and an 'expensive kept woman' and Prince Charles 'a twerp'. Over twenty years Hamilton received nearly 7,000 letters, mostly contesting his views, often aggressively. Having studied the collection, Philip Ziegler concluded:

> Women are more apt to be partisans of the monarchy than men. Money is the most important single element in the minds of those who oppose its existence. The monarch is respected above all as a symbol of stability and the source of glamour in a dingy world. But the impression which one gains most forcefully from the Hamilton letters is the extent to which people are preoccupied by thoughts of the royal family. Obviously nobody would take the trouble to write to an MP if they did not have strong interest in the subject, but these letters reveal that thousands of otherwise apparently sane and well-balanced people feel so passionately on the subject that they consider any point of view but their own as at the best absurd, at the worst vicious or treasonable. For them at least the passing of time has not robbed the monarchy of any of its savour.[23]

This is not to say that the attacks on royalty or on aspects of royalty were entirely ineffectual. At the very least they were part of a trend, which they helped to accelerate away from treating the monarchy as if it had some divine purpose with claims to infallibility.

In his classic sociological study, *The Uses of Literacy*, Richard Hoggart detected a contrast between 'the fervours of London crowds on special occasions' and the provinces where the working man was 'either quite uninterested in royalty or vaguely hostile'.[24] There was always an audience for a royal opening of a public building or attendance at a civic function. But as Tom Harrison, the pioneer of Mass Observation, pointed out, 'celebrations do not necessarily betoken zeal'.[25]

A striking portent was the change of attitude to the playing of the National Anthem in cinemas at the end of the evening. In the early 1950s it was axiomatic that the audience would stand rigidly to attention. Just a few years later, the opening note was the signal for a rush to the doors.

No longer was it customary for the average home to display a picture of the Queen or another favourite royal, or for state schools to include prayers for the Queen as part of their morning assembly. Children's books and comics might still feature a royalist story, but the tone was more light-hearted, with less of the nostalgia for an imagined imperial past.

Prince Philip (he was elevated in 1957) saw which way the wind was blowing:

> In 1953, the situation in this country was entirely different. And not only that – we were a great deal younger. And I think young people, a young Queen and a young family are infinitely more newsworthy and amusing ... I don't know, but I would have thought we were entering probably the least interesting period of the kind of glamorous existence ... I think there is a change. I think people have got more accustomed to us.[26]

This was true enough, but there was another, more significant sea change in progress. Throughout the fifties the royal family was moving away from its role as the personification of the nation, except in a purely formal sense, to being part of the entertainment industry.

The old aristocracy had set the trend. 'Peers may be, as legislators, at a heavy discount,' wrote Malcolm Muggeridge 'but socially they are booming':

> Their marriages and divorces, their travels and real-estate deals, their feasting and their fasting, are eagerly reported. In the days when Dukes of Bedford appeared in history books, they never had anything like the present Duke who gets on television when he opens a nudist camp in his ancestral seat or joins Mr Perry Como on a merry-go-round. Everyone wants to speak like a BBC announcer, to dress like the Windsors, to experience, if only through the lush prose of women's magazine fiction, the sense of being socially superior.

The hollowness of what was on offer was all too apparent. Everybody knew about Moss Bros, specialising in renting out dress for formal occasions. 'It would be a fair guess to say that three-quarters of the men who wore morning dress at Ascot this week were not wearing their own clothes,' reported the *Economist* in 1955, adding, 'It is difficult to believe in the permanence of a social convention that requires people to wear clothes that hardly anyone nowadays even pretends to own.'

The social round, from the Royal Academy's Summer Exhibition and the Chelsea Flower Show to Royal Ascot and the Henley Regatta, was opened up to the aspirational middle class, who were flattered by their acceptability into a social circle hitherto denied to them. With the boom in stately home visiting (over 2 million punters in 1955) the aristocracy made themselves part of the act, with the owner or National Trust occupant of the grand pile happy to be on duty at the souvenir counter exchanging pleasantries with his paying guests.

The humbling of the upper crust was the grist for long-running jokes. As one of P.G. Wodehouse's happiest creations, Lord Emsworth, who made his first appearance in 1915, was the archetype for all amiable, woolly minded peers (he was still ambling along in 1969), while on stage and screen the veteran actor A.E. Mathews, specialised in portraying bumbling patricians, as in *The Chiltern Hundreds*, a political satire based by its author William Douglas Home on his upbringing among the Scottish gentry. (His brother, Alec Douglas-Home, was to be the last indisputably aristocratic occupant of 10 Downing Street.)

In the *Express*, the pocket cartoons of Osbert Lancaster, featuring the pithy comments on topical affairs by the glamorous, if dotty, Lady Maudie Littlehampton, wife of an impoverished Earl, delighted readers who might otherwise have drifted to rival newspapers.

Standing apart from his fellow peers and making no concessions to egalitarian tendences was Bernard Fitzalan-Howard, 16th Duke of Norfolk KG, GCVO, GBE, TD, PC and coronation impresario. After a job well done, the Earl Marshal retreated to his Sussex estates for the rest of the decade while living on in folk memory with his portrayal on Player's cigarette cards in full coronation regalia.

When he next came to public attention it was as manager for the English cricket tour of Australia in the winter of 1962–63. His qualifications were minimal. He was a keen cricketer of village green standards. He had his own cricket ground at Arundel Castle and had managed his own Duke of Norfolk's XI for a tour of the West Indies in 1956–57, but his chief virtue was in smoothing the way for the team when it was called upon to attend society events.

The Duke's grand manner did not go down well with the players. The mercurial and blunt-speaking Yorkshireman Fred Trueman was not best pleased when the Duke, wishing to introduce himself, called out, 'Trueman!

Over here!', beckoning him with his finger. But there was fun to be had at the Duke's expense. Ian Wooldridge recalled the team's initial encounter:

> It was the first time that most of us had met the portly, florid aristocrat ... we hardly knew what to expect: he hadn't exactly sprung to mind as a front-running candidate for the job. It was a black-tie affair, of course, and none of us dared to get drunk. Eventually, over the port, the Duke rose, cleared his throat and delivered himself of a sentence I shall treasure till the end of my days: 'Gentlemen,' he said, 'I wish this to be an entirely informal tour. You will merely address me as "Sir".'

The Earl Marshal was wheeled out for two more state occasions: Churchill's funeral and, in 1969, the investiture of Prince Charles as Prince of Wales. He died, aged 66, in 1975, a veteran of four reigns.

While retaining much of its social cachet, not to mention its wealth, the old aristocracy lost any claim to political influence. Though the three prime ministers after Churchill were from the upper reaches – Eden from the gentry, Macmillan married to the daughter of a Duke and Home from a long line of Scottish landowners – their lesser brethren were mostly fobbed off with minor jobs or left to bluster, usually for lost causes, in the House of Lords.

It was Macmillan who knocked away the foundations of heredity by introducing life peerages, allowing heredity peers to disclaim their titles and phasing out hereditary titles, though Macmillan himself left office with an earldom, the last non-royal to be thus distinguished. A new political elite, based more on money than tradition, came to prominence, forming a network 'of the right people who had been to the right schools, with the right accents, the right beliefs, and a conviction in their divine right to rule'.[27]

After the 1955 election, up to a quarter of Tory MPs had been to Eton and the rest to a handful of socially prestigious institutions. With a succession of Conservative prime ministers – Eden, Macmillan, Douglas-Home – their Cabinets contained more Etonians than ever before in British political history. By 1960, the House of Lords was practically an Old Etonian Club.

The same dominance could be seen in the Brigade of Guards, the Diplomatic Corps and the Stock Exchange. The magic of the old school tie could still carry the least-distinguished chinless wonder into a cosy sinecure. As for those who had adjusted to a reduced role, a heredity peer told me,

'There are at best two advantages in having a title. It gets you a decent table in a restaurant and an upgrade on British Airways.'

Yet, despite an increasingly heavy pounding from the media as a succession of royal scandals caught the headlines and inspired the satirists from *Private Eye* to *Spitting Image*, to ever wilder representations of regal life, the Queen and her family managed, for the most part, to remain above the fray. Outspoken republicans such as Tom Nairn find it hard to understand how it has been possible. The anti-monarchist Stephen Hasler spent much of his academic life puzzling, fruitlessly, over this question. Yet the answer is not hard to detect. For all its claims to be a thoroughly modern state, Britain is still locked in its past. A burgeoning heritage industry with its multifarious by-products, is now the dominant part of the economy. The National Trust, one of the country's largest landowners with a membership of over 5 million, makes a fantasy heritage a substitute for history, while television's costume dramas such as *Downton Abbey* suggest the past is more impressive and exciting than the future.

The royal family is central to the image. The remarkable duration of Elizabeth II's reign and her devotion to conservative values has made her a living symbol of Britain's glory days. She has managed the role with consummate skill:

> On delicate matters, she would let events unfold, not take sides, and – if a decision was unavoidable – make scrupulously certain that any blame for a mistake would be taken by 'advisers', if not in Downing Street, then at the Palace.[28]

There have been errors of judgement, such as the tepid reaction to the death of Princess Diana in 1997, that have put the Queen in an unfavourable light. In the month after Diana's funeral, opinion polls showed 71 per cent were of the view that the monarchy would not exist in fifty years' time. For the republican *Observer* newspaper, the mourners in the Mall denoted a nation united against tradition. But a year later, a large majority believed that the royal family had learned from the public reaction to her death.[29] For the most part, the scandals involving the Queen's family have emphasised her ascendancy over the troubles of ordinary life. Now, as much as at the time of the coronation, many people see in the Queen 'their better selves ideally reflected'.[30]

While the formal powers of the monarchy have all but disappeared, the social influence of the royal family remains considerable. With the solid backing of the nouveau riche craving recognition beyond a well-paid job, the honours system, with one of the senior royals bestowing the baubles, grows ever more extensive. A visit to the Palace, even for an event as mundane as a summer garden party, is widely regarded as one of life's highlights. Across the country there is hardly a charity, a public institution or commercial enterprise that is unaware of the value of the imprimatur of royal patronage. For a good cause to boast a royal name on the letterhead is guaranteed to boost donations and clear the way to powerful backers. In this way, says David Cannadine, 'even the least admirable members of the royal family have been able to win respect and support'. He adds, 'Charitable activity has become the place where the royal culture of hierarchical condescension and the popular culture of social aspiration have completely and successfully merged.'[31]

It may all be different after Elizabeth's reign comes to an end. She will be a hard act to follow and there are serious doubts that her successor will be able to retain the magic of her office. The proof will be in the next coronation. That there will be one is beyond doubt. That it will be radically different from the 1953 bonanza is also axiomatic. But whether it succeeds as an act of national unity or is the spark that sets off a bonfire of the vanities, the crystal ball has nothing to show.

# NOTES

## Chapter 1

1   Kate Williams, *Young Elizabeth* (2012) p.44.
2   *Ibid.*, p.68.
3   Frank Prochaska, *Royal Bounty: The Making of the Welfare Monarchy* (1995) p.143.
4   Henry 'Chips' Channon, *The Diaries 1918–38*, Simon Heffer (ed.) (2021) p.157.
5   George Orwell, *The English People* (1947).
6   J.B. Booth, *The Days We Knew* (1943) p.124.
7   Gordon Cosmo Lang, Archbishop of York, preaching at George V's coronation.
8   Kingsley Martin, *The Crown and the Establishment* (1962) p.19.
9   A.J.P. Taylor, *Essays in English History* (1977) p.205.
10  Henry 'Chips' Channon, *The Diaries 1918–38*, p.626.
11  Harold Nicolson, *Diaries and Letters 1945–1962* (1968) p.167.
12  Frances Havergal, *Royal Bounty: The Making of the Welfare Monarchy*, p.213.
13  David Cannadine, *History in Our Time* (1998) p.65.
14  Henry 'Chips' Channon, *The Diaries 1918–38*, p.629.
15  John (Jock) Colville, *The Fringes of Power* (2004) p.224.
16  Sarah Bradford, *Queen Elizabeth II: Her Life in Our Times* (2012) p.45.
17  *Observer*, 10 February 1952.
18  A.J.P. Taylor, *Essays in English History*, p.288.
19  Hugh Dalton, *High Tide and After Memoirs 1945–1960* (1962) p.9.
20  *The British Way and Purpose: Citizens of Empire* (1943) p.127.
21  Robert Rhodes James, *A Spirit Undaunted* (1998) p.295.

## Chapter 2

1   Ben Pimlott, *The Queen* (2002) p.127.
2   *New York Times*, 20 August 1947.
3   Ingrid Seward, *Prince Philip Revealed* (2020).

4    MOA2253. Quoted in Edward Owens, *The Family Firm. Monarchy, Mass Media and the British Public, 1932–1953* (2019) p.322.
5    *Daily Mail*, 27 December 1947.
6    John Colville, *The Fringes of Power: Downing Street Diaries 1939–1955* (2004) p.583.
7    *The Times*, 4 May 1951.
8    Richard Aldous, *Tunes of Glory: The Life of Malcolm Sargent* (2001) p.154.
9    *The Memoirs of Lord Ismay* (1960) p.457.
10   John Colville, *The Fringes of Power*, p.601.
11   David Cannadine, 'Churchill and the British Monarchy', *Transactions of the Royal Historical Society*, Vol. 2 (2001).
12   *The Times*, 13 February 1952.

# Chapter 3

1    *The Macmillan Diaries: The Cabinet Years 1950–1957*, ed. Peter Cotterall (2003).
2    George Orwell, *The Lion and the Unicorn* (1941).
3    *The Economist*, 25 April 1953.
4    Julie Summers, *Our Uninvited Guests: The Secret Life of Britain's Country Houses 1939–1945* (2018) p.172.
5    John Harris, *No Voice from the Hall* (1998) pp.6–7.
6    Harold Nicolson, *Diaries and Letters 1945–1962* (1968) p.124.
7    David Cannadine, *The Decline and Fall of the British Aristocracy* (1990) p.650.
8    Peter Mandler, *The Fall and Rise of the Stately Home* (1997) p.347.
9    *Ibid.*
10   David Cannadine, *The Decline and Fall of the British Aristocracy*, p.163.
11   Evelyn Shuckburgh, *Descent to Suez* (1987) p.141.
12   John Pearson, *Citadel of the Heart* (1991) p.362.
13   Roy Jenkins, *Churchill* (2001) p.860.
14   *The Macmillan Diaries*, 6 March 1952.
15   Philip Murphy, *Monarchy and the End of Empire* (2013) pp.50–3.
16   Royal Titles Bill, Second Reading, 3 March 1953. Hansard, Vol. 512, cc. 193–257.

# Chapter 4

1    Ian Bradley, *God Save the Queen: The Spiritual Dimension of Monarchy* (2002, pp.82–3.
2    Rev. Henry Hunter, *History of London and its Environs* (1811).
3    Quoted by Christopher Hibbert, *George II: A Personal History* (1998) p.499.
4    Roy Strong, *Coronation* (2005) p.378.
5    C.C.E. Greville, *A Journal of the Reign of Queen Victoria*, Vol. 1 (1887) pp.106–7.
6    Elizabeth Longford, *Victoria RI* (1966) pp.102, 103.
7    Michael Diamond, *Victorian Sensation* (2003) p.9.
8    Cecil Woodham-Smith, *Queen Victoria* (1972) p.205.
9    J.B. Booth, *Palmy Days* (1957) p.321.
10   *Ibid.*
11   Harold Nicolson, *King George V* (1952) p.205.
12   Tom Bradley, *God Save the Queen*, pp.60, 69.
13   Frank Prochaska, *Royal Bounty*, p.6.

14  *Ibid.*

15  Robert Beaken, *Cosmo Lang: Archbishop in War and Crisis* (2012).

16  Lang Papers, Vol. 271, folio 217. Quoted in Beaken, *Cosmo Lang*, p.78.

17  *The Times*, 12 May 1937.

18  Roy Strong, *Coronation*, pp.493, 494.

19  Henry 'Chips' Channon, *The Diaries 1918–38*, pp.678–81.

20  Mass Observation Archive. Quoted in Philip Ziegler, *Crown and People* (1978) p.56.

21  W. Macqueen-Pope, *Goodbye Piccadilly* (1960) pp.307, 308.

22  *Daily Herald*, 13 May 1937.

23  Sarah Bradford, *Elizabeth: A Biography of Her Majesty the Queen* (1997) p.65.

24  Kingsley Martin, quoted in Paul Greenhalgh, *Ephemeral Vistas* (1998) p.82.

# Chapter 5

1  *The Times*, 5 May 1952.

2  Edward Carpenter, *Archbishop Fisher: His Life and Times* (1991) p.250.

3  Paul Bradshaw, *Coronations Past, Present and Future* (2010) pp.29–30.

4  Kingsley Martin, *The Crown and the Establishment*, p.118.

5  Brian Harrison, *Seeking a Role: The United Kingdom 1951–1970* (2009) p.49.

6  Edward Carpenter, *Archbishop Fisher*, p.253.

7  *Ibid.*, p.259.

8  Hansard, 27 January 1953, Vol. 510, cc. 841–2.

9  Hansard, 17 March 1953, Vol. 512, cc.177.

10  Richard Viner, *National Service: A Generation in Uniform 1945–1963* (2014) pp.399–400.

11  Sir Anthony Eden, *Full Circle* (1960) pp.383, 384.

12  Philip Murphy, *Monarchy and the End of Empire* (2013) p.57.

13  *Ibid.*, p.59.

14  Harold Holt's Coronation Diary, 9 May–23 July 1953. National Archives of Australia. NAA: M2608,3.

15  *Ibid.*, p.46.

16  James Lees-Milne, *A Mingled Measure: Diaries 1953–1972* (1994) p.28.

17  Kate Williams, *Young Elizabeth* (2012) p.283.

18  *The Noël Coward Diaries*, Graham Payn and Sheridan Morley (eds) (1982) p.213.

19  Philip Ziegler, *Crown and People* (1978) p.101.

20  *The Saturday Book*, John Hadfield (ed.) (1952) p.45.

21  Jan Morris, *Coronation Everest* (1958) p.57.

22  *Ibid.*, p.137.

# Chapter 6

1  Harold Nicolson, *King George V*, pp.670, 671.

2  J.C.W. Reith, *Into the Wind* (1947) p.169.

3  *The Reith Diaries*, Charles Stuart (ed.) (1975) p.197.

4  Jeffrey Richards, 'The Coronation of Queen Elizabeth and Film', *Court Histories* 9 (2004) pp.69–79.

5  Joe Moran, *Armchair Nation* (2013) p.36.

6   J.C.W. Reith, *Into the Wind*, p.280.

7   *Ibid.*

8   *The Harold Nicolson Diaries 1907–1963* (2005) pp.182–3.

9   Nicholas Faith, *A Very Different Country* (2002) p.65.

10   Joe Moran, *Armchair Nation* (2013) p.73.

11   Douglas Bridson, *Prospero and Ariel* (1971) p.154.

12   *Ibid.*, p.225.

13   Michael Tracey, *A Variety of Lives: A Biography of Sir Hugh Greene* (1983) p.120.

14   Denis Norden, *Clips from Life* (2008) pp.118, 119.

15   Lambeth Palace Library, Fisher 123, 'Diary of Coronation Events', Folios 3–4.

16   Edward Owens, *The Family Firm: Monarchy, Mass Media and the British Public 1932–1953* (2018) p.337.

17   Douglas Bridson, *Prospero and Ariel*, p.183.

18   Lambeth Palace Library, Fisher 123, Folio 8.

19   *The Scotsman*, Peter Dimmock obituary, 24 November 2015.

20   Joe Moran, *Armchair Nation*, p.75.

21   *Ibid.*, p.75.

22   *Ibid.*, p.76.

# Chapter 7

1   David Egerton, *The Rise and Fall of the British Nation* (2018) p.149.

2   Doris Lessing, *Walking in the Shade* (1997) pp.122, 123.

3   Ted Hughes, *Birthday Letters* (1998).

4   Lindsay Anderson, *Never Apologise: The Collected Writings* (2004).

5   Articles relating to the survey appeared in *The People* between August and September 1951. Gorer's book, *Exploring British Character*, was published in 1955.

6   *Ibid.*

7   Bill Williamson, *The Temper of the Times* (1990) p.64.

8   Hugh Dalton, *High Tide and After* (1962) p.233.

9   John Newsom, *The Education of Girls* (1948) pp.12, 25.

10   Colin McInnes, *Absolute Beginners* (1959).

11   John Montgomery, *The Fifties* (1965) p.154.

12   *The Listener*, 14 August 1969.

# Chapter 8

1   *Richard Dimbleby Broadcaster*, Leonard Miall (ed.) (1966) p.86.

2   Mass Observation Archive. Quoted in Philip Ziegler, *Crown and People* (1978) p.108.

3   Joe Moran, *Armchair Nation* (2013) p.76.

4   Geoffrey Grigson, *Country Life*, 6 June 1953.

5   *Ibid.*

6   Harold Holt, Coronation Diary, National Archives of Australia, 172608, 3.

7   *Richard Dimbleby Broadcaster*, Leonard Miall (ed.) (1966) p.869.

8   Katherine Whitehorn, *Selective Memory* (2007) p.50.

9   *Manchester Guardian*, 4 April 1933.

10   *First Over Everest: The Houston-Mount Everest Expedition* (1933).

11   *The Reunion: Coronation Maids*, BBC4, 1 April 2013.
12   Cecil Beaton, *The Strenuous Years: Diaries 1948–55* (1973) p.144.
13   *Ibid.*
14   Elizabeth Longford, *The Pebbled Shore* (1986) p.286.
15   Harold Holt, Coronation Diary, National Archives of Australia, 172608, 3.
16   Richard Dimbleby, *Sunday Dispatch*, 7 June 1953.
17   Brian Harrison, *Seeking a Role: The United Kingdom 1951–1970* (2009) p.49.
18   Richard Dimbleby, *Sunday Dispatch*, 7 June 1953.
19   *Manchester Guardian*, 3 June 1953.
20   James Lees-Milne, *A Mingled Measure: Diaries 1953–1972* (1994) pp.29–30.
21   Harold Nicolson, *Diaries and Letters 1945–1962*, pp.241–2.
22   John Montgomery, *The Fifties* (1965) p.88.
23   *Manchester Guardian*, 3 June 1953.
24   Birmingham History Forum.
25   Cecil Beaton, *The Strenuous Years*, p.146.
26   *Ibid.*, p.147.
27   *The Year that Made a Day*, BBC Publications (1953).
28   BBC Memoryshare Project.
29   Maurice Broady, 'The Organisation of Coronation Street Parties', *Sociological Review* (1956), Vol. 4, No. 2 (December) pp.223–43.
30   *Leamington Spa Courier*, 12 June 1953.
31   Frances Partridge, *Diaries 1939–1972* (2002) p.200, 4 June 1953.
32   Edward Owens, *The Family Firm* (2018).
33   *Richard Dimbleby: Broadcaster*, Leonard Miall (ed.) (1966) p.78.
34   *The Times*, 4 June 1953.

# Chapter 9

1    *Manchester Guardian*, 3 June 1953.
2    Edward Shils and Michael Young, 'The Meaning of the Coronation', *Sociological Review* (1953) Vol. 1, No. 2 (December), pp.63–81.
3    John Colville, *The Fringes of Power* (2004) p.666.
4    *Ibid.*
5    Michael John Law, *Not Like Home, American Visitors to Britain in the 1950s* (2019) p.125.
6    Willard Price, *Innocents in Britain* (1958) p.129.
7    *Ibid.*, p.131.
8    John Betjeman, 'Beside the Seaside', *Collected Poems*.
9    J.B. Morton, *Merry-Go-Round* (1959) pp.110, 111.
10   Author's collection.
11   Doris Lessing, *Walking in the Shade* (1997) p.5.
12   John Metcalf, *London A to Z* (1953) p.44.
13   Leonard Kendall, *Visit to Britain* (1951) p.42.
14   Drew Middleton, *The British* (1957) p.14.
15   Kenneth Tynan, *A View of the English Stage* (1975) pp.126, 128.
16   *Theatre World Annual*, Frances Stephens (ed.), Vol. 4, June 1952–May 1953.
17   *Theatre World*, July 1952.

18   Randolph S. Churchill, *The Story of the Coronation* (1953) p.9.
19   Peter Vansittart, *In the Fifties* (1995) pp.39, 40.


# Chapter 10

1    Robert Bruce Lockhart, *Your England* (1955) p.288.
2    A. James Hommerton and Alistair Thomson, *The Ten Pound Poms* (2005) p.62.
3    *The Noël Coward Diaries*, Graham Payne and Sheridan Morley (eds) (1982) p.222.
4    *Royal Gazette*, 26 November 1953.
5    *Daily Herald*, 26 November 1953.
6    *Country Life*, 13 May 1954.
7    *Ibid.*
8    *Ibid.*
9    *Ibid.*
10   *The Age*, 4 February 1954.
11   *Courier Mail*, 17 March 1954.
12   *The Age*, 4 March 1954.
13   Philip Murphy, *Monarchy and the End of Empire* (2013) p.62.
14   A. James Hommerton and Alistair Thomson, *The Ten Pound Poms* (2005) p.325.
15   Quoted by Ewan Morris, 'Australia and the Queen, 1954', *Journal of Australian Studies*, 18 May 2009.
16   A. James Hommerton and Alistair Thomson, *The Ten Pound Poms*, p.341.
17   Ewan Morris, *Journal of Australian Studies*, 18 May 2009.
18   Philip Murphy, *Monarchy and the End of Empire*, p.62.
19   Philip Ziegler, *Mountbatten* (1985) pp.514–15.
20   *Ibid.*, p.515.
21   Robert Bruce Lockhart, *Your England*, p.289.
22   Caryl Phillips, *Times Literary Supplement*, 18 December 2020.
23   W.R. Louis, *Imperialism at Bay* (1987) p.14.
24   Edmund Dell, *A Strange Eventful History* (2001) p.187.


# Chapter 11

1    Cecil Beaton, *The Strenuous Years*, p.147.
2    Kate Williams, *Young Elizabeth*, p.275.
3    Cecil Beaton, *The Strenuous Years*, p.134.
4    Ben Pimlott, *The Queen* (2002) p.237.
5    Edward Carpenter, *Archbishop Fisher: His Life and Times* (1991) p.389.
6    *Daily Mirror*, 26 October 1955.
7    Ben Pimlott, *The Queen*, p.239.
8    *Ibid.*
9    Edward Carpenter, *Archbishop Fisher*, p.290.
10   Oliver McGregor, *Divorce in England* (1957).
11   *They Stand Apart,* Tudor Rees and Harry Usill (eds) (1955) p. vii.
12   *Ibid.*, p.273.

# Chapter 12

1   Nicholas Faith, *A Very Different Country* (2002) p.9.
2   Fiona McCarthy, *Last Curtsey* (2006) p.7.
3   *Ibid.*, p.9.
4   *This England: Selections from the New Statesman Column 1934–1948*, Michael Bateman (eds) (1969) p.103.
5   Hansard, 9 July 1952, Vol. 503.
6   Quoted in Kingsley Martin, *The Crown and the Establishment*, p.138.
7   Sarah Bradford, *Queen Elizabeth II: Her Life in Our Time* (2012) p.169.
8   John Colville, *The Fringes of Power*, Vol. 2 (1986) p.376.
9   Evelyn Shuckburgh, *Descent to Suez* (1986) p.141.
10  Richard Ingrams, *Malcolm Muggeridge: The Biography* (1995) p.167.
11  *New Statesman*, 22 October 1955.
12  *This England: Selections from the New Statesman Column 1934–1948*, pp.79, 99.
13  Jacob to Richard Ingrams, 3 September 1986. Richard Ingrams, *Malcolm Muggeridge: The Biography*, p.183.
14  *Ibid.*, p.185.
15  'The Monarchy Today', *National and English Review*, Issue 149, pp.63–5.
16  Cecil Beaton, *The Strenuous Years*, p.114.
17  Quoted by Henry Fairlie, *Spectator*, 8 November 1957.
18  Ben Pimlott, *The Queen*, pp.280, 281.
19  Peter Whitebrook, *John Osborne* (2015) p.140.
20  *Ibid.*, p.141.
21  John Osborne, *Almost a Gentleman* (1991) p.92.
22  Kingsley Martin, *The Crown and the Establishment*, p.12.
23  Philip Ziegler, *Crown and People*, p.154.
24  Richard Hoggart, *The Uses of Literacy* (1957) p.111.
25  Tom Harrison, *Britain Revisited* (1961) p.231.
26  Television interview, 1968.
27  Jeremy Paxman, *Friends in High Places* (1990) p.12.
28  Ben Pimlott, *The Queen*, p.239.
29  Andrzej Olechnowicz, *The Monarchy and the British Nation: 1780 to the Present* (2007) p.293.
30  *The Times*, 24 October 1955.
31  David Cannadine, *History in Our Time*, p.30.

# ACKNOWLEDGEMENTS

Having benefited from the wisdom and insight of many fellow historians, I give special thanks to Sir David Cannadine, the pre-eminent chronicler of recent times. His books and articles are never dull and always illuminating, particularly when it comes to the foibles and failings of royalty.

For original archives and first-hand information, I am indebted to the London Metropolitan Archive, Lambeth Palace Library, the National Archives of Australia, BBC Memoryshare and the Birmingham History Forum, not to mention all those citizens of a certain age who have recorded their memories of the coronation on many and varied websites.

A stand-alone credit attaches to the London Library, that magnificent subscription library with its friendly and helpful staff, who are ever ready to guide the way along miles of shelves to find rare volumes that we, the privileged members, are able to take out on loan.

My commissioning editor, Mark Beynon at The History Press, has given encouragement and support, as too has my agent, Michael Alcock, who wins prizes for patience and good cheer. My one-time PA, Jill Fenner, now in happy retirement, has lent her skill to helping me make sense of unstructured thoughts, avoiding repetition and keeping it short, while Jezz Palmer at The History Press has done a great job in seeing the book to press.

Above all, I thank Mary Fulton, my wife and sternest – but always constructive – critic, who makes life such fun.

# INDEX